Test-Driven Development: A J2EE Example

THOMAS HAMMELL

WITH RUSSELL GOLD AND TOM SNYDER

Test-Driven Development: A J2EE Example

Copyright © 2005 by Thomas Hammell

ISBN (pbk): 1-59059-327-8

Printed and bound in the United States of America 9 8 7 6 5 4 3 2 1

Lead Editor: Steve Anglin
Technical Reviewer: Dilip Thomas
Contributing Authors: Russell Gold and Tom Snyder
Editorial Board: Steve Anglin, Dan Appleman, Ewan Buckingham, Gary Cornell, Tony Davis,
     Jason Gilmore, Chris Mills, Dominic Shakeshaft, Jim Sumser
Project Manager: Beth Christmas
Copy Edit Manager: Nicole LeClerc
Copy Editor: Ami Knox
Production Manager: Kari Brooks-Copony
Production Editor: Beth Christmas
Compositor: Dina Quan
Proofreader: Sue Boshers
Indexer: Carol Burbo
Artist: Kinetic Publishing Services, LLC
Cover Designer: Kurt Krames
Manufacturing Manager: Tom Debolski

Distributed to the book trade in the United States by Springer-Verlag New York, Inc., 233 Spring Street, 6th Floor, New York, NY 10013, and outside the United States by Springer-Verlag GmbH & Co. KG, Tiergartenstr. 17, 69112 Heidelberg, Germany.

In the United States: phone 1-800-SPRINGER, fax 201-348-4505, e-mail orders@springer-ny.com, or visit http://www.springer-ny.com. Outside the United States: fax +49 6221 345229, e-mail orders@springer.de, or visit http://www.springer.de.

For information on translations, please contact Apress directly at 2560 Ninth Street, Suite 219, Berkeley, CA 94710. Phone 510-549-5930, fax 510-549-5939, e-mail info@apress.com, or visit http://www.apress.com.

The source code for this book is available to readers at http://www.apress.com in the Downloads section.

Contents at a Glance

Contents

About the Author

TOM HAMMELL is a senior developer and currently works on the development of telecom network infrastructure software for the Open Call Business Unit of Hewlett-Packard. Tom has been developing software for over 18 years and has worked on software in many different fields such as satellite navigation, financial news wires, telecom, and J2EE application server development. Tom has published a number of articles on Java topics ranging from Swing development to unit testing and speaks frequently on technical topics. Tom holds a Bachelor of Science degree in Electrical Engineering and Master of Computer Science degree from Stevens Institute of Technology.

About the Technical Reviewer

DILIP THOMAS is an open source enthusiast who keeps a close watch on LAMP technologies, open standards, and the full range of Apache Jakarta projects. He is co-author of *PHP MySQL Website Programming: Problem, Design, Solution* (Apress, 2003) and a technical reviewer on several open source/open standard book projects.

Dilip resides in Bangalore with his beautiful wife, Indu, and several hundred books and journals. Reach him via e-mail: dilip.thomas@gmail.com.

Acknowledgments

Writing a book, especially a technical one, is not an easy task and would be impossible without the help of a lot of dedicated people who assisted me in bringing this book to you.

First, I would like to thank all the people at Apress for all their work in transforming my ideas and words into an actual book. I would especially like to thank Beth Christmas and Steve Anglin for their constant guidance and patience during the process.

I want to thank my technical reviewer, Dilip Thomas, for his help in ensuring the accuracy and clarity of the material presented in this book. His comments were always precise and relevant and really helped me improve the book.

I also have to thank Russell Gold and Tom Snyder for contributing some of the writing for the first few chapters. Tom Snyder contributed most of the material in Chapter 2, and Russell Gold contributed a good part of Chapter 3. Not only do I appreciate the work they did for the book, but our discussions helped me clarify my ideas about TDD.

Lastly, I would like to thank my wife for her constant support and encouragement during the writing process. She never complained about all the time I spent working on the book or all the chores I neglected to do. Now that the book is finished, I promise her that I will catch up on my chores and find a way to thank her for letting me write this book.

Preface

Tell me and I forget. Teach me and I remember. Involve me and I learn.

—Benjamin Franklin

Anyone who has tried to teach knows how hard it is. Words are often not enough to explain the concepts being taught. Even the most eager students who can respond to the teacher's questions with perfectly correct answers will not truly understand the concepts until they experience them in their own way. For example, it is easy enough to explain to most students the concepts of object-oriented design, such as inheritance, encapsulation, and polymorphism, but it takes years of experience to appreciate and understand how to really apply these ideas.

The concepts of Test-Driven Development (TDD) are very easy to explain and understand. However, its actual application in the real world requires more than just an understanding of the concepts of TDD. It requires knowledge of certain tools needed to run the tests, proper setup of the development environment, and an understanding of how to use the tests to improve the design of the software. This type of knowledge can only be gained with experience. There are no words or diagrams that could be used to impart this knowledge fully to a reader. The best a book can do is to inspire you to explore the concepts on your own and get involved.

That is why I am taking a step-by-step approach to teaching TDD. Each chapter will introduce a new set of concepts that will be explained with several examples that will lead you through the material in a logical way. Each of the chapters will contain some exercises that you can use to explore what has been taught. This will serve to get you involved as well as show you how well you have learned the concepts. Complete answers to the exercises will be given in Appendix B so you will be able to compare your results to the correct answer. Many of the exercises don't have right or wrong answers, or may have many different right answers. The important thing to remember is that doing the exercises is the best way to get involved and learn.

Book Organization

Although this book was written for J2EE developers who want to learn TDD, a lot of the concepts introduced will be useful to all Java developers. The chapters in this book are arranged in the order that would be used to teach a student TDD. Here's a brief summary of what is explained in each chapter:

- Chapter 1: Introduces the concepts of TDD and explains the benefits of TDD.

- Chapter 2: Describes how to create a TDD environment. This includes a discussion of what type of tools are needed as well as some discussion of how to organize the environment. The chapter also presents the requirements and architecture of a simple application that will be used throughout the rest of the book to illustrate the concepts being taught.

- Chapter 3: Teaches you how to create and run unit tests and use them to drive the development of your code. It also includes some information about the best way to organize and run the unit tests.

- Chapter 4: Explains how to use TDD to develop servlets.

- Chapter 5: Explains how to use TDD to develop GUIs.

- Chapter 6: Shows how to use TDD to integrate the different parts of a J2EE application. This includes examples of how to integrate databases, EJBs, servlets, JSPs, and GUIs into a finished application.

- Chapter 7: Presents a series of discussions that explain how to organize your tests and make them easier to run. This chapter will also explain some of the finer details of how to use TDD to improve the design of an application.

- Chapter 8: Gives you some advice on how to transition from your current development environment to a TDD one.

- Appendix A: Contains information on how to download and run the example code presented in this book.

- Appendix B: Contains the answers for the hands-on exercises.

- Appendix C: Contains a list of references and recommended web sites.

I have tried to make the individual topics as self-contained as possible to make it easier for you to explore the book in your own way. Chapter 2 is the only prerequisite for reading the later chapters since it explains the example application that is used throughout the rest of the book.

The importance of downloading and running the example code cannot be emphasized enough. Although the text in the book explains each code example presented, you will not truly understand the concepts until you run the code for yourself. I have tried to make the code examples as easy as possible to run by not only providing the source code for the examples, but also providing an Ant build file that can be used to run the examples. As long as you have the required jar files, running the code examples should not take a lot of effort. (See Appendix A for complete instructions on how to download and run the code examples.)

The examples in this book are geared toward teaching you how to use TDD to develop a J2EE application. I have tried to keep the examples for this book just complicated enough to be useful while at the same time keeping them simple so that they easily illustrate the concepts being presented. This means that I have simplified, as much as possible, the configuration and application server setup so that you can concentrate on the example code.

The examples will also show you how to use tools like JUnit and some of its extensions to develop the various parts of the application. Although I do not explain all of the nuances of each of these tools, the examples presented should help you understand the basics of each tool. After that, it should be easy to explore them on your own and learn how to use them in your particular development environment.

Feedback

A lot of work has been put into this book to try and present the ideas of TDD to you in the best possible way. I have also worked hard to ensure that the source code is easy to run. I am always looking to improve my ability to teach these topics, so I would appreciate any feedback, positive or negative, on the concepts or code presented in this book. You can post your comments on the forum at http://www.apress.com or you can reach me at thomashammell@apress.com.

CHAPTER 1

■■■

Introduction to Test-Driven Development

The problem with software development is that it is too success oriented. Just like the criminal justice system, whereby a man is innocent until proven guilty, most software is considered working until bugs are found.

Most developers believe that to create good software you have to have a good design. The problem is that it's very hard to come up with a good software design by just thinking about it. You can go through requirement analysis and create data models and all kinds of great theoretical constructs, but the minute you start coding, a lot of that stuff gets thrown out the window and forgotten.

Thousands of decisions have to be made to create a piece of software. To make all those decisions correctly *before* you start writing the code is an impossible task. It's easy to make a decision, but it's hard to make the right decision, especially when developing software. Test-First Development or Test-Driven Development (TDD) is a methodology that uses tests to help developers make the right decisions at the right time. TDD is not about testing, it's about using tests to create software in a simple, incremental way. Not only does this improve the quality and design of the software, but it also simplifies the development process.

The beauty of TDD is that with a little change in your development methodology and some additional tools you can produce better software faster. The purpose of this chapter and the rest of this book is to show how the ideas of TDD can be used to radically improve software development.

What Is Test-Driven Development?

TDD is one of the core practices of Extreme Programming (XP).[1] The XP practices were formulated by Kent Beck and Ron Jeffries from their experience in developing a payroll system for Chrysler. The main ideas behind XP are to make the development process simpler and have short, continuous development cycles that allow constant feedback as to the state of the software. Although not all developers believe in all of the XP practices, the ideas of TDD have started to gain wide acceptance.

TDD represents a simple evolution in the way software can be developed. It's the realization that complex software systems can be developed in small simple increments that use

---

1. For an introduction to Extreme Programming, see http://www.xprogramming.com/.

tests to drive the design and implementation of the software. Adopting the TDD philosophy will not require you to make major changes to your development environment. With the addition of a few tools, it's easy to create a TDD environment, as you'll see in Chapter 2.

The hardest part of TDD is changing the way you think about writing code. Instead of creating a design to tell you how to structure your code, you create a test that defines how a small part of the system should function. This test drives the design of the code needed to implement the functionality. This frees you from having to make design decisions up front and allows you the freedom to discover the design as you code so that you can make better decisions about the way the code is structured. TDD also makes you focus on creating the software in an incremental fashion. It's not important to get the code right the first time, because using TDD you continually refactor the code and tests until the software meets the requirements—akin to a carpenter who continually planes a piece of molding to slowly scribe it to an uneven floor.

The ideas of TDD may sound a little vague when you first hear them, but the basic techniques of TDD are easily understood. Once you start practicing these techniques, you'll realize that TDD is more than a nice idea: it's a practical way to improve the development process.

The Test-Driven Development Methodology

On the surface, TDD is a very simple methodology that relies on two main concepts: unit tests and refactoring. TDD is basically composed of the following steps:

1. Write a test that defines how you think a small part of the software should behave.

2. Make the test run as easily and quickly as you can. Don't be concerned about the design of code, just get it to work.

3. Clean up the code. Now that the code is working correctly, take a step back and refactor to remove any duplication or any other problems that were introduced to get the test to run.

TDD is an iterative process, and you repeat these steps a number of times until you are satisfied with the new code. TDD doesn't rely on a lot of up-front design to determine how the software is structured. The way TDD works is that requirements, or use cases, are decomposed into a set of behaviors that are needed to fulfill the requirement. For each behavior of the system, the first thing you do is to write a *unit test* that will test this behavior. The unit test is written first so that you have a well-defined set of criteria that you can use to tell when you have written just enough code to implement the behavior. One of the benefits of writing the test first is that it actually helps better define the behavior of the system and answer some design questions.

For example, suppose you are asked to write some software that will be used to calculate statistics like batting average, ERA, on base percentage, and so on for a softball league. One of the requirements of the system may be something like "The software must be able to calculate the batting average of every player by game and for the season." If you think about this requirement, you can come up with a number of behaviors the software needs to have in order to implement this requirement:

- The software has to be able to identify each player.

- There must be a way to input the data needed to calculate the batting average.

- The software has to be able to identify a game.

- There must be a way to get a player's batting average for a particular game.

- There must be a way to get a player's batting average for the season.

After making some assumptions, such as players will be identified by their name and games by their date, you could write the following unit test:

```
Player wally = PlayerList.getPlayer("Wally Wiffer"); // Get player
// Add batting stats for wally hitting 1 for 5 on 8/9
wally.addGameBA("8/9/2003",1,5);
// Add batting stats for wally hitting 2 for 5 on 8/16
wally.addGameBA("8/16/2003",2,5);
// Add batting stats for wally hitting 0 for 4 on 8/23
wally.addGameBA("8/23/2003",0,4);
float gameBA = wally.getGameBA("8/9/2003"); // Get batting average for game on 8/9
float seasonBA = wally.getBA(); // Get batting average season
assertEquals(200, gameBA);  // Check game batting average calculation
assertEquals(214, seasonBA);  // Check season batting average calculation
```

Because you wrote the unit test first, you now know that you will need a PlayerList class and Player class. The PlayerList class will need a getPlayer() method, and the Player class will need addGameBA(), getGameBA(), and getBA() methods. You also know the type of arguments for each of these methods. Not only has this unit test given you a way to verify that your code works once you write it, it has also helped you define the exact classes and methods required to write just enough code to implement this behavior.

Once the unit test is written, it's executed to verify it fails when it's run. It fails because the code to implement the behavior has not yet been written, but this is an important step because this will verify that the unit test is working correctly. Once the unit test has been verified, then the code to implement the behavior is written, and the unit test is run against it to make sure that the software works as expected.

Now that you have a test that tells you how the code should behave and code that behaves correctly, it's time to clean up the code. We as developers all know that the first pass at writing a piece of code is usually not the best implementation. Usually, we would like to go back and clean it up a little but are afraid that any cleanup we do might break something that works. You don't have to worry about breaking the code using TDD, because if you break something, the unit test will let you know immediately.

Once you finish implementing one behavior, you move on to the next one and go through the same steps—write a test, write the code, refactor—to implement that behavior. In this way the design grows from the actual implementation of the code as the tests are used to drive the development of more and more functionality in a simple, incremental way. This incremental approach also allows for constant refactoring along the way. So as problems are discovered with the current implementation, it's easy to refactor the code and then run all the unit tests to make sure everything still works as expected.

One result of this methodical approach is that it's hard to overdesign the software and create bloated code because you add just enough code to implement the required behavior. This means that it's easy to meet the requirements in a timely manner because you don't waste time developing code that will never be used.

As more and more code is developed, the number of tests grows rapidly into a whole suite of tests that can be run at any time. These test suites are important to the TDD process because you can use them to constantly monitor the software and immediately tell you when problems occur. Since you run these test suites continually during development, you can find and fix bugs much quicker. This adds confidence to the development process.

The Pillars of Test-Driven Development

TDD relies on two main concepts: unit tests and refactoring.

Unit tests allow you to test the software in a more detailed way than you would with functional tests. With unit tests, you can test small units of the code at the application programming interface (API) level. Unit tests are also much easier to run than functional tests since they don't require a full production environment to run, and you can run them quickly as you are developing. Unit tests help developers become more productive because it makes it easier to track down bugs and run regression tests to monitor the state of the software.

To create effective unit tests, you first need to understand the behavior of the unit of software that you are creating. This can usually be done by decomposing the software requirements into simple testable behaviors as illustrated in the batting average example earlier in this chapter. You may define software requirements in a number of different ways, such as a formal requirement spec, use cases, or maybe just some simple user stories. For TDD, it doesn't matter how the requirements are specified, as long as they can be translated into tests.

Refactoring is the process of changing code for the sole benefit of improving the internal structure of the code without changing its function. Refactoring is basically cleaning up bad code. Most developers refactor code on a daily basis using basic common sense. However, a catalog of refactoring methods has been defined and explained in *Refactoring: Improving the Design of Existing Code*, by Martin Fowler et al. (Addison-Wesley, 1999). Since refactoring is an important part of TDD, you need to develop an understanding of these methods so that you can quickly recognize the patterns of bad code and refactor them to improve your code.

The other important thing you need to learn to use TDD is how to write effective tests that can be used to drive the development of the software. Most developers understand how to write tests to test code that has already been written, but writing tests before writing the code takes a different approach. To write tests that drive the development of code, you must concentrate on how to test the functionality of the code rather than its implementation. This may seem a backward way of developing code at the beginning, but with practice it gets easier and more natural.

The Benefits of Test-Driven Development

TDD has many benefits, some that are obvious and others that are more subtle. Let's explore some of the benefits of TDD so you can understand why you would want to use TDD.

Simple, Incremental Development

TDD takes a simple, incremental approach to the development of software. One of the main benefits to this approach is that you have a working software system almost immediately. The first iteration of this software system is very simple and doesn't have much functionality, but the functionality will improve as the development continues. This is a less risky approach than trying to build the entire system all at once, hoping it will work when all the pieces are put together.

Simpler Development Process

Developers who use TDD have less to worry about and are more productive because they are more focused. The only thing that you as a TDD developer have to worry about is getting the next test to pass. You focus your attention on a small piece of the software, get it to work, and move on. This is better than trying to create the software by doing a lot of up-front design. Thousands of decisions have to be made to create a piece of software. To make all those decisions correctly before you start writing the code is hard. It's much easier to make those decisions as you develop the code, which is what TDD lets you do.

Constant Regression Testing

The domino effect is well known in software development. Sometimes a simple change to one module may have unforeseen consequences throughout the rest of the project. This is why regression testing is important. Regression testing is like self-defense against bugs. It's usually done only when a new release is sent to quality assurance (QA). By then it's sometimes hard to trace which code change introduced a particular bug and makes it harder to fix.

TDD runs the full set of unit tests every time a change is made to the code, in effect running a full regression test every time a minor change is made. This means any change to the code that has an undesired side effect will be detected almost immediately and be corrected, which should prevent any regression surprises when the software is handed over to QA. The other benefit of constant regression testing is that you always have a fully working system at every iteration of development. This allows you to stop development at any time and quickly respond to any changes in requirements.

Improved Communication

Communicating the ideas needed to explain how a piece of software should work is not always easy with words or pictures. Words are often imprecise when it comes to explaining the complexities of the function of a software component. The unit tests can serve as a common language that can be used to communicate the exact behavior of a software component without ambiguities.

Improved Understanding of Required Software Behavior

The level of requirements on a project varies greatly. Sometimes requirements are very detailed and other times they are so vague that you don't even know what you don't know. Writing unit tests before writing the code helps you focus on understanding the required behavior of the software. As you write a unit test, you are adding pass/fail criteria for the behavior of the software. Each of these pass/fail criteria adds to the knowledge of how the software must behave. As more unit tests are added because of new features or new bugs, the set of unit tests come to represent a set of required behaviors of higher and higher fidelity.

Centralization of Knowledge

We all have a collective consciousness that stores ideas we all have in common. Unfortunately, programming is mostly a solitary pursuit. Modules are usually developed by a single individual, and a lot of the knowledge that went into designing the module is usually stuck in the head of the person who wrote the code. Even if it's well-documented, clean code, it's sometimes hard to understand some of the design decisions that went into building the code.

With TDD, the unit tests constitute a repository that provides some information about the design decisions that went into the design of the module. Together with the source code, this provides two different points of view for the module. The unit tests provide a list of requirements for the module. The source code provides the implementation of the requirements. Using these two sources of information makes it a lot easier for other developers to understand the module and make changes that won't introduce bugs.

Improved Software Design

One of the less obvious benefits of TDD is the way it can help improve the design of the software. Being required to write the unit tests for the module before the code helps you define the behavior of the software better and helps you to think about the software from a user's point of view. This change in focus forces you to ask some questions about the behavior that you won't have thought about if you didn't have to write the unit tests. This process of discovery helps improve the design in many different ways as described in the next few sections.

Better Encapsulation and Modularity

Encapsulation and modularity help contain the chaos that is software development. Developers cannot think about all the factors of a software project at one time. A good design will break up software into small, logical, manageable pieces with well-defined interfaces. This encapsulation allows you to concentrate on one thing at a time as the application is built. The problem is that sometimes during the fog of development you may stray from the ideas of encapsulation and introduce some unintended coupling between classes. Unit tests can help you detect when you have not fully encapsulated a module.

For example, let's say that you are writing a class that is responsible for calculating the odds for each horse in a race. In order to do this, you need a list of horses in the race as well as how much money was bet on each horse. This information is stored in a database. The first thing you do is to write a unit test to test the calculations needed to determine the odds for the horses. You make no assumptions as to how the calculations will be performed, you only set up a set of pass/fail criteria for the calculation.

Then you start to write the class needed to perform the calculation. When you do, you realize that the database is not yet set up, and the schema has not yet been finalized. Your original intention was to make SQL calls directly from the methods doing the calculation. This means you can't test the calculation class until the database has been set up. Instead of waiting for the database to be set up, you create a mock database class that can be called by the calculation class to get enough information to perform the calculations needed to pass its unit tests. At a later time, the mock database class can be replaced with a real class that actually reads data from the database, but for now the mock database class allows you to complete the development of the calculation class. This has the effect of isolating the calculation class from the database, which increases the encapsulation and results in a better design.

One of the principles of TDD says that the unit tests should be easy to run. This means that you should try to minimize the requirements needed to run any of the unit tests. Focusing on making testing easier will drive you to make more modular classes that have fewer dependencies.

Simpler Class Relationships

A well-designed piece of software will have well-defined levels that build upon each other and clearly defined interfaces between the levels. One of the results of having software that has well-defined levels is that it's easier to test.

The corollary to this is also true. If you design your code by writing tests, your focus will be very narrow, so you will tend not to create a test that has complex class relationships. As you write the unit tests and code, you will create small building blocks that fit neatly together. Of course, not everything will go smoothly; sometimes you will write a test that exposes a problem with the relationship between the different classes that have already been written. If a unit test is hard to write, then this usually means there is a problem in the design of the code. Code that is hard to test is usually bad code. Since the creation of the unit tests help point out the bad code, this allows you to correct the problem and produce better designed, more modular code.

Reduced Design Complexity

Developers try to be forward looking and build flexibility into software so that it can adapt to the ever-changing requirements and requests for new features. Developers are always adding methods into classes just in case they may be needed. This flexibility comes at the price of complexity. It's not that developers want to make the software more complex, it's just that they feel that it's easier to add the extra code up front than make changes later.

Having a suite of unit tests allows you to quickly tell if you have made a change that has unforeseen consequences. This will give you confidence to make more radical changes to the software. In the TDD process, you will constantly be refactoring code. Refactoring in itself is neither good nor bad, so you need a way to measure the effect that the refactoring has on the code. This is what the suite of unit tests gives you.

Having the confidence to make major code changes any time during the development cycle will prevent you from overbuilding the software and allow you to keep the design simple.

The approach to developing software using TDD also helps reduce software complexity. With TDD you only add the code you need to satisfy the unit tests. This is usually called *developing by intention*. Using TDD, it's hard to add extra code that isn't needed. Since the unit tests are derived from the requirements of the system, the end result is that you develop just enough code to have the software work as required.

Can Test-Driven Development Work on J2EE Projects?

TDD is more than an interesting academic idea. It's a set of techniques that can help to radically improve the development of any software project. Although there has been a lot written about TDD, still more needs to be said. The ideas of TDD have been well explained, but using it to build J2EE applications requires some special application of these ideas. J2EE applications have some characteristics that actually make them well suited for TDD.

The J2EE platform promotes an architecture built on interfaces and the separation of logical concerns within a system. As illustrated in *Core J2EE Patterns: Best Practices and Design Strategies* by Deepak Alur et al. (Prentice Hall PTR, 2001), Figure 1-1 shows the multitiered J2EE platform broken down by tiers. Each tier represents the responsibility of the underlying components within the system.

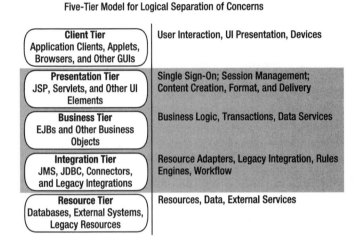

Five-Tier Model for Logical Separation of Concerns

Client Tier Application Clients, Applets, Browsers, and Other GUIs	User Interaction, UI Presentation, Devices
Presentation Tier JSP, Servlets, and Other UI Elements	Single Sign-On; Session Management; Content Creation, Format, and Delivery
Business Tier EJBs and Other Business Objects	Business Logic, Transactions, Data Services
Integration Tier JMS, JDBC, Connectors, and Legacy Integrations	Resource Adapters, Legacy Integration, Rules Engines, Workflow
Resource Tier Databases, External Systems, Legacy Resources	Resources, Data, External Services

Figure 1-1. *Five-tier model*

By implementing recommended J2EE design patterns and refactoring techniques, we logically partition components within the system, and create a design that is easier to test. Instead of creating a coupled system that cannot be tested without the entire system running, you create a system with clear interfaces and encapsulation boundaries that support unit-level tests. Components within one tier get tested with stubbed out implementations of interfaces representing the runtime components from another tier. Later chapters give detailed examples of this approach using many of the J2EE APIs.

Using a TDD approach makes large J2EE projects more manageable. The benefits of TDD tends to increase as the size of the project increases. Most development projects break systems up into multiple components that get developed by different teams. Combine geographically dispersed groups with the increased number of developers, and interteam communication and the integration of components become critical success factors. TDD helps mitigate this risk. It provides a mechanism for teams to share working, testable code. Teams can even share the tests as concrete examples of how the code works. Following this type of TDD approach could have prevented many of the project failures I've witnessed in my career—project failures caused by long development processes that push integration and testing out until late in the project schedule. How many times have you seen project schedules report "on track" during development and then fall apart when system and integration testing begins? By that time, the project is in crunch mode and has little room for missed requirements or failing components. With TDD, progress is tangible on a daily basis. Shared tests and source code help keep development teams honest and schedules on track.

Some practitioners fear this approach, citing concerns with the maintenance of test code in addition to production code. While TDD statistics do show that the number of lines of test code is often equal to the number of lines of production code, the comparison is a misleading statistic. Unit test code is generally very simple. Take the following test case for example. Class Foo has a read(Bar bar) method that throws a BarException if the instance of Bar is null or invalid.

```
public void testNullBar() throws Exception
{
    try {
        Foo foo = new Foo();
        foo.readBar( null );
        fail("Expected BarException" );
    } catch ( BarException ) {}
}
```

This test fails the first time a developer mistakenly changes the implementation of Foo to permit a null Bar reference. In most cases, developers will never even look at the lines of test code, unless a test fails. With the test, you can question coworkers when the test fails to see why Foo does not permit a null Bar reference. Without the test, however, you may waste days tracking down bugs that a simple unit test could have prevented.

Another concern for large projects is the total quantity of tests, and the increased number of test scenario paths through the system. As the number of tests increases, the longer it takes for regression and system testing cycles to run. The unit test focus of TDD is a faster alternative to functional tests. With functional tests, the test system becomes more complex. With a typical J2EE application, a functional test environment probably requires but is not limited to the following running processes:

- J2EE application server

- Database

- Mail server

With a TDD unit test approach, you can test pieces of the system individually. You can achieve reasonable coverage through selecting specific test combinations without causing the test suite to grow prohibitively.

The TDD process can be effectively applied to J2EE projects. I will show you how to do this by demonstrating step by step how to create a real J2EE application. The construction of this application will help show how TDD can be applied to real-world projects.

Some Misconceptions About Test-Driven Development

This introduction to TDD would not be complete unless we discussed some of the misconceptions about implementing the TDD process.

Some people may think that the process of creating unit tests may add time to the overall development cycle, but this is usually not the case. Like any other new technique, TDD has a learning curve, and this will initially add to the development time. Creating unit tests does take time. It will also take extra time to set up the testing framework itself. Some unit tests like those that test servlets and EJBs will require special test harnesses to be configured and maintained, and this is not always a simple job. The extra time spent creating unit tests and the testing framework should produce higher quality, better designed software with fewer bugs, which means you can deliver the software faster. Most schedules do not include the time and cost of the many changes and bug fixes that occur toward the end of a software project, so even though it may look like the project takes longer using TDD, the reality is that software is in a deliverable state faster when using TDD.

Also, as you get familiar with TDD, you will become better at it and produce the code faster than before. There have been no studies that I know of on the effect of TDD on the development time for a project, but from my experience, introducing TDD does not add any time to the development process. In fact, TDD can shorten the development process once all the benefits are realized.

Some people believe that using TDD makes the developer's focus too narrow and prevents the developer from seeing the big picture. While it is possible to make some invalid assumptions about the way the software should behave, thereby invalidating some of the unit tests, this is not a major problem. In fact, TDD provides the ability to constantly refactor the software as developers come to better understand the requirement of the software. So if some testing assumptions were made that led the development team down the wrong path, then those assumptions can be changed and the code refactored until it works correctly. Also, it's important to understand that TDD does not prevent up-front design when it is needed.

Summary

The purpose of this chapter was to introduce the theory of TDD and explain its basic concepts and benefits. TDD is more than a nice idea—it's a proven methodology that can be used to simplify the development environment and help developers produce better software. Of course, some things that sound good in theory are hard to put into practice. TDD is not that hard to put into practice, but it does take some new knowledge and experience to properly implement. The rest of this book will be dedicated to explaining how to use TDD on a real project. The example application presented throughout the following chapters will be a J2EE application, but most of the techniques presented could be used on any software project.

Chapter 2 will show you how to set up a TDD development environment. Chapters 3 through 6 will show how to use TDD to develop different parts of the example application. Chapters 7 and 8 will present some advanced material that will show you how to make the TDD process more efficient and also show you the best way to transition a project to using TDD. The book contains a lot of example code and a number of hands-on exercises. The example code will help give you the knowledge of how to implement TDD, and the hands-on exercises should give you the experience and confidence you need to start practicing TDD on your own projects.

CHAPTER 2

■ ■ ■

Getting Started

I once worked on a project that placed a low priority on process improvement. Everyone complained that building various components of the system took too long, and running regression tests took too long, but no one was willing to change the process. The most common excuse was, "Yes, we know that is a problem, but we are too busy to fix it right now." What amazed those of us working on this project most was the complete lack of value placed on the amount of time it took a developer to complete everyday development tasks.

Compiling and testing are tasks developers perform almost every single day—these tasks should be quick and painless. On this project, however, building just one jar file consisting of a few thousand source files took over 15 minutes. Running tests involved pulling specific versions of libraries from the CM system, reading directions on multiple web sites, and running five to ten different shell and Perl commands. Once the tests were finished, the developer had to manually decipher test failures hidden in text files with cryptic names. I don't even like to recall how long it took for developers on this project to run the tests.

After a little investigation, the team discovered the build mechanism for that "slow building" library was a poorly written collection of make files. The make files were written such that a separate javac process was forked to compile each source file in the entire library. A simple conversion from the make files to an Ant build file dropped the build time to under a minute. When we looked into the acceptance tests, we discovered the entire regression test suite consisted of functional tests. By converting the functional tests to unit tests, we were able cut regression tests that ran for hours down to less than a half hour.

As software engineers, we often deal with performance requirements and end-user acceptance requirements. Why should the development process be any different? Quite frankly, it shouldn't. Development projects should have realistic requirements for how long a build and test cycle should take. Metrics should be collected on a regular basis, so corrective action can be taken as soon as the build and test times exceed requirements.

Selecting the Right Tools

Chapter 1 gave a brief introduction to the philosophy and methodologies of TDD, but how does one go about implementing a TDD process? What do you need to practice TDD? The key to TDD is automating the code ➤ compile ➤ test process with the right set of tools! We've all heard the expression, "Use the right tool for the job." This expression definitely holds true for TDD. Without the right tools, implementing and maintaining a TDD process can be time consuming and painful. It's a standard practice for development teams to use common build scripts or make files for compiling source code. A good TDD process takes this practice a step further by implementing common scripts that combine the compile and test steps into a standard development process. So, what are the right tools?

First and foremost is the test framework itself. A test framework supplies a class hierarchy, convenience APIs, and a common language for writing and running repeatable tests. Development teams would probably end up implementing such a framework if they do not use one that is publicly available. Without such a framework, developers would have to re-create common test harnesses and utility classes just to run their own tests. Depending on the requirements of the application you are building, your test and development process may also require additional framework extensions to cover protocols such as HTTP.

The sample application built throughout the remainder of this book is a J2EE-based Football Pool application for automating your favorite office pool. It must run on multiple operating systems and multiple application servers. The application itself is described in more detail later in this chapter in the section "The Sample Application: J2EE Football Pool." For now, you only need to be concerned with how the type of application drives requirements for the TDD process. Since the application is a J2EE application, you know your development and test environment must include a J2SE SDK and a J2EE application server. Adding the application-specific elements to your process requirements of an automated code ➤ compile ➤ test process results in the following TDD requirements:

1. A Java test framework supporting common assertions

2. A cross-platform scripting tool to start/stop tests and dependent processes

3. A cross-platform mechanism for building and packaging Java source code

4. An integrated development environment (IDE) that supports refactoring

5. A J2EE application server

6. A J2SE SDK

Almost every development project goes through a tool analysis process to determine what tools are needed to develop the software. Unfortunately, spending a few chapters comparing tool choices for each of the preceding requirements would severely limit the amount of TDD material I could cover in this book. The following section lists some recommended tools for implementing the preceding TDD requirements. Each tool is briefly described along with a short explanation of why the tool was chosen for the given requirement. I will mention several alternative approaches related to some of these tools, with a sentence or two on why those approaches weren't used here.

Recommended Tools

Following the Keep It Simple, Stupid (KISS) and You Aren't Gonna Need It (YAGNI) rules of Extreme Programming (XP), each tool listed in the following sections fits into the TDD process by meeting one or more of the requirements in its simplest form. The following sections contain a brief description of each tool along with a URL where it can be found.

JUnit

JUnit (`http://www.junit.org`) is the primary test tool for satisfying the first requirement for a Java test framework. JUnit is the Java version of the xUnit architecture for unit and regression-testing frameworks. Written by Erich Gamma and Kent Beck, it's distributed as an open source project, includes the core test framework class hierarchy, and defines a common language for writing and running repeatable tests. JUnit uses reflection to examine the tests and code under tests. This allows JUnit to execute any method of any class and examine the results. With this framework, all developers on the project know how to write and execute tests, and interpret test results using the following nomenclature:

- `TestCase`: Abstract class for implementing a basic unit test

- `TestSuite`: Composite class for organizing and running groups of tests

- `Assertions`: For testing expected results (`assertNotNull(..)`, `assertEquals(..)`, `assertSame(..)`, etc.)

- `TestRunner`: Graphical and text-based test runners

- `Failure`: Indicates a checked test assertion failed (i.e., `assertNotNull(..)` returned false)

- `Error`: Indicates an unexpected exception or setup failure that stopped the test

JUnit is widely accepted as a standard for unit testing in Java. Many of the available testing products on the market are either based on or extend JUnit. Also, many IDEs currently have built-in support for JUnit. The majority of unit tests written in this book are JUnit tests.

JUnit framework will be discussed in more detail in Chapter 3.

HttpUnit

HttpUnit (`http://www.httpunit.org`), written by Russell Gold, is an open source Java library for black-box testing HTTP-based web applications and servlets. The library supports testing applications containing the following:

- Basic and form-based authentication

- State management with cookies

- JavaScript

- Automatic page redirection

HttpUnit easily integrates with JUnit for fast development of HTTP-based functional tests. In fact, using HttpUnit with JUnit allows you to write tests for web applications and entire web sites. HttpUnit provides methods that allow JUnit TestCases to examine returned HTML content as text, an XML DOM, or containers of forms, tables, and links, as well as provide a way to submit forms, press buttons, and follow links. It also contains a servlet test framework, ServletUnit, which can be used to help develop servlets.

ServletUnit will be discussed in more detail in Chapter 4, and HttpUnit will be discussed in further detail in Chapter 6.

Ant

You can meet requirements #2 and #3 (a cross-platform scripting tool to start/stop tests and dependent processes, and a cross-platform mechanism for building and packaging Java source code) by using Ant. Ant (http://ant.apache.org/index.html) is a cross-platform build and scripting tool. It was developed as a Java and XML-based open source project by the Apache Software Foundation. Similar to make, gnumake, and nmake files, Ant build files define project dependencies, class paths, and build targets. Unlike make, however, Ant is designed for Java with build scripts written as XML files, which can be validated with an XML editor. Also unlike make, Ant dependencies are simple dependencies and are not used to bring targets up to date like make does. Ant is written in Java and can easily be extended to create custom tasks whenever necessary. A default Ant install supports a number of Java-specific tasks (a task being like a command) plus many platform-independent file management tasks for automating the entire build process. Following is a brief list of some of the useful tasks available:

- Compile and run Java.

- Create, copy, delete, and move files and directories (with regular expression pattern matching).

- Create archive files (.jar, .war, .ear, .zip, etc.).

- Connect to Configuration Management systems (CVS, StarTeam, Visual SourceSafe, etc.).

- Run JUnit tests.

A key feature of Ant is its integration with the JUnit test framework listed previously. With Ant, you can run multiple sets of JUnit and HttpUnit tests, aggregate the test results, and publish HTML test reports for the entire process to a web server for immediate viewing by clients or management. Ant scripts control the build and test process for the majority of examples throughout this book.

You could make an argument for using a combination of Perl and make files to control the build process, but I see no reason to introduce two different tools to accomplish what Ant can do by itself. This is a Java project, staffed by Java developers. While Perl is a powerful programming language, and make has been used in software for decades, they are two additional specialized skill sets that are not required for this project. Remember that the development and test environment must be maintained over time just as are the product source and test code.

Refactoring IDE

All of the following IDEs meet requirement #4—an IDE that supports refactoring. This is not an exhaustive list, just a list of popular IDEs that you may be familiar with and meet our needs.

- *JDeveloper*: http://technet.oracle.com/software/products/jdev/content.html

- *IDEA*: http://www.intellij.com/idea

- *Eclipse*: http://www.eclipse.org

While Java development can certainly be accomplished with any text or Java source code editor, maintaining a large base of source code and the accompanying tests is easier to accomplish with an IDE that supports automated refactoring (see *Refactoring: Improving the Design of Existing Code*, by Martin Fowler et al. [Addison-Wesley, 1999]). One of the common arguments for writing tests is the amount of work required to create and maintain such tests. An IDE that supports refactoring gives developers the necessary tool to accomplish tasks that would otherwise be tedious and time consuming.

Take changing a method signature, for example. Assume that a change in requirements forces a change to the method signature in a common interface. If this method is used in over 100 lines in various source files, this change could take hours. With a refactoring IDE, this change is completed and tested in just minutes. All three IDEs listed previously have automated features for accomplishing common refactoring techniques such as the following:

- Extract method.

- Introduce variable.

- Rename/move package.

- Extract superclass.

- Change method signature.

The list of IDEs shown earlier is not intended to be all encompassing. There may be other IDEs on the market that support refactoring. The three listed are either open source or are available as a free trial download.

J2EE Application Server

Requirement #5 (the application server) is a development, testing, and production requirement. Since the sample application is a J2EE application, it must ultimately run on a J2EE application server. From a unit testing purist standpoint, the goal for developers should be to write all tests as unit tests, and limit tests that run on the application server to functional tests and end-user acceptance tests. The examples covered in this book will be tested on the JBoss application server.

The sample application should be capable of running on other J2EE application servers with few or no changes.

J2SE Java Development Kit

Requirement #6 is met by any 1.4.x version of the J2SE Java Development Kit, or JDK (http://java.sun.com/downloads). It goes without saying that Java development requires a JDK. It is listed here for completeness, and to avoid e-mails from angry first-time developers complaining that their build script fails to execute.

TDD Tool Summary

Why use these tools? Simply put, all of the examples throughout the remainder of this book are implemented and illustrated using the preceding tools. These tools are not absolutely required to practice TDD. The selection of tools does, however, prove that a development team can implement a TDD process in a cost effective and efficient manner. I would further argue that a typical development team would unnecessarily waste a huge chunk of development time building a fraction of the functionality provided by these tools in any attempt to implement a homegrown TDD solution. Why reinvent the wheel, when there is a perfectly good set of supported products to kick around for FREE?

Setting Up Your TDD Environment

In the preceding section, I provide the URLs of download locations and documentation for all of the recommended tools. For your convenience and to help speed up the initial setup process, a prepackaged archive of the TDD environment for the sample application is available for download on the book's companion website (http://www.apress.com/TDD). For complete instructions on how to download and run the code for this book, see Appendix A. Ant will be the main tool used to build and run the examples, so the next section provides a brief introduction to Ant in case you're not familiar with it.

A Quick Introduction to Ant

Writing and running an Ant build file is similar to writing and running a Perl, batch, or shell script. The major difference with Ant is that build files (scripts) are written in XML. The following build file is the ubiquitous "Hello World" example written as an Ant script:

```
<project name="HelloWorld" default="say-hello" basedir=".">
    <property name="hello.message"  value="Hello World"/>
    <target name="say-hello" depends="set-time">
        <echo message="${hello.message} today is a beautiful ${time.of.day}"/>
    </target>
    <target name="set-time">
        <tstamp>
            <format property="time.of.day" pattern="hh:mm aa " locale="en"/>
        </tstamp>
    </target>
</project>
```

Each build file contains one `project` element and at least one (default) `target` element. The preceding example build file defines the `project` "HelloWorld" with a default target named "say-hello" and a second target named "set-time". The project also defines a property (Ant's version of a variable) named "hello.message". The "say-hello" target contains one `task` element named echo. The echo task, believe it or not, echoes (prints out) the value in its `message` attribute. The "set-time" target contains the `tstamp` task, which is Ant's mechanism for creating date and time stamps. The result of the `tstamp` task is set in the property "time.of.day". The echo `message` attribute in the example contains the string

```
"${hello.message} today is a beautiful ${time.of.day}"
```

Ant uses a UNIX syntax style to represent the "value of" a variable. Referencing ${hello.message} results in the value "Hello World". The `message` attribute also contains a reference to the property ${time.of.day}, but "time.of.day" is not set in the target "say-hello".

If the property "time.of.day" is set in the target "set-time", will the "say-hello" target have access to this property? What does the echo task print at runtime? The answer lies in how the depends attribute of the target element works within Ant. The "say-hello" target is declared as follows:

```
<target name="say-hello" depends="set-time">
```

The depends attribute in Ant means "run the target(s) listed here first." Since depends="set-time", the "set-time" target gets run before the "say-hello" target, resulting in the following message being printed:

```
Hello World the time is: 11:01 PM
```

If the depends attribute was not set to "set-time", the output would have been

```
Hello World the time is: ${time.of.day}
```

The complete output from executing ant with no arguments or executing ant say-hello on this example build file results in the same message being printed out at runtime:

```
// no arguments - runs the default target in the build.xml file
<install-dir>/TDD/examples/ch2>ant
Buildfile: build.xml
set-time:
say-hello:      [echo] Hello World the time is: 11:12 PM
BUILD SUCCESSFUL
Total time: 1 second
// passing "say-hello" as the target argument
> ant say-hello  // runs the "say-hello" target in the build.xml file
Buildfile: build.xml
set-time:
say-hello:      [echo] Hello World the time is: 11:12 PM
BUILD SUCCESSFUL
Total time: 1 second
```

Two final important facts concerning Ant properties:

- *Properties are immutable:* Once a property is set, its value cannot be changed.

- *Properties are global:* Once a property is set in a project file, its value is accessible to all targets and tasks executing after the value is set.

Ant Summary

Comparing Ant to other programming or scripting languages, targets are similar to methods or functions. They get named by the author of the file, and contain one or more logic and/or command statements such as a condition or task that control the actual work executed within the target. Variables can be defined globally within a project, or within a target by property elements. A target is invoked directly or implicitly when running the ant shell from the command line. There are many features of Ant not covered in this basic introduction. Refer to the official Ant documentation on Ant's web site, http://ant.apache.org/manual/index.html, for additional information, or purchase a copy of *Java Development with Ant* by Erik Hatcher and Steve Loughran (Manning Publications, 2002) for a more thorough Ant education.

The Sample build.xml File

Now that you have a basic understanding of what an Ant script looks like and how it executes, it's time to review the build.xml script for the sample application. A compressed view of the samples build file shows the following targets:

```
<project name="tdd_build" default="test">
    <target name="init">
    <target name="clean">
    <target name="compile-tests" depends="compile-src">
    <target name="compile-src" depends="init">
    <target name="test" depends="compile-tests">
    <target name="all" depends="clean,test"/>
</project>
```

The default target is "test", which depends on "compile-tests", which in turn depends on "compile-src", which itself depends on "init". Therefore the execution order is

1. init

2. compile-src

3. compile-tests

4. test

You should see the same execution order of targets in the build output when the default Ant target is run:

```
<install-dir>/TDD>ant
Buildfile: build.xml
init:
compile-src:    [javac] Compiling 6 source files to
                                        <install-dir>/TDD\build\classes
compile-tests:  [javac] Compiling 1 source file to
                                        <install-dir>/TDD\build\testclasses
test:                   [junit] TEST tdd.TddTestSuite FAILED
BUILD FAILED
```

The compile steps should succeed, but the test and overall build should fail because you haven't yet implemented the functionality needed to make the test pass. What is important at this point is the simplicity and power of this little Ant script. A few Ant targets and dependency settings are the building blocks for this automated compile and test development process. The Ant targets define what gets run, and the dependencies control the order of execution. Setting the default target to "test" ensures that all tests get run every time the build file is executed. You have to manually run another target in the build file to bypass the execution of the tests.

The Sample Application: J2EE Football Pool

In this example, imagine you are a consultant working for AllBetsROff Software Inc. The company makes software for running football pools on the web. Your assignment is to develop a J2EE football pool. Just in case you have never heard of a football pool, it is a form of gambling whereby players pick which teams they think will win from a list of up to 16 scheduled games. Whoever picks the most number of games correctly wins the pool. One game, usually the Monday night football game, is marked as a tiebreaker, and players enter their best guess of the total points (each team's score added together) for the game. If two players tie with the same number of winning picks, the player closest to the total points of the game without going over wins the tiebreaker.

The Football Pool web application gives players access to the game schedules for the season, team records, and weekly and season rankings for all Football Pool players. Figure 2-1 shows the Football Pool conceptual model.

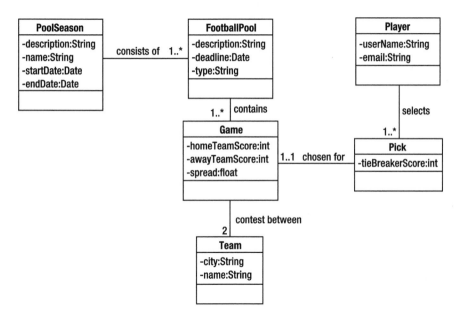

Figure 2-1. *Football Pool conceptual model*

One or more players are designated as administrators to manage the pool. The administrator opens and closes a pool for betting and posts game results. Players select a winner for each scheduled game in a pool. Players also guess the total score for the tiebreaker game. The winner of the pool is the one who picked the most winners, with any ties going to the person who has the best predicted total score in the tiebreaker. If by chance there is a tie in the tiebreaker score, the winner is the player who posted his or her picks to the system first. Or maybe you'll decide to implement a rule that no two players can submit the same tiebreaker score.

Use Cases

Now that you have a basic understanding of the application, let's create a set of use cases to better define the requirements. The football pool has two types of users: an administrator who runs the pool and players who make the picks. The use cases for each of these users is fairly easy to create from the description of the application. Figure 2-2 shows the list of use cases for the Football Pool application.

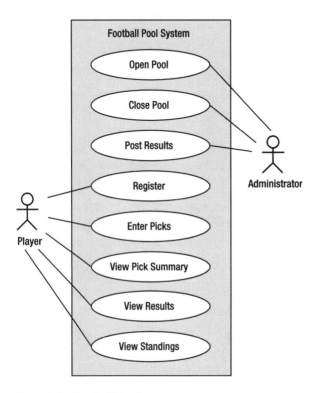

Figure 2-2. *Football Pool use cases*

Use Case 1: Player Registers Self

A player enters his or her desired user name, e-mail address, and password into the system. If the user name already exists, the player is prompted to pick another name. A player may register multiple user names with the same e-mail address. After entering a unique user name, the player receives an e-mail from the system at the e-mail address specified during registration containing a confirmation URL. Upon confirmation of the e-mail address, the user is successfully registered in the system.

Use Case 2: Administrator Opens Pool

The administrator enters the season and weekly pools, specifying the pool type, the pick deadline date and time, the home and away teams for each game, and the game date and time. He or she selects one game as the tiebreaker. Once the data is correct, the administrator opens the pool for betting. When the pool is opened, an e-mail is sent to registered players informing them of the latest available pool. Figure 2-3 shows the GUI used by the administrator to manage the football pool.

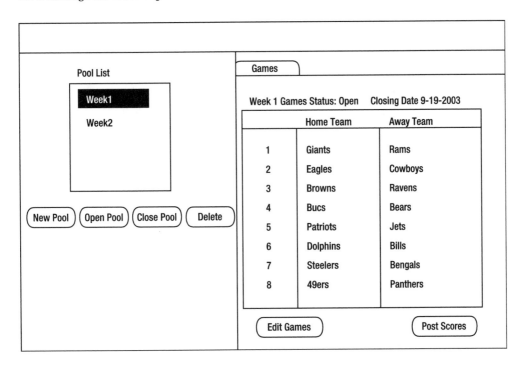

Figure 2-3. *Admin GUI mock-up*

The list on the left side shows the different weekly pools for the football pool. The right side shows the games for the week selected in the list. To add a new week to the football pool, the administrator clicks the New Pool button. This opens a dialog box (Figure 2-4) that allows the administrator to enter a name and closing date for the new pool as well as create a table of games for the week.

The administrator adds the individual games to the pool by selecting a game from the team list and clicking either the Add Home Team or Add Away Team button. This moves the team from the list to the corresponding column in the top row of the table. Once both the home and away teams are filled in for the top row of the table, a new empty row is inserted at the top of the table and the original row moves down. In this manner the Games table grows from the top down as home and away team pairs are added. The administrator is able to drag and drop a team from the team list to the Games table.

If the administrator wants to delete a game in the table he or she selects a row in the table and presses the Delete Game button. To set the tiebreaker game, the administrator selects a row in the Games table and clicks the Set Tie Break Game button. This places a bullet in the row of the tiebreaker game. Once the administrator has filled in all the information for the new pool, he or she clicks the OK button at the bottom of the dialog box to close it and return to the main GUI.

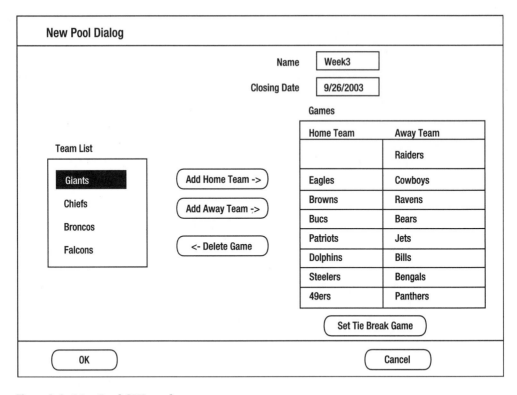

Figure 2-4. *New Pool GUI mock-up*

Once the new pool is added, it will appear in the pool list in the main GUI. The administrator will be able to select the pool from the list and be able to perform the following operations:

- Open the pool by clicking the Open Pool button.

- Edit the pool by opening the pool and clicking the Edit button. This will bring up a dialog box similar to the New Pool dialog box that will allow games of the pools to be modified.

- Close the pool by clicking the Close Pool button.

- Post game results by clicking the Post Scores button. This will bring up a dialog box that will allow the administrator to enter the scores for the games.

- Or delete the pool by clicking the Delete button.

Use Case 3: Administrator Closes Pool

After a pool is open, the administrator may close a pool at any time. A closed pool prevents new picks from being entered into the system or changes to existing picks in the system. When the pool is closed, an e-mail is sent to registered players informing them the pool is closed for new picks.

Use Case 4: Administrator Posts Results

After the pool is closed, the administrator enters actual scores for each of the games played. Once all scores have been entered, the administrator posts the results. When the results are published, an e-mail is sent to registered players containing the name of the winning player and a URL to the pool results.

Use Case 5: Player Enters Picks

After a pool is open, a player may sign on and enter picks predicting the winner of each game and the total score of the tiebreaker game. The players may change their picks until the pool is closed. Figure 2-5 shows an initial mock-up of the web page players will use to select picks.

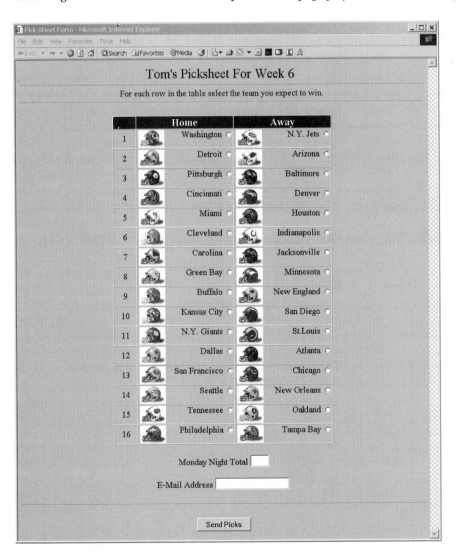

Figure 2-5. *Web page mock-up*

Use Case 6: Player Views Pick Summary

Once the pool has been closed by the administrator, the player will be able to sign on to the system and view a summary of all the picks that have been made by all of the players.

Use Case 7: Player Views Results

Once the results have been posted, players may examine their pick results. The system will indicate their winning and losing predictions and display each player's rank for the pool.

Use Case 8: Player Views Standings

When at least one set of results has been posted, a player may view the list of players ranked by the number of correct predictions. The list only includes players who have entered at least one pool for the current season. Players may also view the records for each team.

Use Case 9: Player Views Home Page

The Football Pool application will have a home page that will be customized for each user. It will show information about this week's pool, last week's winner, and statistics about how well the player did in previous weeks' pools. Figure 2-6 shows a mock-up of the home page.

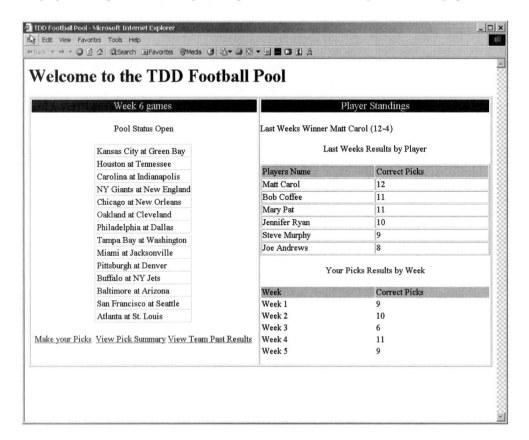

Figure 2-6. *Home page mock-up*

Summary

The purpose of this chapter was to introduce the tools needed to effectively perform TDD and also to introduce the requirements for the Football Pool application that will be used throughout the rest of the book. As described in the beginning of the chapter, taking the time to set up your development environment properly will make it easier to develop software. There are enough problems producing good software, so you don't want your development environment to get in the way.

Although TDD requires a few more tools to use than normal software development, it is worth the time to learn how to apply these tools because they will enhance the development experience and make it easier to produce better code in a more efficient manner. Chapter 3 will explain how to use the tools described in this chapter to start developing the Football Pool application.

CHAPTER 3

■ ■ ■

Unit Testing: The Foundation of Test-Driven Development

This chapter and the next three chapters will show you how to develop the Football Pool application using TDD. Each chapter will concentrate on a different aspect of the application, demonstrating along the way how the tools and TDD methodologies can be used to quickly and easily create a well-designed, high-quality application.

In order to organize this information in a logical manner, each chapter will contain topics on the following:

- *Use case analysis*: As tests and code are developed, I'll discuss what behavior is being implemented.

- *Test creation*: Once the behavior is explained, I'll show you how to create tests for the expected system behavior.

- *Code implementation*: After the tests are written, you'll see how to develop code to get the test to pass.

- *Ant automation*: As new classes and packages are created, I'll walk you through creating and modifying Ant scripts to automate the build test code cycle.

- *Refactoring*: After the tests and code are written, I'll discuss refactoring to help improve the quality of the tests and code.

- *Design patterns discussion*: After the refactoring discussion, I'll point out and discuss the design patterns that emerge.

In some chapters, these topics will be repeated several times as the application changes through the chapter. Each chapter will complete only a part of the application, and will contain a hands-on exercise that allows you to try and use TDD to complete part of the application. These exercises will enable you to implement another system behavior, following another design pattern, or modify the existing design to meet a change in the requirements. Complete answers to the exercises will be given in Appendix B so that you will be able to compare your results to a sample implementation.

The Role of Testing in Software Development

As discussed in Chapter 1, creating good software takes more than creating a good up-front design. If it was possible to create good software through good design, then most software wouldn't need multiple QA cycles, it would just work like a car coming off the assembly line.

But software does need multiple QA cycles to improve it to the point where it can be released. So the question is, If testing software is a good way to find bugs and improve it, why not test it as often as possible? Software testing does more than just check that the software meets the requirements; it often points out defects in the design or structure of the software that need to be fixed. This testing actually helps improve the software. Most developers realize this and try to test as they develop software. But what is the most effective way to test as you develop software?

The purpose of this chapter is to show you how to use simple unit tests to drive the development of software. But before I can do this, you have to understand the different types of tests that you can use to develop software. This will help you understand what unit testing is and where it fits in the process.

Manual Tests

The most common way that developers test is manually. Developers write some code that they believe should work, and then try it out. In some cases this is done by building a portion of the actual user interface, in other cases by writing a test rig that provides a fake interface—often via a series of command line programs. Such tests rely on the developer to recognize when the system response is correct and when it is not. The test rig may or may not be discarded once the code is checked in; in any case, it is difficult for other developers or testers to use the manual tests to verify the correctness of the code. Manual tests are mostly used to verify that the code just written works. The results are usually not repeatable, and there is usually little thought given to regression testing.

Functional Tests

To address the shortcomings of manual tests, developers and dedicated testers often write automated tests that work against the official supported application interface. In the case of a J2EE application, this means, of course, going through the standard J2EE APIs, talking to web applications via HTTP, EJBs through RMI, and so on. This kind of test is called a *functional test*.

Functional testing is also referred to as *black-box testing* because functional testing is only concerned with applying an input to the system and seeing what the resultant output is. Functional testing can tell you that the application is doing the right thing, but it does not give any detailed insight as to whether the individual modules are working correctly.

Functional tests have a clear advantage in that they make no assumptions about the internal structure of the application, and emulate fairly closely what a user would actually do to use the system. They are in effect the automation of a manual test. This makes regression testing feasible, as anyone can rerun the tests, and they can be accumulated into suites.

The problem with functional tests is that they require a lot of time and overhead to run. Every time you make a change to a J2EE application, you have to deploy the new code to the server. To run the functional test, you need to have a full production environment with all the associated databases, message queues, etc. This is not always possible, especially early in the development phase. Also, it can be hard to simulate some of the error conditions that need to be tested. Therefore, although functional testing is better than manual testing, the overhead associated with it will make it hard to run on a regular basis.

In-Container Tests

Application servers typically provide an environment, or *container*, in which small user-written program components can run, interact with users through well-defined interfaces, and also interact with each other. You can design a component so that it actually runs tests against other components in the same container. Such tests are called *in-container tests*. Like functional tests, in-container tests require a running server. Unlike functional tests, in-container tests let you write your tests directly against the API of the code you want to validate, without the need to go through all of the associated I/O or other protocols. You still have to start up and shut down the server between code updates, but the tests themselves can be much faster and lighter weight. You also have a fair bit more flexibility in controlling the environment for your tests, so you can simulate some error conditions without excessive difficulty.

In-container tests may let you do a lot that would otherwise be difficult; however, there are many parts of the environment that you still cannot control, you still require a good copy of the production environment, and the startup time can make it inconvenient to run fast code-compile-test cycles. These tests are easier to run than functional tests, but still require too much overhead to run very often.

Unit Tests

It would be nice if it were possible to test individual parts or *units* of software as they are written to make sure that they work as expected without the overhead required to run functional or in-container tests. This is what unit testing is. Unit testing allows you to test your code at the API level. Unit tests are written from the developer's point of view as opposed to functional tests, which are written from the user point of view. This allows you to fully test all parts of an individual unit of code in isolation. Unit testing usually involves setting up some kind of test framework. Although the test framework may take a little time to set up, once it is set up it becomes easy for you to start practicing the build a little, test a little philosophy.

An interesting thing happens when developers start writing unit tests. Because unit testing is relatively easy to run, developers run tests more often, which leads to quicker detection of problems with the software. In fact, once there is a good set of unit tests in the software, these tests are usually run after the nightly builds to ensure that the code that was checked in that day didn't break anything. This is good because it provides instant feedback as to the state of the code and allows you to fix bugs as they occur instead of waiting until the next QA cycle. Clearly, unit testing is a good way to add more testing to the software process.

As you get better at writing unit tests, you will not only write tests that test the normal operation of the software, but also start adding tests for boundary conditions such as what happens if an input parameter is zero. This leads to discovery of bugs that point out problems with the structure and design of the code. This forces you to change the structure of the software to make it better, hence improving the design. Another nice benefit of unit testing is that if you know that all the code you write will have to be unit tested, you will tend to structure your code so that it is easier to test. This usually leads to cleaner, more modular code, which again shows that testing can not only help find bugs but also actually be used to improve design.

Reconsidering the Role of Testing in Software Development

Testing is usually an afterthought in the development process, but as you have seen, testing is an important part of software development. Testing can be used not only to find bugs but also to point out errors in the structure and design of the software. If testing can help you determine how well the software is designed, can it be used to drive the design of the software? The answer is yes, and this is the basic idea behind the Test-Driven Development philosophy.

Driving Development with a Simple Unit Test

Now that you have your development environment set up, your high-level architecture defined, and a set of use cases created, how do you get started? There are many different places you could start. Let's start by examining Use Case 2 (Administrator Opens Pool), defined in Chapter 2, as it sets up the data needed for everything else. Use Case 2 says

> *The administrator enters the season and weekly pools, and the home and away teams for each game. He or she selects one game as the tiebreaker. Once the data is correct, the administrator opens the pool for betting.*

You can look at this use case from a number of different angles, depending on which layer of the architecture you are working on. If you are working on the client tier, then this use case helps define the functions of the administrator interface. If you are working on the business tier, then this use case helps define the structure of the football pool. Let's start at the business tier and combine this use case with the initial data model. From that, we can infer the following behaviors. We need a way to

- Specify a list of games, each consisting of a home team and an away team.

- Select a tiebreaker game.

- Verify the data.

- Open the pool.

Let's start with the first behavior and decide how to test it (remember that you want to write the test first). The test will be written as a JUnit test. If you are not familiar with JUnit, see the sidebar "JUnit Overview" for a quick primer. For now, let's ignore user interface issues, and treat the data model as descriptive, rather than prescriptive.

```java
public void testPoolCreate() throws Exception {
FootballPool pool = new FootballPool("9/07/2003");
    pool.addGame("New York Jets", "Miami Dolphins" );
    pool.addGame("San Francisco 49ers","New York Giants"  );
    assertEquals( "Game 1 away team", "Miami Dolphins", pool.getHomeTeam(0) );
    assertEquals( "Game 2 away team", "New York Giants", pool.getHomeTeam(1) );
    assertEquals( "Game 1 home team", "New York Jets", pool.getAwayTeam(0) );
    assertEquals( "Game 2 home team", "San Francisco 49ers", pool.getAwayTeam(1) );
}
```

JUNIT OVERVIEW

As described in Chapter 2, JUnit is the Java version of the xUnit architecture for unit and regression testing. To get you started, here is a simple example that explains how JUnit works. The code shown here tests a few methods of the Java String class:

```java
import junit.framework.*;
public class StringTester extends TestCase  {
  String testStr1;
  String testStr2;

  public StringTester(String name)  {
     super(name);
  }

  protected void setUp()  {
     testStr1 = "unit testing";
     testStr2 = " isn't that hard";
  }
  public void testLength()  {
     int length = testStr1.length();
     assertEquals(11,length);
  }
  public void testSubString()  {
     String subStr = testStr1.substring(5);
     assertEquals("testing", subStr);
  }
  public void testConcat()  {
     String newStr = testStr1.concat(testStr2);
     assertEquals("unit testing isn't that hard", newStr);
  }

  public static Test suite()  {
    TestSuite suite= new TestSuite(StringTester.class);
     return suite;
  }

  public static final void main(String[] args)  {
     junit.textui.TestRunner.run(suite());
  }
}
```

The class, called StringTester, is a subclass of JUnit's TestCase class. The constructor has one argument, name. This argument will be the name of the unit test being run and will be used in any messages displayed by JUnit. The next method in the listing, setUp(), is used to initialize a couple of strings. The next three methods (testLength(), testSubString(), and testConcat()) are the actual tests. The test methods must be no-argument methods that test a specific condition using one of JUnit's assert methods.

If the conditions of the assert are true, then JUnit marks the test as passed; otherwise, the test is marked as failed.

The `suite()` method is used by JUnit to create a collection of tests. There are two ways to create a suite. The first is to create an instance of the `TestSuite` and then add the individual tests to the suite. The other is to create an instance of `TestSuite` by passing in the test class in the constructor. This creates a suite containing all the methods in the test class that start with the word "test". This is the preferred way to create a suite, since it is simpler and helps prevent accidental omission of tests.

The class has a main method that can be used to run the unit tests. The main method calls the `junit.textui.TestRunner.run` method to run all the tests of the suite. The main method is not required, but it is useful if the unit tests are going to be run by a batch file. The JUnit test can also be run through the JUnit GUI. For complete updated information about JUnit, check out its web site at `http://www.junit.org`.

Note the test helps you make some simplifying design decisions here:

- Games are treated as an ordered list.

- The pool will be uniquely identified by a date. This date is the Sunday that most of the games will be played.

- Teams are treated as a string representing the team name.

- You can tell the number of games in the pool.

- You can retrieve the name of the home or away team for any game in the pool.

If we were to now try to compile this test, it would of course fail miserably, since we haven't yet written the code! That's fine. It drives us to write a skeleton for the new class:

```
public class FootballPool {
    public FootballPool(String date) {}
    public void addGame( String awayTeam, String homeTeam ) {}
    public int size() { return 0; }
    public String getHomeTeam( int gameNum ) { return ""; }
    public String getAwayTeam( int gameNum ) { return ""; }
}
```

Note that we do not specify anything that was not required by the test. We can now compile and run our test, which should fail, thus telling us that we need to implement something. The test is driving us, as planned. Before we implement the behavior this test calls for, we need to make a decision. There are a few obvious implementation possibilities: we could create parallel lists for the home and away teams or create a new class to represent a game and maintain a single list of games. Either will allow us to pass the test, and, of course, we can always change our minds later.

So let's add a new class to represent a game as follows:

```
Class Game {
    private String _homeTeam;
    private String _awayTeam;

    Game( String awayTeam, String homeTeam ) {
        _homeTeam = homeTeam;
        _awayTeam = awayTeam;
    }

    String getHomeTeam() { return _homeTeam; }
    String getAwayTeam() { return _awayTeam; }
}
```

This lets us begin to make the tests pass. First, since the size check fails, we add the following:

```
private Vector gameList = new Vector();

public void addGame( String awayTeam, String homeTeam ) {
    gameList.addElement(new Game(awayTeam, homeTeam));
}

public int size() { return gameList.size(); }
```

The size check now passes, but the retrieval of home team fails, so we add

```
public String getHomeTeam( int gameNum ) {
    Game game = (Game)gameList.elementAt(i);
    return game.getHomeTeam();
}
```

This gets us to the final assertion, which we fix similarly.

```
public String getAwayTeam( int gameNum ) {
    Game game = (Game)gameList.elementAt(i);
    return game.getAwayTeam();
}
```

To review: we selected an expected behavior of the system, wrote a test that expressed that expectation, and then wrote *just enough code* to make the test pass. We did not deliberately leave "hooks" for features that we expect to add later. It is not necessary and it wastes time.

Having checked off the first behavior from the list, we'll next move on to the specification of a tiebreaker game. Expecting that our user interface will refer to the games consistently by their index in the pool, we can use basically a simple setter; however, we want to make sure that the game specified really exists, so we want the setter to throw an exception if it does not. We state that by the following test:

```
public void testTiebreakerSelect() throws Exception {
    FootballPool pool = new FootballPool("9/7/2003");
    pool.addGame( "Jets", "Falcons" );
    pool.addGame( "Giants", "49ers" );
    pool.setTiebreakerGame( 1 );

    try {
        pool.setTiebreakerGame( 3 );
        fail( "Permitted selection of non-existent game as the tiebreaker" );
    catch (NoSuchGameException e) {}
}
```

This test begins much as the first one did, by adding some games to the pool. It then tries to set the tiebreaker game twice: once to a good value and once to a bad value. Note that when you expect a test statement to throw an exception, you follow it with a call to Assert.fail (inherited by your test case), which will only be reached if no exception is thrown. You then catch the expected exception.

As before, once the test is written, we have to make it compile by adding the skeleton code to our class:

```
public void setTiebreakerGame( int num ) {}
```

We also have to create the appropriate exception class. Although this allows us to run both of our tests and confirm that the original still works, the new one fails (no exception is thrown from the attempt to set a bad game number). Armed with a failing test, we make it work by implementing the method properly:

```
public void setTiebreakerGame( int num ) throws NoSuchGameException {
    if((num < 0) || (num > gameList.size()) ){
        throw(new NoSuchGameException());
    }
    _tieBreakerGame = num;
}
```

The last behavior that we have to implement for this use case is to add the ability to set the status of the pool to "Open". So we write the following test:

```
public void testSetPoolToOpen() {
    FootballPool pool = new FootballPool("9/07/2003");
    pool.addGame("Jets", "Dolphins");
    pool.addGame("49ers","Giants");
    pool.openPool();
    assertEquals("Open", pool.getStatus());
}
```

which just creates a pool, calls the openPool() method, then uses the getStatus() to make sure the openPool() method was successful. We then add the following code to the FootballPool class to get the test to pass:

```
public void openPool(){
      m_status = "Open";
   }

   public String getStatus() {
      return(m_status);
   }
```

The basic techniques I have shown to implement this use case can be used to handle all kinds of situations, and in many cases are all that is needed. Once you have built a set of classes, you can build other classes that depend on them and slowly, step-by-step, build up your system.

Automating the Test ➤ Code ➤ Build Cycle

As you continue to write more tests and code, you want to automate the compilation of the code and the running of the tests. You want to make this as easy as possible since you will need to run the tests on a continual basis to develop your code.

There are a couple of ways that you can choose to automate the test ➤ code ➤ build cycle. One way to do it is to rely on your favorite IDE. Most IDEs have support for running JUnit tests, so it is fairly easy to create and run the tests from inside the IDE as you are developing the code. Although this is convenient for the person developing the tests and code, it makes it hard for other developers to run the tests on a regular basis, since it requires that they add new tests created by other developers to their own IDE environment. A better way would be to have a centralized script that all developers could use to run all the unit tests developed by all developers. This way, as new tests are created, the developer who created the scripts would add them to the centralized script. This can easily be done with Ant, but before we create the Ant script for our football pool application, we should first create a test suite.

A TestSuite is a JUnit class that is used to run multiple test cases. Although we only have one test case at the moment (FootBallPoolTester), we will soon be adding more, and in order to be able to run all the test cases from a single point, we are going to create a test suite. A test suite is easy to create. Let's create a test suite that will run our current test case (see Listing 3-1).

Listing 3-1. *Test Suite for the Unit Tests*

```
public class Ch3TestSuite extends TestSuite {
    public Ch3TestSuite(){
    }

    public static Test suite(){
        TestSuite suite = new TestSuite();
        suite.addTestSuite(FootBallPoolTester.class);
        return suite;
    }

    public static final void main(String[] args){
        junit.textui.TestRunner.run(suite());
    }
}
```

There is really nothing to this test suite class; it only contains one method, suite(), which is used to create a list of tests to run. There are two ways to add tests to the suite. In this case, we are using the addTestSuite() method to add all the tests from the FootBallPoolTester class to the suite. It is also possible to add individual tests to the suite by using the addTest() method of the TestSuite class as follows:

```
suite.addTest(new FootBallPoolTester("testSetPoolToOpen"));
```

For the moment we only have one test case, the FootBallPoolTester, so running the test suite is the same as running the FootBallPoolTester; however, as we add more test cases, they will be added to the test suite so that we can use it to run all the tests that we have created. Large projects usually have more than one test suite: one test suite for the entire project as well as a test suite per package. This allows developers to focus on testing each of the packages of the project separately if needed.

Now that we have the test suite, we can create the Ant script that can be used to run the tests. For our project, we already have an Ant script that is used to compile the code and create a jar file; all we have to do is to add a couple of tasks to the build file to be able to run the tests. The first test we need to add is a JUnit task as shown in Listing 3-2.

Listing 3-2. *Ant Task to Run Test Suite*

```
<target name="run-all-tests" depends="jar, jartest">
    <junit printsummary="yes">
        <classpath>
            <fileset dir="${dependencies.dir}">
                <include name="**/*.jar"/>
            </fileset>
            <fileset dir="${dist.dir}/lib">
                <include name="**/*.jar"/>
            </fileset>
        </classpath>
        <formatter type="xml"/>
        <test name="com.apress.tddbook.Ch3TestSuite" todir="${testdata.dir}"/>
    </junit>
</target>
```

The JUnit task is an option task that is built into Ant. Make sure you have your class path set up properly in order to run this task. See the Ant documentation for the full details on this task.

What this task does is to run the test specified by the test tag (com.apress.tddbook.Ch3TestSuite) and writes the results of the test to the directory defined by the todir tag. The results are formatted as an XML file as defined by the formatter tag, but they can also be formatted as plain text. If you run this task, you will see the following output:

```
TddBook>ant -buildfile ch3-build.xml run-all-tests
Buildfile: ch3-build.xml

prepare:

compile:
```

```
[javac] Compiling 7 source files to
                          C:\Java\Projects\TddBook\build\Chapter3\classes
[javac] This version of java does not support the
                          classic compiler; upgrading to modern

jar:
    [jar] Building jar: C:\Java\Projects\TddBook\dist\lib\Ch3.jar

test-compile:
    [javac] Compiling 9 source files to
                    C:\Java\Projects\TddBook\build\Chapter3\test-classes
    [javac] This version of java does not support the classic compiler;
                          upgrading to modern

jartest:
    [jar] Building jar: C:\Java\Projects\TddBook\dist\lib\Ch3Test.jar

run-all-tests:
    [junit] Running com.apress.tddbook.Ch3TestSuite
    [junit] Tests run: 3, Failures: 0, Errors: 0, Time elapsed: 0.27 sec


BUILD SUCCESSFUL
```

This task first compiles the source files, and then creates the Ch3.jar file. The next thing that is done is that all the test classes are compiled and put into the Ch3Test.jar file. Once the source code jar and test jar are built, then the tests are run and the results printed out. As you can see, the task is easy to run and produces immediate feedback as to the state of the code. If a test had failed, you could look into the output file that was created by the task to see what the cause of the failure was. You can also use the output file generated by this task to generate a report that can be viewed as a series of web pages. This report is trivial at this point in the project, but as the number of test cases and test suites grow, this report can be useful. To generate the report, you have to add another Ant task to the build file as shown in Listing 3-3.

Listing 3-3. *Ant Task to Generate Unit Test Report*

```
<target name="unit-test-report" depends="run-all-tests">
      <junitreport todir="${testdata.dir}">
          <fileset dir="${testdata.dir}">
              <include name="TEST-*.xml"/>
          </fileset>
          <report todir="${testdata.dir}"/>
      </junitreport>
</target>
```

What this task will do is generate a series of web pages that will be put into the directory specified by the report tag. Figure 3-1 shows the main page of the report. At the moment, it's not a very exciting report, but as more test cases and test suites are added, it will become more interesting.

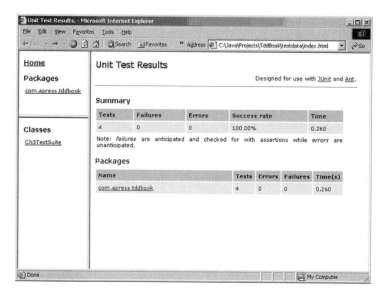

Figure 3-1. *Main page of the unit test report generated by the Ant task*

One other task we may want to add to the Ant script is the ability to run just the FootBallPoolTester set of tests. This way, if we are working on adding functionality to the FootballPool class, we will be able to just run FootBallPoolTester instead of the entire suite of tests. To do this, we simply add the task shown in Listing 3-4.

Listing 3-4. *Ant Task to Run Individual Set of Unit Tests*

```
<target name="run-footballpool-tests" depends="jar, jartest">
    <junit printsummary="yes">
        <classpath>
            <fileset dir="${dependencies.dir}">
                <include name="**/*.jar"/>
            </fileset>
            <fileset dir="${dist.dir}/lib">
                <include name="**/*.jar"/>
            </fileset>
        </classpath>
        <formatter type="xml"/>
        <test name="com.apress.tddbook.FootBallPoolTester"
        todir="${testdata.dir}"/>
    </junit>
</target>
```

The only thing different than the run-all-tests task is the argument in the test tag.

Now we have an Ant script that can not only compile the code for the project but also run some or all of our unit tests in one easy step. This will make it easier to run regression testing and continue our development.

Developing Around Dependencies

As we continue developing the Football Pool application, there are going to be times when the test and code we develop may depend on other classes that have not yet been developed. There will also be times when using the real classes for our tests will require so many resources or so much overhead as to make our tests slow or hard to run. Since we want to make the writing and running of tests easy and efficient, we need some way to simulate these dependent classes as we continue our development.

So far we have implemented most of Use Case 2 from a business tier point of view. The result of this implementation was the development of the `FootballPool` class that is used to store a list of games for a particular week of play. The next step in our development is to implement part of Use Case 5 (Player Enters Picks) from the business tier point of view. Use Case 5 says

> *After a pool is open, a player may sign on and enter picks predicting the winner of each game and the total score of the tiebreaker game. The players may change their picks until the pool is closed.*

From this use case, we can infer a number of behaviors. We need a way to

- Provide a way for a player to sign in to the football pool and be identified.

- Get the list of games from the football pool that is currently open.

- Store the player's picks for a particular football pool.

- Allow players to view and edit their picks for a particular football pool.

We are going to ignore the first behavior for the moment because the client tier will more than likely be responsible for authenticating the user. We assume that the user will be identified by a unique user name. So let's start with the implementation of the second behavior, getting a list of games from the currently open football pool. As always, we start by writing a test (see Listing 3-5).

Listing 3-5. *Test for Getting the Currently Open Pool*

```
public void testGetOpenPoolGameList() {
        PoolData poolData = new PoolData();
        FootballPool pool = poolData.getOpenPool();
        assertEquals("Kansas City",pool.getAwayTeam(0));
        assertEquals("Green Bay",pool.getHomeTeam(0));
        assertEquals("Houston",pool.getAwayTeam(1));
        assertEquals("Tennessee",pool.getHomeTeam(1));
        assertEquals("Carolina",pool.getAwayTeam(2));
        assertEquals("Indianapolis",pool.getHomeTeam(2));
        assertEquals("NY Giants",pool.getAwayTeam(3));
        assertEquals("New England",pool.getHomeTeam(3));
        assertEquals("Chicago",pool.getAwayTeam(4));
```

```
        assertEquals("New Orleans",pool.getHomeTeam(4));
        assertEquals("Oakland",pool.getAwayTeam(5));
        assertEquals("Cleveland",pool.getHomeTeam(5));
        assertEquals("Philadelphia",pool.getAwayTeam(6));
        assertEquals("Dallas",pool.getHomeTeam(6));
        assertEquals("Tampa Bay",pool.getAwayTeam(7));
        assertEquals("Washington",pool.getHomeTeam(7));
        assertEquals("Miami",pool.getAwayTeam(8));
        assertEquals("Jacksonville",pool.getHomeTeam(8));
        assertEquals("Pittsburgh",pool.getAwayTeam(9));
        assertEquals("Denver",pool.getHomeTeam(9));
        assertEquals("Buffalo",pool.getAwayTeam(10));
        assertEquals("NY Jets",pool.getHomeTeam(10));
        assertEquals("Baltimore",pool.getAwayTeam(11));
        assertEquals("Arizona",pool.getHomeTeam(11));
        assertEquals("San Francisco",pool.getAwayTeam(12));
        assertEquals("Seattle",pool.getHomeTeam(12));
        assertEquals("Atlanta",pool.getAwayTeam(13));
        assertEquals("St. Louis",pool.getHomeTeam(13));
    }
```

This test simply gets the currently open football pool from the PoolData class and checks to make sure it contains the correct games. It doesn't compile at the moment because the PoolData class doesn't yet exist, so let's stub it out.

```
public class PoolData
{
    public FootballPool getOpenPool() {
        FootballPool fbPool = null;
        return(fbPool);
    }
}
```

This gets our test to compile and run, but it fails the test. Now we have to add some code to get the test to pass. The PoolData class is meant to be the central class that is used to read, update, and delete data from the football pool. This class will have to somehow interact with the data store that is used to store the data. In this case, the data store will be a database.

To get the getOpenPool() method to work, we could just make some SQL calls from the method and then use the result set to create the FootballPool object, but there are a couple of problems with this approach. The first problem is the database has not yet been designed and doesn't exist. We could stop the development for a moment and design and create a database to use for development, but this would be a bad idea. The trouble is that it would be hard to design a database at the moment since we haven't yet decided how to arrange all the data into database tables, and we probably don't even know exactly all the types of data that we need to store. Any database we design now will need to be continually changed as we discover new data that needs to be added to it. This will add a lot of overhead to the development environment, since this database will have to be continually updated, which is not the TDD way.

Using TDD means keeping the tests as easy to run as possible, and this means isolating each test as much as possible from dependent classes. Therefore, we need to isolate the PoolData class from the database as much as possible. The best way to do this is to hide the database-specific calls from the PoolData class. This way, the PoolData class just contains the logic that validates the data going to and from the database. To isolate the database-specific calls from the PoolData class, we will create an interface for these calls to allow us to have multiple implementations for the database calls. We can have one implementation for our development that will make it easy to run our tests, and another one for production that will use the real database. Let's update the getOpenPool() method using the new interface (see Listing 3-6).

Listing 3-6. *PoolData Class*

```
public class PoolData
{
    /** handle to the database access methods */
    PoolDatabase _poolDB;
    public PoolData() {

    }
    public FootballPool getOpenPool() {
        FootballPool fbPool = null;
        Vector poolList = _poolDB.getPoolWithStatus("Open");
        if(poolList.size() == 1) {
            fbPool = (FootballPool)poolList.elementAt(0);
        }
        return(fbPool);
    }

    public PoolDatabase get_poolDB(){
        return _poolDB;
    }

    public void set_poolDB(PoolDatabase _poolDB){
        this._poolDB = _poolDB;
    }
}
```

If you look at the updated PoolData class, you will see that it now has a private variable, _poolDB of type PoolDatabase, that is used to access the database-specific calls. Since we are going to have multiple implementations for this class, we provide a setter method so the implementation can be set programmatically. The PoolDatabase interface is defined as follows:

```
public interface PoolDatabase {
    public Vector getPoolWithStatus(String status);
}
```

We still have to do one more thing to get our test to work, and that is to implement the PoolDatabase class. Since we don't want to take the time or overhead to create a real database, we are going to have to simulate access to the database in order to make our test work. There are two basic types of objects we can use to simulate our PoolDatabase implementation: a *stub* or a *mock object*.

Testing with Stubs

A *stub* is a class that looks like the production class but does not contain the full functionality of the production class. It only works for a limited set of criteria and is used only during development. For example, if we wanted to use a stub to implement our PoolDatabase interface, we could write the stub class shown in Listing 3-7.

Listing 3-7. *PoolDatabaseStub Class*

```java
public class PoolDatabaseStub implements PoolDatabase {
    public Vector getPoolWithStatus(String status) {
        Vector poolList = new Vector();
        FootballPool pool = new FootballPool("9/17/2003");
        pool.addGame("Kansas City", "Green Bay");
        pool.addGame("Houston", "Tennessee");
        pool.addGame("Carolina", "Indianapolis");
        pool.addGame("NY Giants", "New England");
        pool.addGame("Chicago", "New Orleans");
        pool.addGame("Oakland", "Cleveland");
        pool.addGame("Philadelphia", "Dallas");
        pool.addGame("Tampa Bay", "Washington");
        pool.addGame("Miami", "Jacksonville");
        pool.addGame("Pittsburgh", "Denver");
        pool.addGame("Buffalo", "NY Jets");
        pool.addGame("Baltimore", "Arizona");
        pool.addGame("San Francisco", "Seattle");
        pool.addGame("Atlanta", "St. Louis");
        poolList.addElement(pool);
        return (poolList);
    }
}
```

The problem with stubs is that they are hard to maintain. The PoolDatabaseStub class will allow our test to pass, but the next test we write will probably require us to modify the stub. Also, if a stub becomes complex, it may be hard to determine if a regression test is failing because of an error in the code undergoing the test or an error in the stub. Stubs are useful in some situations where the code being tested has many interactions with the dependent class. Chapter 6 will use a stub class to help develop the Admin GUI in isolation. For our `PoolDatabase` class, however, there is an easier way to simulate the required behavior using mock objects.

Testing with Mock Objects

The idea of mock objects came out of the Extreme Programming practice of trying to make writing unit tests as simple and easy as possible. Tim Mackinnon, Steve Freeman, and Philip Craig gave the first presentation on mock objects at the XP2000 conference. A copy of their paper is available at `http://www.connextra.com/aboutUs/mockobjects.pdf`. Mock objects are similar to stubs in that they can be used to simulate the functionality of a production class. They overcome some of the problems and limitations of stubs by allowing developers to define very fine-grain dependent objects needed for a test to pass from within the test code.

Unlike stubs, you don't create a class to simulate the dependent class you need. You usually use a mock object framework that allows you to specify the behavior of the dependent class through an API. The API usually allows you to define the methods of the dependent class and the behavior of each of the methods in a simple a straightforward way. Since mock objects are defined in the test code, this means that the behavior of a particular method can be different for each test. This is different from implementing a stub because the stub method cannot be changed for each test but must be written so it works for all tests all the time. A few well-established mock objects frameworks are available to use. Check out `http://www.mockobjects.com` for a complete list of available frameworks as well as more information on mock objects.

Although different frameworks exist for creating mock objects, the way that they are used in testing follows this pattern:

1. Create an instance of a mock object.

2. Set the state of the mock object.

3. Set expected behavior for the mock object.

4. Use the mock object as a parameter in the test.

5. At the end of the test, verify the mock object was used correctly.

To demonstrate how to use mock objects, I'll show you how to implement the `PoolDatabase` using the EasyMock framework. (See the sidebar "Using EasyMock" for a quick explanation of EasyMock.)

USING EASYMOCK

EasyMock is a mock object framework that can be used to generate mock objects dynamically at runtime from an interface class. It requires Java 1.3.1 or higher to run. You specify the behavior expected by actually calling the methods yourself, passing in the desired parameters. The first step in using EasyMock is creating a control object for the mock from the *interface* class as follows:

```
MockControl control = MockControl.createStrictControl( interface.class );
```

You then create the mock object itself with the getMock() method. This creates an implementation of the interface that is used to create the control.

```
interfaceImpl mockImpl = (interface) control.getMock();
```

The getMock() call creates a dynamic proxy associated with the control that implements the desired interface. This object starts in programmable mode in which any call is permitted and is remembered. The programmable mode is used to train the new mock object so that when its methods are called, it knows how to respond. To train a mock object, you simply call one of the methods yourself now in the same way it would be called in the test:

```
mockImpl.method1("Hello");
```

This specifies that you expect this method1 to be called with a value of "Hello" as its only parameter. If this method returns a value, then you can set the return value as follows:

```
control.setReturnValue("How are you");
```

If this method does not return a value, you do not need to do anything else.

Once you have trained all of the methods of the mock object, you need to turn the mock object on using the replay() method.

```
control.replay();
```

At this point, the mock object is ready to be used by the test and should act like a real object as long as its methods are called with the values that were used in the training mode; any calls other than those expected will result in a test failure. When you are all done, you call

```
control.verify();
```

The verify() method will report a failure if any of the expected methods were not called. For more information, see the documentation at http://www.easymock.org/Documentation.html.

Using the EasyMock framework, we can rewrite our test as shown in Listing 3-8 (**changes in bold**).

Listing 3-8. *Get Open Pool Test Using Mock Objects*

```
public void testGetOpenPoolGameList() {
        //Get mock object
        PoolDatabase mockPoolDB = (PoolDatabase)poolDBMockcontrol.getMock();
```

```
//Train the mock object
mockPoolDB.getPoolWithStatus("Open");
//Create return value for mock method
Vector mockPoolList = createFbPoolList();
poolDBMockcontrol.setReturnValue(mockPoolList);
//Training over. Set the mock to replay trained behavior when called
poolDBMockcontrol.replay();
PoolData poolData = new PoolData();
//Set PoolDB to mock Object
poolData.set_poolDB(mockPoolDB);
FootballPool pool = poolData.getOpenPool();
assertEquals("Kansas City",pool.getAwayTeam(0));
assertEquals("Green Bay",pool.getHomeTeam(0));
assertEquals("Houston",pool.getAwayTeam(1));
assertEquals("Tennessee",pool.getHomeTeam(1));
assertEquals("Carolina",pool.getAwayTeam(2));
assertEquals("Indianapolis",pool.getHomeTeam(2));
assertEquals("NY Giants",pool.getAwayTeam(3));
assertEquals("New England",pool.getHomeTeam(3));
assertEquals("Chicago",pool.getAwayTeam(4));
assertEquals("New Orleans",pool.getHomeTeam(4));
assertEquals("Oakland",pool.getAwayTeam(5));
assertEquals("Cleveland",pool.getHomeTeam(5));
assertEquals("Philadelphia",pool.getAwayTeam(6));
assertEquals("Dallas",pool.getHomeTeam(6));
assertEquals("Tampa Bay",pool.getAwayTeam(7));
assertEquals("Washington",pool.getHomeTeam(7));
assertEquals("Miami",pool.getAwayTeam(8));
assertEquals("Jacksonville",pool.getHomeTeam(8));
assertEquals("Pittsburgh",pool.getAwayTeam(9));
assertEquals("Denver",pool.getHomeTeam(9));
assertEquals("Buffalo",pool.getAwayTeam(10));
assertEquals("NY Jets",pool.getHomeTeam(10));
assertEquals("Baltimore",pool.getAwayTeam(11));
assertEquals("Arizona",pool.getHomeTeam(11));
assertEquals("San Francisco",pool.getAwayTeam(12));
assertEquals("Seattle",pool.getHomeTeam(12));
assertEquals("Atlanta",pool.getAwayTeam(13));
assertEquals("St. Louis",pool.getHomeTeam(13));

    poolDBMockcontrol.verify();
}
```

As you can see, the first part of the test has been changed to create the mock object for the PoolDatabase class. The first thing that happens in the test is that a mock object is created to implement the PoolDatabase class using the poolDBMockcontrol class that was created in the test setup method as follows:

```
poolDBMockcontrol = MockControl.createControl(PoolDatabase.class);
```

Once the mockPoolDB object is created, its behavior is specified by training it to respond to the various method calls. In our case, there is only one method that needs to be trained: getPoolWithStatus(). For our test, we expect the method to be called with the parameter "Open" and expect this method to return a Vector of FootballPools of size one. The expected return value is created by a private method in the test's class (see Listing 3-9).

Listing 3-9. *Creation of Expected Return Value for the Mock Object*

```
private Vector createFbPoolList()
    {
        Vector poolList = new Vector();
        FootballPool pool = new FootballPool("9/17/2003");
        pool.addGame("Kansas City", "Green Bay");
        pool.addGame("Houston", "Tennessee");
        pool.addGame("Carolina", "Indianapolis");
        pool.addGame("NY Giants", "New England");
        pool.addGame("Chicago", "New Orleans");
        pool.addGame("Oakland", "Cleveland");
        pool.addGame("Philadelphia", "Dallas");
        pool.addGame("Tampa Bay", "Washington");
        pool.addGame("Miami", "Jacksonville");
        pool.addGame("Pittsburgh", "Denver");
        pool.addGame("Buffalo", "NY Jets");
        pool.addGame("Baltimore", "Arizona");
        pool.addGame("San Francisco", "Seattle");
        pool.addGame("Atlanta", "St. Louis");
        poolList.addElement(pool);
        return (poolList);
    }
```

Once the mockPoolDB object has had its method trained, it is ready to be used in the test by calling its poolDBMockcontrol replay() method. Now that we have an object that implements the PoolDatabase interface, we can use it to run our test. At the end of the test, the poolDBMockcontrol calls the verify() method. This method will throw an exception if one of the trained methods was not called. If a trained method was not called, this means that the test did not exercise its expected path, so the test should fail.

The nice thing about using EasyMock over a stub is that all the code used to simulate the dependent class is in the test code and can grow and change as the test evolves. Mock objects also make it easier to test certain error conditions. In general, mock objects are usually better to use than stubs because they provide a finer-grain object that can be tailored to each individual test without a lot of overhead or maintenance. Another feature of mock objects that is useful is that a true mock object usually provides a way to verify itself. For example, EasyMock provides a verify() method that is used to verify that the mock object was called. If the mock object wasn't called by the code being tested, this would indicate an error.

Let's write a test for testing whether PoolDatabase.getPoolWithStatus("Open") returns an empty list or a list that has more than one FootballPool in it. First we write the tests (see Listing 3-10).

Listing 3-10. *Error Tests for the Get Open Pool Behavior*

```
public void testGetOpenPoolEmptyListError() {
        //Get mock object
        PoolDatabase mockPoolDB = (PoolDatabase)poolDBMockcontrol.getMock();
        //Train the mock object
        mockPoolDB.getPoolWithStatus("Open");
        //Create return value for mock method that will cause an error
        //because the list is empty
        Vector mockPoolList = new Vector();
        poolDBMockcontrol.setReturnValue(mockPoolList);
        //Training over. Set the mock to replay trained behavior when called
        poolDBMockcontrol.replay();

        PoolData poolData = new PoolData();
        //Set PoolDB to mock object
        poolData.set_poolDB(mockPoolDB);

        FootballPool pool = poolData.getOpenPool();
        assertEquals(null, pool);

        poolDBMockcontrol.verify();
    }
    public void testGetOpenPoolListSizeError() {
        //Get mock object
        PoolDatabase mockPoolDB = (PoolDatabase)poolDBMockcontrol.getMock();
        //Train the mock object
        mockPoolDB.getPoolWithStatus("Open");
        //Create return value for mock method that will cause an error
        // because the list is too big
        Vector mockPoolList = new Vector();
        mockPoolList.addElement("element1");
        mockPoolList.addElement("element2");
        poolDBMockcontrol.setReturnValue(mockPoolList);
        //Training over. Set the mock to replay trained behavior when called
        poolDBMockcontrol.replay();

        PoolData poolData = new PoolData();
        //Set PoolDB to mock object
        poolData.set_poolDB(mockPoolDB);

        FootballPool pool = poolData.getOpenPool();
        assertEquals(null, pool);

        poolDBMockcontrol.verify();
    }
```

As you can see, it's very easy to simulate error conditions by changing the expected return value of the mock object for both tests; we just change the value of the mockPoolList to generate the error condition. If we run these tests, they pass because we were already smart enough to check for these errors in our original code. Now that we understand how to use mock objects, let's work on implementing the rest of the behaviors for this use case.

The next behavior we are going to implement is storing the player's picks for a particular football pool. We begin by writing the test (see Listing 3-11).

Listing 3-11. *Test for Saving Player Picks*

```java
public void testStorePlayersPicks()
    {
        //Get mock object
        PoolDatabase mockPoolDB = (PoolDatabase)poolDBMockcontrol.getMock();
        //Train the mock object
        mockPoolDB.getPoolWithStatus("Open");
        //Create return value for mock method
        Vector mockPoolList = createFbPoolList();
        poolDBMockcontrol.setReturnValue(mockPoolList);
        //Training over. Set the mock to replay trained behavior when called
        poolDBMockcontrol.replay();

        PoolData poolData = new PoolData();
        //Set PoolDB to mock object
        poolData.set_poolDB(mockPoolDB);
        //Get list of games for the open pool
        FootballPool pool = poolData.getOpenPool();
        Vector gameList = pool.getGameList();
        //For each game make a pick
        PlayersPicks playerPicks = new PlayersPicks("EddyC", "9/17/2003",gameList);
        for(int i = 0; i < gameList.size(); i++)
        {
            Game game = (Game) gameList.elementAt(i);
            playerPicks.makePick(i, game.getHomeTeam());
        }
        PoolData.savePlayersPicks(playerPicks);
        //Get the user picks and verify that they were set correctly
        PlayerPicks savedPicks = PoolData.getPlayersPicks("EddyC");
        for(int i = 0; i < savedPicks.size(); i++)
        {
            String homeTeam = savedPicks.getHomeTeam(i);
            assertEquals(homeTeam, savedPicks.getPickedTeam(i));
        }
    }
```

As you can see, the test helps us make some design decisions about how we are going to create and store the player picks. We are going to need a PlayersPicks class that will contain the list of the player's pick for a particular pool. To construct the player's pick list, we are going to need the player's name, pool date, and the list of games for the pool. We are going to get the list of games from the FootballPool class. The FootballPool class doesn't have a getter for the list of games, so we will have to add this method. The PlayersPicks class will also require makePick(), getHomeTeam(), and getPickedTeam() methods.

The test also requires some new methods for the PoolData class. We need to add the savePlayerPicks() and getPlayerPicks() methods.

Now that we have the test written, we can write the code to get the test to pass. We first write the PlayersPicks class as shown in Listing 3-12.

Listing 3-12. *PlayersPicks Class*

```
public class PlayersPicks
{
    private Vector _gameList = new Vector();
    private String _playersName;
    private String _poolDate;


    public PlayersPicks(String playersName, String poolDate, Vector gameList) {
        _gameList = gameList;
        _playersName = playersName;
        _poolDate = poolDate;
    }


    public void makePick( int gameNum, String pickTeam ) {
        Game game = (Game)_gameList.elementAt(gameNum);
    }


    public String getHomeTeam( int i ) {
        Game game = (Game)_gameList.elementAt(i);
        return game.getHomeTeam();
    }


    public String getAwayTeam( int i ) {
        Game game = (Game)_gameList.elementAt(i);
        return game.getAwayTeam();
    }

    public String getPickedTeam( int i ) {
        Game game = (Game)_gameList.elementAt(i);
        return game.getPickedTeam();
```

```
    }

    public int size(){
        return(_gameList.size());
    }
    public String getPlayersName(){
        return _playersName;
    }
    public String getPoolDate(){
        return _poolDate;
    }
}
```

The PlayersPicks class is similar to the FootballPool class in the way it manages the games. We decide to use the same Game class to store the games and picks. To store the picks, we have to update the Game class to include this information by adding the chosen team to the class and adding a setter and getter.

Now that we have the PlayersPicks class complete, we have to add two new methods to the PoolData class.

```
public void savePlayersPicks(PlayersPicks playerPicks)
    {
        String name = playerPicks.getPlayersName();
        String date = playerPicks.getPoolDate();
        _poolDB.savePlayersPicks(playerPicks);
    }
    public PlayersPicks getPlayersPicks(String playersName, String poolDate)
    {
        return(_poolDB.getPlayersPicks(playersName, poolDate));
    }
```

This causes us to add two more methods to the PoolDatabase interface. At this point we can compile and run the test, but it fails because we did not train mockPoolDB for the two new methods we just added. So we have to add the code shown in Listing 3-13 to the beginning of the test (**changes in bold**).

Listing 3-13. *Test for Saving Player Picks with Mock Objects*

```
public void testStorePlayersPicks()
    {
        //Get mock object
        PoolDatabase mockPoolDB = (PoolDatabase)poolDBMockcontrol.getMock();
        //Train the mock object
        mockPoolDB.getPoolWithStatus("Open");
        //Create return value for mock method
        Vector mockPoolList = createFbPoolList();
        poolDBMockcontrol.setReturnValue(mockPoolList);
        PlayersPicks mockplayerPicks = createPlayersPicks();
        mockPoolDB.savePlayersPicks(mockplayerPicks);
```

```
    poolDBMockcontrol.setMatcher(MockControl.ALWAYS_MATCHER);
    mockPoolDB.getPlayersPicks("EddyC", "9/17/2003");
    poolDBMockcontrol.setReturnValue(mockplayerPicks);
    //Training over. Set the mock to replay trained behavior when called
    poolDBMockcontrol.replay();

    PoolData poolData = new PoolData();
    //Set PoolDB to mock object
    poolData.set_poolDB(mockPoolDB);
    //Get list of games for the open pool
    FootballPool pool = poolData.getOpenPool();
    Vector gameList = pool.getGameList();
    //For each game make a pick
    PlayersPicks playerPicks =
                        new PlayersPicks("EddyC", "9/17/2003", gameList);
    for(int i = 0; i < gameList.size(); i++)
    {
        Game game = (Game) gameList.elementAt(i);
        playerPicks.makePick(i, game.getHomeTeam());
    }
    poolData.savePlayersPicks(playerPicks);
    //Get the user picks and verify that they were set correctly
    PlayersPicks savedPicks = poolData.getPlayersPicks("EddyC", "9/17/2003");
    for(int i = 0; i < savedPicks.size(); i++)
    {
        String homeTeam = savedPicks.getHomeTeam(i);
        assertEquals(homeTeam, savedPicks.getPickedTeam(i));
    }

    poolDBMockcontrol.verify();
}
```

As you can see, we updated the mockPoolDB object to train the two new methods we added to the PoolDatabase interface: savePlayersPicks() and getPlayersPicks(). To train the savePlayersPicks() method, we have to create a PlayersPicks object and pass it in to the method. However, there is a problem with the default behavior of EasyMock that needs to be fixed for this training to work. The problem is in the way EasyMock determines whether the trained method was called correctly. The default behavior of EasyMock uses a simple equals comparison to determine whether the arguments passed in during the real call are the same as the ones passed in during the training. For simple arguments, such as Strings and ints, the equals comparison works fine, but in the savePlayersPicks() method we are passing in an actual object when we train it and another object at the same time when we call it during the test. Since the two objects are not the same, the equals comparison fails, and EasyMock throws an exception. To prevent EasyMock from throwing this behavior, we can change the way that the comparison is done using the setMatcher method of the MockControl. Setting it to ALWAYS_MATCHER prevents EasyMock from comparing the arguments passed in to the method and solves the problem.

The getPlayersPicks() method is trained in the usual way. With this the test now passes, and we are done with implementing this use case. The process that we just went through illustrates one of the benefits of using mock objects. Mock objects allow you to implement dependent methods just as you need them. This allows you to develop your code in a simple, incremental way. Because of this, you can discover the design of certain classes as you continue to develop your tests. For example, the PoolDatabase is an interface that we have decided not to implement at this time, but to use mock objects for now to let us test it. Although we did implement the PoolDatabase interface, the tests help us discover what methods this interface should contain.

Now that you understand stubs and mock objects, you have a basic understanding of the tools needed to develop your code in isolation in a simple, incremental way. As with all methods and tools, it is only through experience with these that you will gain a complete understanding.

Hands-On Exercises

You're on your own now. It's time to test your knowledge of TDD (and how well I explained it) and try to add some more functionality to the application on your own. Your assignment is to implement the core functionality needed to implement part of Use Case 4 (Administrator Posts Results). You need to implement the behavior necessary to post the results for weekly picks for the football pool. Don't worry about anything to do with the user interface or the actual database implementation at this point.

An example solution for this exercise can be found in Appendix B.

Unit Testing Best Practices

So far, you have learned how to use tests to drive the development process. You have also learned how to use stubs and mock objects to create placeholder classes that are needed to simulate classes that have not yet been developed. You now have the basic tools and knowledge to write unit tests, but there are some rules and best practices you should follow when writing them to help make them more effective.

- *Keep it simple*: Keep each individual test as simple as possible. This KISS principle applies to testing just like it applies to coding.

- *Make it easy to run*: Tests that are easy to run will be run more often.

- *Minimize the test dependencies*: This is an extension of the last point. The fewer things a test depends upon, such as a database connection, message queue, etc., the easier it will be to run.

- *Keep a test self contained*: If a test uses a database or a set of files or any other resource, then that test should initialize the resource at the beginning of the test and free it at the end of the test.

- *Properly document the unit tests*: Like any code being developed, it is important that the unit tests be properly documented. Just as it is easier to maintain well-documented code, well-documented test cases will be easier to update.

Organizing and Running Your Unit Tests

As you continue to develop, you will start to accumulate a lot of unit tests that you will want run on a regular basis. It's important that the unit tests be organized and packaged in a way similar to the code of the project. This project has an src directory that contains the source code needed to implement the application. The unit tests are contained in the test directory, which is at the same level as the src directory. Both these directories will have the same package structure to make it easy to relate the classes and tests. For example, the source code for this chapter is in the directory /src/com/apress/tddbook/ and the tests for this chapter are in /test/com/apress/tddbook.

Besides keeping the tests and code well organized, it's important to make the tests easy and quick to run. This means following the best practices for unit tests as stated previously and keeping the tests simple and self-contained. The tests used to develop the code will not be thrown away after the code is developed, but instead used to do regression testing and refactoring of the code. To make this testing as easy as possible, it's important to take the time and do some housekeeping as new tests are developed. Earlier in the chapter we showed you how to create a test suite and how to run tests and test suites using Ant. As new tests are created, they need to be added to a suite, since this makes it easy to run a large number of tests. Also, it is important to add new tasks to the Ant build file so all the tests can be run as part of the test ➤ code ➤ build cycle. This will allow you to run all the tests developed as part of a nightly build. Chapter 7 will have more details about organizing, maintaining, and running the unit tests, but the simple things described here will go a long way to helping keep the tests manageable and easy to run.

Summary

In this chapter, I have tried to put the theory of Chapter 1 and the tools in Chapter 2 into practice. We started out by developing a simple unit test that helped us write the code for a base class for the Football Pool application. This example showed you how the JUnit testing framework works and allowed you to see how to go through the test ➤ code ➤ build cycle the TDD way. You then learned how to use JUnit's TestSuite to run a set of tests and also how Ant can be used to make the tests easier to run.

The last main topic discussed is how to develop around dependent classes. There will be times when the classes that you need to write tests for depend on other classes. In order to keep the tests as independent as possible, you need a way to simulate dependent classes so you can test in isolation. I discussed the use of both stubs and mock objects as ways to simulate dependent classes and showed how to use EasyMock mock object framework. I also discussed some of the advantages of using mock objects and why they are preferred over stubs.

Hopefully this chapter has shown you how the ideas and tools of TDD can be used to create good, well-designed software in a simple, incremental way. The TDD process of writing isolated unit tests helps you build an application with good modularity that is easy to test and refactor. Because of the simple, incremental development of the application, hidden dependencies are avoided, the application is better designed, and the code is simpler, with fewer bugs. This in general helps improve the reliability and robustness of the application.

Although this chapter has provided a good base for understanding the TDD process, there is still a lot more to the process that needs to be explained. Chapter 4 will cover how TDD can be used to develop servlets, Chapter 5 will explore how TDD can be applied to developing GUIs, and Chapter 6 will show how to use TDD to integrate the pieces of the application into the finished product. Each of these chapters will help you expand your knowledge of TDD and help you become a better developer.

■ ■ ■

CHAPTER 4

Test-Driven Development for Servlets and JSPs

In the last chapter, I explained how to apply the basic tools and techniques of TDD to develop the core of the Football Pool application. Although the techniques described in the last chapter can be used to develop a lot of the application, other sections of the application, like parts of the user interface, require some special techniques and tools in order to practice TDD. In this chapter, we are going to develop parts of the user interface that are used by the players to enter their picks and view the results. This user interface will be a web interface driven by servlets and JSPs.

The Problem Developing Servlets and JSPs Using TDD

Servlets and JSPs are different from the code that we have developed so far. The code that we developed in Chapter 3 was generic Java code that could easily be run in isolation with the help of some simple mock objects. Servlet and JSP code require a container to run that is harder to simulate. There are a number of ways that you can test servlets and JSPs as you develop them:

- Use mock objects to simulate the parts of the servlet container needed by the servlets being developed.

- Use an already developed simulated servlet container like Mockrunner or ServletUnit.

- Use a real servlet container and develop the servlet and JSP using in-container testing.

Using Mock Objects to Simulate the Servlet Container

It is possible to use mock objects to simulate the servlet container; consider the servlet code in Listing 4-1 and the simple test in Listing 4-2 that is used to test its getUser() method.

Listing 4-1. *SimpleServlet*

```java
public class SimpleServlet extends HttpServlet
{
    public void doGet(HttpServletRequest request, HttpServletResponse response)
          throws ServletException, IOException
    {
        String user = getUser(request, response);
        response.getWriter().print("User that call this servlet is " + user);
    }
    public void doPost(HttpServletRequest request, HttpServletResponse response)
          throws ServletException, IOException
    {
        doGet(request, response);
    }

    private String getUser(HttpServletRequest request,
                           HttpServletResponse response)
    {
        return((String)request.getAttribute("UserName"));
    }
}
```

Listing 4-2. *SimpleServlet Tester*

```java
public class SimpleServletTester extends TestCase
{
    MockControl HttpServletReqMockCntl;
    MockControl HttpServletRespMockCntl;

    public SimpleServletTester(String s) {
        super(s);
    }

    public void testServletGetUser(){
        StringWriter strWriter = new StringWriter();
        //Mock out the servlet request and response objects
        HttpServletRequest mockServletRequest =
                    (HttpServletRequest)HttpServletReqMockCntl.getMock();
        HttpServletResponse mockServletResponse =
                    (HttpServletResponse)HttpServletRespMockCntl.getMock();
        //Train the request object
        mockServletRequest.getAttribute("UserName");
        HttpServletReqMockCntl.setReturnValue("TimmyC");
        HttpServletReqMockCntl.replay();
        try
        {
```

```java
            mockServletResponse.getWriter();
            HttpServletRespMockCntl.setReturnValue(new PrintWriter(strWriter));
        }
        catch (IOException e)
        {
            System.out.println(
                    "Error mocking out response.getWriter() exception is " + e);
        }
        HttpServletRespMockCntl.replay();
        SimpleServlet simpleServlet = new SimpleServlet();
        String user = null;
        try
        {
            simpleServlet.doGet(mockServletRequest, mockServletResponse);
        }
        catch (ServletException e)
        {
            e.printStackTrace();
        }
        catch (IOException e)
        {
            e.printStackTrace();
        }
        assertEquals("User that call this servlet is TimmyC",
                    strWriter.toString());
    }

    public void setUp() {

        HttpServletReqMockCntl =
                        MockControl.createControl(HttpServletRequest.class);
        HttpServletRespMockCntl =
                        MockControl.createControl(HttpServletResponse.class);
    }

    public static Test suite() {
        TestSuite suite = new TestSuite(SimpleServletTester.class);
        return suite;
    }


    public static final void main(String[] args) {
        junit.textui.TestRunner.run(suite());
    }
}
```

As you can see, in order to test just one method of the servlet, we have to mock out a couple of functions of the `request` and `response` object. We use a `StringWriter` for the `response` object's `PrintWriter` so that the test will be able to check any output the servlet would produce. Doing this allows us to create and run tests, but as the servlet gets more and more complex, it will take more and more work to mock out the methods that would normally be provided by the servlet container. The other problem with this approach is that mock methods that are implemented may not be able to fully simulate the real ones provided by the servlet container, so the servlet may pass the tests but not work when it is actually deployed to the container.

Using mock objects to simulate the servlet container is a good idea only if your servlets use a small subset of the methods provided by the servlet container API, because simulating the entire container would be a very complex task. If you continue with the approach that we started with in our simple example here to develop mock objects, as you develop more servlets you may eventually reach a realization that the mock objects have become too complicated to maintain or properly simulate a complex object like a servlet container. This means you will have to find other ways to develop around dependent objects.

Using In-Container Testing to Develop Servlets

To get around the problems with using mock objects to simulate a servlet container, you could run your tests inside a real servlet container during development. This would eliminate the overhead of mocking out all the methods of the container and allow you to test the servlets in an environment very close to the production environment in the actual container. To run the tests inside the container, you could deploy the application to a real application server and then write some code to exercise the servlet. This would work, but would take a lot of effort.

Luckily, there is a testing framework called Cactus[1] that provides an easy way to run tests inside the container of any application server. Cactus is a simple testing framework that allows you to run in-container tests for a number of different J2EE containers like servlets, JSPs, and EJBs. Cactus is a good framework and has a lot of support in the Java community, but it has some disadvantages. The main disadvantage is the overhead and complexity that Cactus adds to the process. In order to run tests using Cactus, you first have to package your application like you would if you were deploying it to a real J2EE application server, which means putting the servlets in a war file with the corresponding web.xml file.

Cactus also requires some configuration in order to run the tests. Setting up Cactus is not hard, but it is an extra step in the development process. All this extra overhead adds time to the test-code cycle and makes it harder to make changes to the code and quickly see the results. Although in-container testing with tools like Cactus can be used for TDD, there is another way that you need to consider.

Using a Simulated Servlet Container to Develop Servlets

Between EasyMock and Cactus are tools that allow developers to test servlets using a simulated servlet container. Simulated servlet containers like the ones provided by ServletUnit or

---

1. Information on Cactus can be found at `http://jakarta.apache.org/cactus/`. I will discuss the use of Cactus in the TDD process further in Chapter 6.

Mockrunner allow developers to test servlets without the overhead of in-container tests or the complexity of having to mock out all the methods of the servlet container. These tools are relatively easy to use and don't require a lot of overhead. The only drawback to using a simulated servlet container for testing servlets is that when the servlet is deployed to the real container, it may show some problems that were not caught in the tests because the simulated servlet container works slightly differently from the real one. For the most part, though, the simulated servlet container is the best way to start developing servlets because of its low overhead and complexity; it provides the easiest solution to the problem of testing servlets. This is the TDD way, since one of the goals of TDD is to keep the tests as simple as possible. As the project progresses, we may need to use in-container testing to fully test all aspects of the servlets, but for now the simulated servlet containers will allow us to make a quick start.

Developing a Servlet the TDD Way

To understand how to develop a servlet the TDD way, let's continue the development of the Football Pool application. The players of the football pool will use a web interface to make their picks and check the results. This will require us to develop a number of different servlets and JSPs. Let's start first with trying to understand the behavior of one aspect of the web interface by reexamining one of the use cases from the client's point of view. In Chapter 3, we implemented Use Case 5 (Player Enters Picks) from the business tier point of view. Let's look at this use case again from a client tier perspective. Use Case 5 says

> *After a pool is open, a player may sign on and enter picks predicting the winner of each game and the total score of the tiebreaker game. The players may change their picks until the pool is closed.*

From this use case, we can infer a number of behaviors. We need a way to

- Provide a means for players to sign into the football pool and be identified.

- Display a list of games from the football pool that is currently open to users.

- Provide a means for players to enter and save their picks for the football pool.

- Allow players to view and edit their picks for a particular football pool.

The first behavior will be provided by the application server's authentication mechanism, so we won't worry about it for now. We will assume that the servlet will have a way to get the name of the user when the servlet is run. Let's start with the second behavior and create a test that will help us develop the servlet needed to implement this behavior. We are going to use the ServletUnit framework to develop our test. For a brief overview of ServletUnit, see the sidebar "ServletUnit Overview."

SERVLETUNIT OVERVIEW

ServletUnit is part of the HttpUnit framework and can be used to test servlets without a servlet container. Although HttpUnit can be used to test servlets and JSPs, it is mainly used to do black-box testing (i.e., functional testing) from the web browser's point of view. ServletUnit goes one step further and allows you to not only execute a servlet and verify the results, but also individually test all its methods. ServletUnit includes a simulated servlet container that provides all the functionality of a real servlet container. This means that tests are very quick and easy to set up and run. For example, consider the `SimpleServlet` of Listing 4-1, shown earlier. In order to test this servlet using ServletUnit, you would have to perform the following steps:

1. Create an instance of the `ServletRunner` class. This is the class that simulates the servlet container and allows access to the internal object's servlets being run.

2. Register the servlet(s) that you plan to test with the `ServletRunner`.

3. Create a `ServletUnitClient`. This client will allow you to access the different parts of the registered servlets.

4. Create a `WebRequest` that is used to call your servlet. (Note: ServletUnit does not really use the host or port part of the URL of the `WebRequest` and only uses the part of the URL starting with the path.)

5. Get the `InvocationContext`. The `InvocationContext` represents the invocation of a servlet. This interface allows you to access the servlet as well as its `request` and `response` objects.

Once you have the `InvocationContext`, you can get a handle to the servlet and execute any of its methods. This allows you to test the servlet a little piece at a time instead of testing just the final result. For example, the code shown in Listing 4-3 tests just the `getUser` method of the `SimpleServlet`.

Listing 4-3. *ServletUnit Test*

```
public void testServletGetUser(){
        ServletRunner sr = new ServletRunner();
        sr.registerServlet("SimpleServlet", SimpleServlet.class.getName());
        ServletUnitClient sc = sr.newClient();
        WebRequest request =
                    new PostMethodWebRequest("http://localhost/SimpleServlet");
        try {
            InvocationContext ic = sc.newInvocation(request);
            SimpleServlet simpleServlet = (SimpleServlet) ic.getServlet();
            assertNull("A session already exists",
                              ic.getRequest().getSession(false));
            HttpServletRequest simpleServletRequest = ic.getRequest();
            simpleServletRequest.setAttribute("UserName", "TimmyC");
            String userName = simpleServlet.getUser(ic.getRequest(),
                                                        ic.getResponse());
            assertEquals("TimmyC", userName);
        }
```

```
        catch (Exception e){
            fail("Error testing getUser exception is " + e);
            e.printStackTrace();
        }
    }
```

Using ServletUnit allows you to develop servlets the TDD way, since it provides a means to test small parts of a servlet as it is being developed. For more detailed information on ServletUnit, see the HttpUnit site at http://httpunit.org.

To implement the second behavior, we are going to have to write a servlet that will be able to get the games of the currently open football pool. Let's write a test that will help us design the servlet (see Listing 4-4).

Listing 4-4. *Test for Displaying Player Picks*

```
public void testDisplayPlayerPicks() {
        //Set up ServletUnit to run the PlayerPickServlet
        ServletRunner sr = new ServletRunner();
        sr.registerServlet("PlayerPickServlet", PlayerPickServlet.class.getName());
        ServletUnitClient sc = sr.newClient();
        WebRequest request =
                new PostMethodWebRequest("http://localhost/PlayerPickServlet");
        try {
            InvocationContext ic = sc.newInvocation(request);
            PlayerPickServlet ppickServlet = (PlayerPickServlet) ic.getServlet();
            assertNull("A session already exists",
                            ic.getRequest().getSession(false));
            // Call the getOpenPool() method of the servlet and
            // check the results
            FootballPool openPool = ppickServlet.getOpenPool(ppickServletRequest);

            assertEquals("Kansas City", openPool.getAwayTeam(0));
            assertEquals("Green Bay", openPool.getHomeTeam(0));
            assertEquals("Houston", openPool.getAwayTeam(1));
            assertEquals("Tennessee", openPool.getHomeTeam(1));
            assertEquals("Carolina", openPool.getAwayTeam(2));
            assertEquals("Indianapolis", openPool.getHomeTeam(2));
            assertEquals("NY Giants", openPool.getAwayTeam(3));
            assertEquals("New England", openPool.getHomeTeam(3));
            assertEquals("Chicago", openPool.getAwayTeam(4));
            assertEquals("New Orleans", openPool.getHomeTeam(4));
            assertEquals("Oakland", openPool.getAwayTeam(5));
            assertEquals("Cleveland", openPool.getHomeTeam(5));
            assertEquals("Philadelphia", openPool.getAwayTeam(6));
```

```
            assertEquals("Dallas", openPool.getHomeTeam(6));
            assertEquals("Tampa Bay", openPool.getAwayTeam(7));
            assertEquals("Washington", openPool.getHomeTeam(7));
            assertEquals("Miami", openPool.getAwayTeam(8));
            assertEquals("Jacksonville", openPool.getHomeTeam(8));
            assertEquals("Pittsburgh", openPool.getAwayTeam(9));
            assertEquals("Denver", openPool.getHomeTeam(9));
            assertEquals("Buffalo", openPool.getAwayTeam(10));
            assertEquals("NY Jets", openPool.getHomeTeam(10));
            assertEquals("Baltimore", openPool.getAwayTeam(11));
            assertEquals("Arizona", openPool.getHomeTeam(11));
            assertEquals("San Francisco", openPool.getAwayTeam(12));
            assertEquals("Seattle", openPool.getHomeTeam(12));
            assertEquals("Atlanta", openPool.getAwayTeam(13));
            assertEquals("St. Louis", openPool.getHomeTeam(13));
        }
        catch (Exception e)
        {
            fail("Error testing PlayerPickServlet Exception is " + e);
            e.printStackTrace();
        }
    }
}
```

If you look at Listing 4-4, you can see that we use ServletUnit to write a test that calls the getOpenPool() method of the servlet to get the currently open football pool and then checks to make sure the pool returned is correct. We do this by first setting up ServletUnit's ServletRunner and ServletUnitClient and then use the InvocationContext object to execute one of the servlet's methods and check the results. From this, we can see that the servlet will require a getOpenPool() method that will take the request object as an argument and return a FootballPool. Now that we understand the requirements of this method, let's implement the servlet so that the test passes (see Listing 4-5).

Listing 4-5. *getOpenPool() Method of the PlayerPickServlet*

```
public class PlayerPickServlet extends HttpServlet
{

    FootballPool getOpenPool(HttpServletRequest request)
    {
        PoolData poolData =
                (PoolData)request.getSession().getAttribute("PoolData");
        FootballPool pool = poolData.getOpenPool();
        return(pool);
    }
}
```

To implement the servlet, we don't worry about how the servlet will be called or how it will display the data; we just concentrate on implementing the getOpenPool() method. In Chapter 3, we developed the PoolData class, which can be used to get data from the football pool. We decide to use an instance of the PoolData class in the servlet since it has the methods we need to get the open football pool. The only problem with using the PoolData class is deciding how this class gets initialized. For now we will assume that the PoolData class will be initialized before this method is called and stored in the session data for this servlet.

Now that we have implemented the servlet, we can run the test. If we do, it fails because the PoolData object hasn't been initialized. We don't want to take the time to implement the initialization of the PoolData because this depends on the database, which we haven't yet implemented. To get the test to pass, we are going to have to mock out the PoolData class. To do this, we update the test as shown in Listing 4-6 (**updated code in bold**).

Listing 4-6. *Test for Displaying Player Picks with Mock Objects*

```
public void testDisplayPlayerPicks() {
        //Get mock object
        PoolData mockPoolData = (PoolData)poolDataMockcontrol.getMock();
        //Train the mock object
        mockPoolData.getOpenPool();
        //Create return value for mock method
        FootballPool fbPool = createFbPool();
        poolDataMockcontrol.setReturnValue(fbPool);
        poolDataMockcontrol.replay();
        //Set up ServletUnit to run the PlayerPickServlet
        ServletRunner sr = new ServletRunner();
        sr.registerServlet("PlayerPickServlet", PlayerPickServlet.class.getName());
        ServletUnitClient sc = sr.newClient();
        WebRequest request =
                new PostMethodWebRequest("http://localhost/PlayerPickServlet");
        request.setParameter("username", "TimmyC");
        try
        {
            InvocationContext ic = sc.newInvocation(request);
            PlayerPickServlet ppickServlet = (PlayerPickServlet) ic.getServlet();
            assertNull("A session already exists",
                            ic.getRequest().getSession(false));
            HttpServletRequest ppickServletRequest = ic.getRequest();
            HttpSession servletSession = ppickServletRequest.getSession();
            servletSession.setAttribute("PoolData", mockPoolData);
            // Call the getOpenPool() method of the servlet and
            // check the results

            FootballPool openPool = ppickServlet.getOpenPool(ppickServletRequest);
```

```
            assertEquals("Kansas City", openPool.getAwayTeam(0));
            assertEquals("Green Bay", openPool.getHomeTeam(0));
            assertEquals("Houston", openPool.getAwayTeam(1));
            assertEquals("Tennessee", openPool.getHomeTeam(1));
            assertEquals("Carolina", openPool.getAwayTeam(2));
            assertEquals("Indianapolis", openPool.getHomeTeam(2));
            assertEquals("NY Giants", openPool.getAwayTeam(3));
            assertEquals("New England", openPool.getHomeTeam(3));
            assertEquals("Chicago", openPool.getAwayTeam(4));
            assertEquals("New Orleans", openPool.getHomeTeam(4));
            assertEquals("Oakland", openPool.getAwayTeam(5));
            assertEquals("Cleveland", openPool.getHomeTeam(5));
            assertEquals("Philadelphia", openPool.getAwayTeam(6));
            assertEquals("Dallas", openPool.getHomeTeam(6));
            assertEquals("Tampa Bay", openPool.getAwayTeam(7));
            assertEquals("Washington", openPool.getHomeTeam(7));
            assertEquals("Miami", openPool.getAwayTeam(8));
            assertEquals("Jacksonville", openPool.getHomeTeam(8));
            assertEquals("Pittsburgh", openPool.getAwayTeam(9));
            assertEquals("Denver", openPool.getHomeTeam(9));
            assertEquals("Buffalo", openPool.getAwayTeam(10));
            assertEquals("NY Jets", openPool.getHomeTeam(10));
            assertEquals("Baltimore", openPool.getAwayTeam(11));
            assertEquals("Arizona", openPool.getHomeTeam(11));
            assertEquals("San Francisco", openPool.getAwayTeam(12));
            assertEquals("Seattle", openPool.getHomeTeam(12));
            assertEquals("Atlanta", openPool.getAwayTeam(13));
            assertEquals("St. Louis", openPool.getHomeTeam(13));

        }
        catch (Exception e)
        {
            fail("Error testing PlayerPickServlet Exception is " + e);
            e.printStackTrace();
        }
    }
```

If you run the test now, it fails because the PoolData class is not an interface, and Easy-Mock can only mock out interfaces. The question is whether we should change the PoolData class to an interface or not. Changing it will help us get our test to pass and may make sense. If the PoolData class is going to be used by numerous web clients, servlets, and EJBs, it should probably be an interface so that the implementation of the PoolData is isolated from the classes that use it. Because of this, we decide to refactor the PoolData class and make it an interface and move the implementation of the class to the PoolDataImpl object. Once we do this, the test passes, which means the servlet can now get a list of games for the open pool.

Our servlet still does not have a way to present them to the player yet, but at the moment we are concentrating on adding methods to the servlet that will allow it to manage the data needed for the football pool. This is because we plan on using the Model View Controller (MVC) Model 2 pattern for this application, which means that the servlet will act as the controller, the business logic classes such as the PoolData class will be the model, and the view will be implemented by JSPs. This is a common pattern that is used in some way in most web applications. Using the MVC Model 2 pattern helps break up the application into small logical pieces with well-defined interfaces, which are not only easier to develop, but also easier to test. It's important that as we continue to develop the servlet, we keep the MVC Model 2 pattern in mind and keep the servlet free of any model or view logic.

Now that we have a way for the servlet to get a list of games for the open football pool, we need to implement the next behavior, which is to be able to provide the players with a way to enter and save their picks. Again, we are not going to worry about how the picks are going to be passed to the servlet, but concentrate on the logic needed to get the picks from the servlet to the model. As always, we start first by writing a test, as shown in Listing 4-7.

Listing 4-7. *Test for Making Player Picks*

```
public void testMakePlayerPicks() {
        // Set up ServletUnit to run the PlayerPickServlet
        ServletRunner sr = new ServletRunner();
        sr.registerServlet("PlayerPickServlet", PlayerPickServlet.class.getName());
        ServletUnitClient sc = sr.newClient();
        WebRequest request =
                new PostMethodWebRequest("http://localhost/PlayerPickServlet");
        // Set up the parameters that will be passed into the servlet
        request.setParameter("username", "TimmyC");
        request.setParameter("poolDate", "9/17/2003");
        request.setParameter("game_1_pick", "Green Bay");
        request.setParameter("game_2_pick", "Houston");
        request.setParameter("game_3_pick", "Indianapolis");
        request.setParameter("game_4_pick", "NY Giants");
        request.setParameter("game_5_pick", "Chicago");
        request.setParameter("game_6_pick", "Cleveland");
        request.setParameter("game_7_pick", "Dallas");
        request.setParameter("game_8_pick", "Washington");
        request.setParameter("game_9_pick", "Jacksonville");
        request.setParameter("game_10_pick", "Pittsburgh");
        request.setParameter("game_11_pick", "Buffalo");
        request.setParameter("game_12_pick", "Baltimore");
        request.setParameter("game_13_pick", "San Francisco");
        request.setParameter("game_14_pick", "Atlanta");
        try {
            InvocationContext ic = sc.newInvocation(request);
            PlayerPickServlet ppickServlet = (PlayerPickServlet) ic.getServlet();
```

```
                assertNull("A session already exists",
                            ic.getRequest().getSession(false));
                HttpServletRequest ppickServletRequest = ic.getRequest();
                ppickServlet.storePlayersPicks(ppickServletRequest);
                // Call the getPlayerPicks() method of the servlet and
                // check the results
                PlayersPicks playerPicks =
                            ppickServlet.getPlayerPicks(ppickServletRequest);
                assertEquals("Green Bay", playerPicks.getPickedTeam(0));
                assertEquals("Houston", playerPicks.getPickedTeam(1));
                assertEquals("Indianapolis", playerPicks.getPickedTeam(2));
                assertEquals("NY Giants", playerPicks.getPickedTeam(3));
                assertEquals("Chicago", playerPicks.getPickedTeam(4));
                assertEquals("Cleveland", playerPicks.getPickedTeam(5));
                assertEquals("Dallas", playerPicks.getPickedTeam(6));
                assertEquals("Washington", playerPicks.getPickedTeam(7));
                assertEquals("Jacksonville", playerPicks.getPickedTeam(8));
                assertEquals("Pittsburgh", playerPicks.getPickedTeam(9));
                assertEquals("Buffalo", playerPicks.getPickedTeam(10));
                assertEquals("Baltimore", playerPicks.getPickedTeam(11));
                assertEquals("San Francisco", playerPicks.getPickedTeam(12));
                assertEquals("Atlanta", playerPicks.getPickedTeam(13));
            }
        catch (Exception e) {
                System.out.println("Error testing PlayerPickServlet Exception is "
                                                                        + e);
                fail("Error testing PlayerPickServlet Exception is " + e);
                e.printStackTrace();
            }
        }
    }
```

If you look at the testMakePlayerPicks test, you will see it starts out the same as the last test by first setting up ServletRunner and ServletUnitClient. It then sets up the parameters that will be passed to the servlet in the request. The parameters needed by this servlet method are the user name, pool data, and pick for each of the games. Once the parameters are set, we then use the InvocationContext to invoke the servlet and call its storePlayersPicks(). Since the storePlayersPicks() method does not return anything, there is no way to check whether the method worked. To get around this problem, we add a call to the getPlayerPicks() method that allows us to get the saved picks and check them for correctness.

Now that we have the test written, we can add the code shown in Listing 4-8 to the servlet to get the test to pass.

Listing 4-8. *storeOpenPool Method of the PlayerPickServlet*

```
void storePlayersPicks(HttpServletRequest request) {
        FootballPool fbPool = getOpenPool(request);
        Vector gameList = fbPool.getGameList();
        PlayersPicks playerPicks =
```

```
            new PlayersPicks(request.getParameter("username"),
                            request.getParameter("poolDate"), gameList);
    for(int i = 0; i < gameList.size(); i++)
    {
        String gameParam = "game_" + (i+1) + "_pick";
        playerPicks.makePick(i, request.getParameter(gameParam));
    }

    PoolData poolData =
                (PoolData)request.getSession().getAttribute("PoolData");
    poolData.savePlayersPicks(playerPicks);

    request.getSession().setAttribute(request.getParameter("username") +
                            "s_PlayerPicks", playerPicks);

}
PlayersPicks getPlayerPicks(HttpServletRequest request){
    PlayersPicks playerPicks = (PlayersPicks)request.getSession().getAttribute
                        (request.getParameter("username") + "s_PlayerPicks");
    return(playerPicks);
}
```

In order to get the test to pass, we have to add two methods to the servlet. The first
method, storePlayersPicks(), takes the request object as an argument and creates and
stores the players' picks. The way this method works is that it first gets a list of games from the
open pool, then creates a PlayerPicks object using the user name and pool date. Once the
PlayerPicks object is created, we loop through the list of games and make a pick for each
game based on the game_x_pick parameter, where x is the game number. After all the picks are
made, the PlayerPicks object is saved using savePlayersPicks() of the PoolData interface.

The picks are also saved to the servlet's session data. The reason we save the picks to the
servlet's session is so we have an easy way to retrieve the picks for our test. If you look at the
getPlayerPicks() method, you will see that it simply returns the PlayerPicks object from
the servlets session data. This is artificial and is only used so we have a way to get stored
PlayerPicks for our tests. Eventually this method will be replaced with better implementation
that will get the data from the actual database, but for now this method allows the test to pass,
which is all that is important at this point.

Now that we have added the servlet's methods needed to get the test to run, we need to
update the test so that it contains the mock objects needed for the servlet, or the test will not
pass. If you look at the new servlet code, you will see that we need to mock out two methods
of the PoolData class, the getOpenPool() method and the savePlayersPicks() method. So we
update the test as shown in Listing 4-9 (**changes in bold**).

Listing 4-9. *Test for Making Player Picks with Mock Objects*

```
public void testMakePlayerPicks()
    {
        //Get mock object
        PoolData mockPoolData = (PoolData)poolDataMockcontrol.getMock();
```

```
//Train the mock object
mockPoolData.getOpenPool();
//Create return value for mock method
FootballPool fbPool = createFbPool();
poolDataMockcontrol.setReturnValue(fbPool);
mockPoolData.savePlayersPicks(null);
poolDataMockcontrol.setMatcher(MockControl.ALWAYS_MATCHER);
poolDataMockcontrol.replay();
ServletRunner sr = new ServletRunner();
sr.registerServlet("PlayerPickServlet", PlayerPickServlet.class.getName());
ServletUnitClient sc = sr.newClient();
WebRequest request =
        new PostMethodWebRequest("http://localhost/PlayerPickServlet");
request.setParameter("username", "TimmyC");
request.setParameter("poolDate", "9/17/2003");
request.setParameter("game_1_pick", "Green Bay");
request.setParameter("game_2_pick", "Houston");
request.setParameter("game_3_pick", "Indianapolis");
request.setParameter("game_4_pick", "NY Giants");
request.setParameter("game_5_pick", "Chicago");
request.setParameter("game_6_pick", "Cleveland");
request.setParameter("game_7_pick", "Dallas");
request.setParameter("game_8_pick", "Washington");
request.setParameter("game_9_pick", "Jacksonville");
request.setParameter("game_10_pick", "Pittsburgh");
request.setParameter("game_11_pick", "Buffalo");
request.setParameter("game_12_pick", "Baltimore");
request.setParameter("game_13_pick", "San Francisco");
request.setParameter("game_14_pick", "Atlanta");
try
{
    InvocationContext ic = sc.newInvocation(request);
    PlayerPickServlet ppickServlet = (PlayerPickServlet) ic.getServlet();
    assertNull("A session already exists",
                    ic.getRequest().getSession(false));
    HttpServletRequest ppickServletRequest = ic.getRequest();
    HttpSession servletSession = ppickServletRequest.getSession();
    servletSession.setAttribute("PoolData", mockPoolData);
    ppickServlet.storePlayersPicks(ppickServletRequest);
    PlayersPicks playerPicks =
                    ppickServlet.getPlayerPicks(ppickServletRequest);
    assertEquals("Green Bay", playerPicks.getPickedTeam(0));
    assertEquals("Houston", playerPicks.getPickedTeam(1));
    assertEquals("Indianapolis", playerPicks.getPickedTeam(2));
    assertEquals("NY Giants", playerPicks.getPickedTeam(3));
```

```
        assertEquals("Chicago", playerPicks.getPickedTeam(4));
        assertEquals("Cleveland", playerPicks.getPickedTeam(5));
        assertEquals("Dallas", playerPicks.getPickedTeam(6));
        assertEquals("Washington", playerPicks.getPickedTeam(7));
        assertEquals("Jacksonville", playerPicks.getPickedTeam(8));
        assertEquals("Pittsburgh", playerPicks.getPickedTeam(9));
        assertEquals("Buffalo", playerPicks.getPickedTeam(10));
        assertEquals("Baltimore", playerPicks.getPickedTeam(11));
        assertEquals("San Francisco", playerPicks.getPickedTeam(12));
        assertEquals("Atlanta", playerPicks.getPickedTeam(13));

    }
    catch (Exception e)
    {
        System.out.println("Error testing PlayerPickServlet Exception is "
                                                                     + e);

        fail("Error testing PlayerPickServlet Exception is " + e);
        e.printStackTrace();
    }
}
```

If we run this test now, it passes and confirms that the save player pick behavior is now working.

The last behavior we have to implement in the servlet is the ability to allow players to edit their picks. To do this, all we have to do is to add a way to get the players' picks from the database. We add this behavior just like the last two behaviors. We first write the test shown in Listing 4-10.

Listing 4-10. *Test for Editing Player Picks*

```
public void testEditPlayerPicks()
    {
        //Get mock object
        PoolData mockPoolData = (PoolData) poolDataMockcontrol.getMock();
        //Train the mock object
        mockPoolData.getOpenPool();
        //Create return value for mock method
        FootballPool fbPool = createFbPool();
        poolDataMockcontrol.setReturnValue(fbPool);
        mockPoolData.savePlayersPicks(null);
        poolDataMockcontrol.setMatcher(MockControl.ALWAYS_MATCHER);
        mockPoolData.getPlayersPicks("TimmyC", "9/17/2003");
        poolDataMockcontrol.setReturnValue(createPlayerPicks());
        poolDataMockcontrol.replay();
        ServletRunner sr = new ServletRunner();
        sr.registerServlet("PlayerPickServlet", PlayerPickServlet.class.getName());
```

```
ServletUnitClient sc = sr.newClient();
WebRequest request =
            new PostMethodWebRequest("http://localhost/PlayerPickServlet");
request.setParameter("username", "TimmyC'");
request.setParameter("poolDate", "9/17/2003");
request.setParameter("game_1_pick", "Kansas City");
request.setParameter("game_2_pick", "Houston");
request.setParameter("game_3_pick", "Indianapolis");
request.setParameter("game_4_pick", "NY Giants");
request.setParameter("game_5_pick", "Chicago");
request.setParameter("game_6_pick", "Cleveland");
request.setParameter("game_7_pick", "Dallas");
request.setParameter("game_8_pick", "Washington");
request.setParameter("game_9_pick", "Miami");
request.setParameter("game_10_pick", "Denver");
request.setParameter("game_11_pick", "Buffalo");
request.setParameter("game_12_pick", "Baltimore");
request.setParameter("game_13_pick", "San Francisco");
request.setParameter("game_14_pick", "St. Louis");
try
{
    InvocationContext ic = sc.newInvocation(request);
    PlayerPickServlet ppickServlet = (PlayerPickServlet) ic.getServlet();
    assertNull("A session already exists",
                    ic.getRequest().getSession(false));
    HttpServletRequest ppickServletRequest = ic.getRequest();
    HttpSession servletSession = ppickServletRequest.getSession();
    servletSession.setAttribute("PoolData", mockPoolData);
    //Get players current picks
    PlayersPicks playerPicks =
                    ppickServlet.getPlayerPicks(ppickServletRequest);
    //Check the present value of the player picks
    assertEquals("Green Bay", playerPicks.getPickedTeam(0));
    assertEquals("Houston", playerPicks.getPickedTeam(1));
    assertEquals("Indianapolis", playerPicks.getPickedTeam(2));
    assertEquals("NY Giants", playerPicks.getPickedTeam(3));
    assertEquals("Chicago", playerPicks.getPickedTeam(4));
    assertEquals("Cleveland", playerPicks.getPickedTeam(5));
    assertEquals("Dallas", playerPicks.getPickedTeam(6));
    assertEquals("Washington", playerPicks.getPickedTeam(7));
    assertEquals("Jacksonville", playerPicks.getPickedTeam(8));
    assertEquals("Pittsburgh", playerPicks.getPickedTeam(9));
    assertEquals("Buffalo", playerPicks.getPickedTeam(10));
    assertEquals("Baltimore", playerPicks.getPickedTeam(11));
```

```
            assertEquals("San Francisco", playerPicks.getPickedTeam(12));
            assertEquals("Atlanta", playerPicks.getPickedTeam(13));

            poolDataMockcontrol.reset();
            //Retrain the mock object
            mockPoolData.getOpenPool();
            fbPool = createFbPool();
            poolDataMockcontrol.setReturnValue(fbPool);
            mockPoolData.savePlayersPicks(null);
            poolDataMockcontrol.setMatcher(MockControl.ALWAYS_MATCHER);
            mockPoolData.getPlayersPicks("TimmyC", "9/17/2003");
            poolDataMockcontrol.setReturnValue(createUpdatedPlayerPicks());
            poolDataMockcontrol.replay();
            //Process the updates from the request
            ppickServlet.storePlayersPicks(ppickServletRequest);
            //Get the updated player picks and check to make sure
            // the updates were made correctly
            playerPicks = ppickServlet.getPlayerPicks(ppickServletRequest);
            assertEquals("Kansas City", playerPicks.getPickedTeam(0));
            assertEquals("Houston", playerPicks.getPickedTeam(1));
            assertEquals("Indianapolis", playerPicks.getPickedTeam(2));
            assertEquals("NY Giants", playerPicks.getPickedTeam(3));
            assertEquals("Chicago", playerPicks.getPickedTeam(4));
            assertEquals("Cleveland", playerPicks.getPickedTeam(5));
            assertEquals("Dallas", playerPicks.getPickedTeam(6));
            assertEquals("Washington", playerPicks.getPickedTeam(7));
            assertEquals("Jacksonville", playerPicks.getPickedTeam(8));
            assertEquals("Denver", playerPicks.getPickedTeam(9));
            assertEquals("Buffalo", playerPicks.getPickedTeam(10));
            assertEquals("Baltimore", playerPicks.getPickedTeam(11));
            assertEquals("San Francisco", playerPicks.getPickedTeam(12));
            assertEquals("St. Louis", playerPicks.getPickedTeam(13));

    }
    catch (Exception e)
    {
        fail("Error testing EditPlayerPicks Exception is " + e);
        e.printStackTrace();
    }
}
```

And we have to update the servlet's getPlayerPicks() method as shown in Listing 4-11.

Listing 4-11. *getPlayerPicks() Method of the PlayerPickServlet*

```
PlayersPicks getPlayerPicks(HttpServletRequest request)
    {
        PoolData poolData =
                        (PoolData)request.getSession().getAttribute("PoolData");
        PlayersPicks playerPicks =
                        poolData.getPlayersPicks(request.getParameter("username"),
                                            request.getParameter("poolDate"));
        return(playerPicks);
    }
```

If you look at the testEditPlayerPicks() test, you will see that it is very similar to the testMakePlayerPicks() test. The main difference is that the testEditPlayerPicks() test has to get the current picks for the specified player before processing the new picks specified in the request. Because of this, we have to update the getPlayerPicks() method of the servlet so that it can get the picks for the specified player from the database instead of the session data. This requires us to add some training steps to the getPlayerPicks() method of the mockPoolData in our test so that the servlet will return the correct value when called. Notice how we have to reset and retrain the mockPoolData object because we have to have mockPoolData.getPlayerPicks() return two different values for the same call depending on when it is called. Doing this gets the test to pass. Unfortunately, the updates to the servlet's getPlayerPicks() method causes the testMakePlayerPicks() test to fail, so we have to go back and add the training for mockPoolData.getPlayerPicks() to the testMakePlayerPicks() test. This is normal and is just part of the iterative process of TDD.

At this point, we have finished implementing the behavior of Use Case 5 from the servlet point of view. There is still more work that needs to be done to the servlet before it can be run in a real servlet container, but most of the core methods are complete. What is missing is the framework needed to process the actual HTTP request and return the HTTP response to the user. We will add the HTTP request logic later; what we need to work on now is how to return the data created in the servlet back to the user through the HTTP response. This means we have to develop the JSPs needed to convert the servlet's data to the HTTP response.

Hands-On Exercises

Before you move on to developing JSPs using TDD, it's time to test your knowledge of servlet development using TDD and try to add some more functionality to the application on your own. Your assignment is to implement the servlet needed to implement part of Use Case 4 (Administrator Posts Results). You need to implement the behavior needed to post the results for weekly picks for the football pool. Don't worry about how the servlet will pass the data to the JSP; just use the core classes developed in this chapter and the hands-on solutions from Chapter 3 to develop a servlet that will get the data you need to post the pool results.

Developing JSPs Using TDD

Developing JSPs using TDD is a little different from developing servlets. JSPs are used to show the user a view of the data being displayed. So not only does a JSP have to function correctly, but some work must also be done to ensure that it looks good and presents the data in a logical way. TDD can only be used to make sure the JSP functions correctly, not that it looks good. The job of creating a good-looking display is left up to the development team. Developing a JSP using TDD does, however, usually produce a better structured JSP with a cleaner interface between the servlet and JSP. This leads to a more reliable application that is easier to maintain.

Unlike a servlet, whose behavior can be defined by looking at use cases, a JSP's behavior is defined by what the page should look like. Therefore the first part of developing a JSP is to come up with the visual design of the page. The visual design of a JSP page is usually in the form of a drawing or picture or maybe even a static HTML mock-up.

There are two main aspects to developing a JSP. The first aspect is determining how to turn the view of the page into a set of HTML elements that can be viewed by the browser. The second aspect is to determine what data the JSP page must have in order to render the page correctly. TDD cannot help in translating the visual design of the page into a set of HTML elements, but it can help determine what data needs to be passed to the JSP page. TDD can also help ensure that changes to the rest of the code do not break the JSP pages.

The development of the JSP page usually begins by translating the visual design of the page into HTML elements that will be used to create the actual page. This can be done with some JSP development tools or manually. Once you know what elements will be used to render the various labels, tables, buttons, etc., of the visual design of the page, you can then start developing tests for the output of the JSP using different data sets and conditions. These tests will not only help you develop the JSP page, but also help you determine how the data will be passed from the servlet to the JSP page.

I'll illustrate the process by developing one of the JSPs we need for the football pool. In the previous section, we developed the servlet that lets players make their football picks for the weekly pool. Let's develop the corresponding JSP for this servlet. The design of the page for this part of the application was presented in Chapter 2 when I described how players would make their picks. Let's review the visual design of the JSP page so we can determine what HTML elements we are going to use for the page and then write the tests we need to finish the development of the page.

If you look at the player pick sheet mock-up as shown in Figure 4-1, you will see that the page has the following elements:

- A title showing what week the picks are for and the name of the player making the picks

- A table with three columns (game number, home team, away team) and a row for each game

- A radio button for each home and away team

- A team icon for each home and away team

- A text field for the player to enter the total score for the Monday night game

- A text field for the player to enter his or her e-mail address

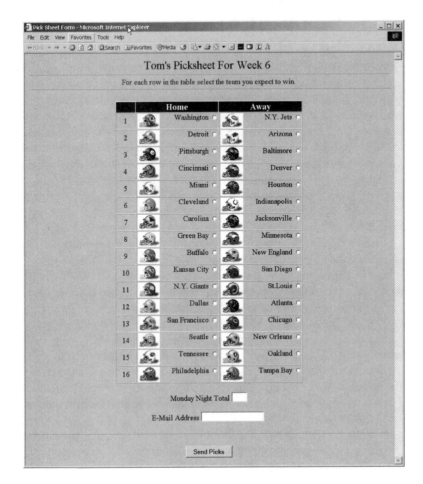

Figure 4-1. *Player pick sheet mock-up*

We then use our favorite JSP development tool to translate each of these elements to HTML elements. We create a JSP called PickPage.jsp that just outputs some static HTML in order to verify that the design of the page looks correct. The resultant JSP is show in Listing 4-12.

Listing 4-12. *Static JSP for Displaying Player Picks*

```
<HTML><HEAD>
<TITLE>Pick Sheet Form</TITLE>
<BODY text=#000000 bgColor=#00FFFF background="" ;>
<FORM name=theForm action=http://localhost:8080/FootBallPool/PlayerPickServlet
     method=post     encType=x-www-form-encoded>
<CENTER>
   <P><BIG>Tom's Picksheet for Week 5</BIG><BR>
   <HR>
      <FONT color=#000080>
      For each row in the table select the team you expect to win.
```

```
      <HR>
      </FONT>
</CENTER><BR>
<DIV align=center>
<CENTER>
<TABLE cellSpacing=0 cellPadding=1 border=1>
  <TBODY>
  <TR align=middle bgColor=#000000>
    <TD align=middle width=50><FONT color=#ffffff><BIG><B></B></BIG></FONT></TD>
    <TD align=middle width=220><FONT
      color=#ffffff><BIG><B>Home</B></BIG></FONT></TD>
    <TD align=middle width=220><FONT
      color=#ffffff><BIG><B>Away</B></BIG></FONT></TD>
</TR>
<TR align=middle bgColor=#000000>
    <TD align=middle width=50> 1</TD>
<TD align=right width=220><IMG src='images/Green Bay.gif' align=left>
<FONT color=#000000> Green Bay
  <INPUT type=radio size=2 name=Game_1 ></FONT>
</TD>
<TD align=right width=220><IMG src='images/Kansas City.gif' align=left>
  <FONT color=#000000> Kansas City
    <INPUT type=radio size=2 name=Game_1 ></FONT>
</TD>
</TR>
 </TBODY></TABLE></CENTER></DIV>
<DIV align=center>
<CENTER><FONT color=#000000>
<P>Monday Night Total <INPUT size=2 name=MNTotal></P></FONT></CENTER></DIV>
<DIV align=center>
<CENTER><FONT color=#000000>
<P>E-Mail Address <INPUT name=email type=text>  </P></FONT></CENTER></DIV>
<HR align=center>
<DIV align=center>
<CENTER>
<P><INPUT type=button value="Send Picks"> </P></DIV></FORM></CENTER></BODY></HTML>
```

Next we will start to develop some tests that will help us make the JSP more dynamic and determine what data the page needs.

Writing tests for JSPs is a little harder than writing tests for servlets. Although a number of tools can be used to test the resultant HTML output by JSPs, there is no good tool for testing JSPs in isolation. We can, however, use ServletUnit to run a servlet and display a JSP. We don't want to develop a servlet for each JSP we want to test because this would be inefficient. Instead we are going to develop a generic servlet that we can use to test any JSP using ServletUnit. We will call this servlet the JSPDispatcherServlet. The code for the JSPDispatcherServlet appears in Listing 4-13.

Listing 4-13. *JSPDispatcherServlet*

```
public class JSPDispatcherServlet extends HttpServlet
{
        public void doGet(HttpServletRequest request, HttpServletResponse response)
                throws ServletException, IOException
        {
            response.setContentType("text/html");
            String jspPage = request.getParameter("JSPPage");
            RequestDispatcher dispatcher =
                            getServletContext().getRequestDispatcher(jspPage);
            dispatcher.include(request, response);
            return;
        }

        public void doPost(HttpServletRequest request,
                            HttpServletResponse response)
                throws ServletException, IOException
        {
            doGet(request, response);
        }
}
```

As you can see, there is not much to the servlet; it simply gets the JSP to display from the request and then just dispatches it. This will allow us to run any JSP without having to develop a specific servlet for each JSP page.

The first test we write will call the JSPDispatcherServlet to display PickPage.jsp. The test, shown in Listing 4-14, will use ServletUnit to verify all the visual elements of the page are there and that they contain the correct data.

Listing 4-14. *Test for PickPage.jsp*

```
public void testDisplayPlayerPicks()
{
    ServletRunner sr = new ServletRunner();
    sr.registerServlet("JSPDispatcherServlet",
                            JSPDispatcherServlet.class.getName());
    ServletUnitClient sc = sr.newClient();
    WebRequest request =
        new PostMethodWebRequest("http://localhost/JSPDispatcherServlet");
    request.setParameter("JSPPage", "/PickPage.jsp");
    try
    {
        InvocationContext ic = sc.newInvocation(request);
        JSPDispatcherServlet jspDispServlet =
                                (JSPDispatcherServlet) ic.getServlet();
        assertNull("A session already exists",
                        ic.getRequest().getSession(false));
```

```
        jspDispServlet.doGet(jspDispRequest, ic.getResponse());
        WebResponse response = sc.getResponse(ic);

        Document pickPageDoc = response.getDOM();
        NodeList h2NodeList = pickPageDoc.getElementsByTagName("h2");
        if (h2NodeList.getLength() > 0)
        {
            Node h2Node = h2NodeList.item(0);
            Node childNode = h2Node.getFirstChild();
            String h2NodeStr = childNode.getNodeValue();
            assertEquals("TimmyC's Picksheet for Week 6", h2NodeStr);
        }
        else
        {
            fail("Can't find h2 element");
        }
        assertNotNull("No response received", response);
        assertEquals("tables", 1, response.getTables().length);
        assertEquals("columns", 3,
                    response.getTables()[0].getColumnCount());
        assertEquals("rows", 15,
                    response.getTables()[0].getRowCount());
        assertEquals("", form.getParameterValue("MNTotal"));
        assertEquals("", form.getParameterValue("email"));
    }
    catch (Exception e)
    {
        System.out.println("Error getting reponse Exception is " + e);
        e.printStackTrace();
    }
}
```

The test is similar to our earlier servlet tests with a couple of differences. The main difference is that we are not testing the servlet but the resultant JSP, so after we set up the servlet we call the doGet method to dispatch the JSP page. Once the JSP page is dispatched, we use the getResponse method of the ServletUnitClient to get the actual HTML that is generated by the JSP. ServletUnit's WebResponse class is used to hold the response from the servlet. The WebResponse class has a number of methods that can be used to parse the response. Basically an element of the WebResponse can be found by doing the following:

- Getting the actual input stream of the response and parsing through it to find the element

- Converting the returned HTML into an XML DOM and then searching for an element as in an XML document

For HTML elements like forms, tables, and links, the WebResponse class contains special methods to find these types of elements.

For more details on the different methods of the WebResponse class, check out the ServletUnit javadocs.

If you look at the test, you will see that once we get the response object we check for the required elements. We first check the title of the page to make sure it's there and contains the correct text. We then check the table to make sure it is the right size. (We should also check the value of each cell of the table, but to keep the example small I chose not to show this.) After we check the table, we check for the Monday Night Total and Email fields to make sure that they are there and are empty. Many other HTML elements can be checked like background color, font size, etc., but these elements only affect the look of the page and not its content. For our tests, we are only concerned that the page contains the required fields to display the data and that the data displayed is correct, so we only need to check a subset of elements for the page.

If you run this test with the PickPage.jsp, it fails because the static page does not contain the correct data. To get the test to pass, we have to make the JSP more dynamic so that it can accept data from the servlet and display the correct data. We also have to update our test to set the values of parameters and attributes of the servlet so that it passes the correct data to the JSP.

First we update the JSP as shown in Listing 4-15 (**changes in bold**).

Listing 4-15. *Updated JSP for Displaying Player Picks*

```
<%@ page import="com.apress.tddbook.FootballPool,
                 com.apress.tddbook.Game"%>

<HTML><HEAD><TITLE>Pick Sheet Form</TITLE>
<BODY text=#000000 bgColor=#00FFFF background="" ;>
<FORM name=theForm action=http://localhost:8080/FootBallPool/PlayerPickServlet
      method=post
encType=x-www-form-encoded>
<CENTER>
<h2><%out.println(request.getParameter("playersName")
+ "'s Picksheet for Week " + request.getParameter("weekNum"));
%></h2> <BR>
<HR>
<FONT color=#000080>For each row in the table select the team you expect to win.

<HR>
</FONT></CENTER><BR>
<DIV align=center>
<CENTER>
<TABLE cellSpacing=0 cellPadding=1 border=1>
  <TBODY>
  <TR align=middle bgColor=#000000>
    <TD align=middle width=50><FONT color=#ffffff><BIG><B></B></BIG></FONT></TD>
    <TD align=middle width=220><FONT
      color=#ffffff><BIG><B>Home</B></BIG></FONT></TD>
```

```
<TD align=middle width=220><FONT
  color=#ffffff><BIG><B>Away</B></BIG></FONT></TD></TR>

<%
        FootballPool pool = (FootballPool)request.getAttribute("openPool");
        if(pool != null)
        {
        int numGames = pool.size();
            for(int i = 0; i < numGames; i++)
            {
                String homeTeamName = pool.getHomeTeam(i);
                String awayTeamName = pool.getAwayTeam(i);

                out.println("<TR align=middle>");
                out.println("<TD align=middle width=50>" + (i + 1) + "</TD>");
                out.println("<TD align=right width=220><IMG src='images/" +
                                homeTeamName + ".gif'" +"align=left>
                    <FONT color=#000000>" +  homeTeamName+
                      "<INPUT type=radio size=2 " +
                        "name=Game_"+ i + " ></FONT></TD>");
                out.println("<TD align=right width=220><IMG src='images/" +
                                awayTeamName + ".gif'" +
                      "align=left><FONT color=#000000>" +  awayTeamName+
                      "<INPUT type=radio size=2 " +
                      "name=Game_"+ i + " ></FONT></TD>");
                out.println("</tr>");
            }
        }
    %>
      </TBODY></TABLE></CENTER></DIV>
<DIV align=center>
<CENTER><FONT color=#000000>
<P>Monday Night Total <INPUT size=2 name=MNTotal></P></FONT></CENTER></DIV>
<DIV align=center>
<CENTER><FONT color=#000000>
<P>E-Mail Address <INPUT name=email type=text>  </P></FONT></CENTER></DIV>
<HR align=center>
<DIV align=center>
<CENTER>
<P><INPUT type=button value="Send Picks"> </P></DIV></FORM></CENTER></BODY></HTML>
```

If you look at the updated JSP, you will see that it needs three pieces of data to display properly: playersName, weekNum, and a FootballPool object.

Now that we understand what data the JSP needs to display the page correctly, we update the test as shown in Listing 4-16 (**changes in bold**).

Listing 4-16. *Test for PickPlayer.jsp with Mock Objects*

```
public void testDisplayPlayerPicks()
    {
        ServletRunner sr = new ServletRunner();
        sr.registerServlet("JSPDispatcherServlet",
                                JSPDispatcherServlet.class.getName());
        ServletUnitClient sc = sr.newClient();
        WebRequest request =
            new PostMethodWebRequest("http://localhost/JSPDispatcherServlet");
        request.setParameter("playersName", "TimmyC");
        request.setParameter("weekNum", "6");
        request.setParameter("JSPPage", "/PickPage.jsp");
        try
        {
            InvocationContext ic = sc.newInvocation(request);
            JSPDispatcherServlet jspDispServlet =
                                (JSPDispatcherServlet) ic.getServlet();
            assertNull("A session already exists",
                            ic.getRequest().getSession(false));
            HttpServletRequest jspDispRequest = ic.getRequest();
            HttpSession servletSession = jspDispRequest.getSession();
            jspDispRequest.setAttribute("openPool", createFbPool());
            jspDispServlet.doGet(jspDispRequest, ic.getResponse());
            WebResponse response = sc.getResponse(ic);

            Document pickPageDoc = response.getDOM();
            NodeList h2NodeList = pickPageDoc.getElementsByTagName("h2");
            if (h2NodeList.getLength() > 0)
            {
                Node h2Node = h2NodeList.item(0);
                Node childNode = h2Node.getFirstChild();
                String h2NodeStr = childNode.getNodeValue();
                assertEquals("TimmyC's Picksheet for Week 6", h2NodeStr);
            }
            else
            {
                fail("Can't find h2 element");
            }
            assertNotNull("No response received", response);
            assertEquals("tables", 1, response.getTables().length);
            assertEquals("columns", 3,
                        response.getTables()[0].getColumnCount());
            assertEquals("rows", 15,
                        response.getTables()[0].getRowCount());
            WebForm form = response.getForms()[0];
```

```
            assertEquals("", form.getParameterValue("MNTotal"));
            assertEquals("", form.getParameterValue("email"));
        }
        catch (Exception e)
        {
            System.out.println("Error getting reponse Exception is " + e);
            e.printStackTrace();
        }
    }
}
```

Now if you run the test, you will see it passes. It is a little strange testing HTML output without actually seeing the resultant output, but these tests help you separate the display of the data from the look and feel of the page. This lets you concentrate on the design of the JSP and how the JSP and servlet exchange data.

As mentioned in the beginning of this section, TDD can help develop only the functional part of the JSP and how it interacts with the servlet. The visual look of the servlet and how the data is presented must still be verified manually. But once the look is created, the tests developed for the JSP will help ensure that the data is always displayed correctly as the code of the JSP and servlets are changed.

Hands-On Exercises

It's time to test your knowledge of JSP development using TDD by trying to add some more functionality to the application on your own. Your assignment is to implement the JSP needed to display the data of the servlet developed in the previous "Hands-On Exercises" section. Your first step should be to turn to the visual design of the results page shown in Chapter 2 in Figure 2-6 and determine the HTML elements needed to render the page. Then develop a test for the JSP page using the JSPDispatcherServlet. After you develop the test, use it to create the dynamic JSP for the results page.

Putting It Together

So far, we have developed the servlet and JSP in isolation. Now it's time to put the two together so that we can finish development. The JSP and servlet have a symbiotic relationship. The servlet needs the JSP to display its data, and the JSP needs the servlet to get the data to display. Our tests for the servlet that we have developed so far have concentrated on developing tests that would satisfy the behavior of the use cases. This led us to create servlets that would be able to get certain types of data for the football pool. The tests we have developed for the JSP using the JSPDispatcherServlet have helped us to define what data each JSP needs. Now what we are going to do is to create an end-to-end test that will help us finish development of the servlet to make sure it will be able to display its data correctly using the associated JSP.

This test should be easy to develop because we already created a test for the JSP output when we developed the JSPs, so all we have to do is to take that test and replace the JSPDispatcherServlet with the PlayerPickServlet that will be used to call the JSP. If we do that, we get the test shown in Listing 4-17.

Listing 4-17. *End-to-End Test for PlayerPickServlet*

```
public void testDisplayPlayerPicksWithRealJSP()
    {
        //Get mock object
        PoolData mockPoolData = (PoolData) poolDataMockcontrol.getMock();
        //Train the mock object
        mockPoolData.getOpenPool();
        //Create return value for mock method
        FootballPool fbPool = createFbPool();
        poolDataMockcontrol.setReturnValue(fbPool);
        poolDataMockcontrol.replay();
        ServletRunner sr = new ServletRunner();
        sr.registerServlet("PlayerPickServlet", PlayerPickServlet.class.getName());
        ServletUnitClient sc = sr.newClient();
        WebRequest request =
                new PostMethodWebRequest("http://localhost/PlayerPickServlet");
        request.setParameter("playersName", "TimmyC");
        request.setParameter("weekNum", "6");
        try
        {
            InvocationContext ic = sc.newInvocation(request);
            PlayerPickServlet ppickServlet = (PlayerPickServlet) ic.getServlet();
            assertNull("A session already exists",
                            ic.getRequest().getSession(false));
            HttpServletRequest ppickServletRequest = ic.getRequest();
            HttpSession servletSession = ppickServletRequest.getSession();
            servletSession.setAttribute("PoolData", mockPoolData);
            ppickServlet.doGet(ppickServletRequest, ic.getResponse());
            WebResponse response = sc.getResponse(ic);

            Document pickPageDoc = response.getDOM();
            NodeList h2NodeList = pickPageDoc.getElementsByTagName("h2");
            if (h2NodeList.getLength() > 0)
            {
                Node h2Node = h2NodeList.item(0);
                Node childNode = h2Node.getFirstChild();
                String h2NodeStr = childNode.getNodeValue();
                assertEquals("TimmyC's Picksheet for Week 6", h2NodeStr);
            }
            else
            {
                fail("Can't find h2 element");
            }
            assertNotNull("No response received", response);
            assertEquals("tables", 1, response.getTables().length);
            assertEquals("columns", 3,
```

```
                        response.getTables()[0].getColumnCount());
            assertEquals("rows", 15,
                        response.getTables()[0].getRowCount());
            WebForm form = response.getForms()[0];
            assertEquals("", form.getParameterValue("MNTotal"));
            assertEquals("", form.getParameterValue("email"));
        }
        catch (Exception e)
        {
            fail("Error getting reponse Exception is " + e);
            e.printStackTrace();
        }
    }
}
```

If you look at this test, it is similar to the test of the JSP alone, except that there is no setup of the parameters needed for the JSP, and the servlet that is called is the real one. Of course, this test fails and causes us to add the doGet() method to the PlayerPickServlet class as shown in Listing 4-18.

Listing 4-18. *doGet Method for PlayerPickServlet*

```
public void doGet(HttpServletRequest request, HttpServletResponse response)
        throws ServletException, IOException
    {
        FootballPool fbPool = getOpenPool(request);
        request.setAttribute("openPool", fbPool);
        RequestDispatcher dispatcher =
                    getServletContext().getRequestDispatcher("/PickPage.jsp");
        dispatcher.include(request, response
        return;
    }
```

With this added code, the test passes. The servlet is still not accessing the real database but using the mockPoolData class. In Chapter 6, we will create a class that the servlet can use to access the real database, but for now the mockPoolData class along with the code we have developed in this chapter has allowed us to create a servlet and JSP that satisfies most of Use Case 5 from a user interface point of view.

There is still some more work that has to be done before we can deploy the servlets and JSPs to a real application server. Besides creating a class that will allow the servlets to access the real database, we also have to understand how the servlets will interact with each other and how they will all be tied together. These topics will be discussed in Chapter 6.

Hands-On Exercises

It's time to test your knowledge of JSP/servlet development using TDD by trying to add some more functionality to the application on your own. Your assignment is to complete the development of the servlet/JSP needed to implement part of Use Case 4. You need to finish implementing the behavior needed to post the results for weekly picks for the football pool.

Use the code developed in the previous "Hands-On Exercises" section to create a test that does an end-to-end test of the servlet and allows you to complete the development of the servlet.

Summary

In this chapter, you have expanded your knowledge of TDD and learned how to apply it to the development of servlets and JSPs. I introduced you to a couple different methods for simulating a real servlet container, and we used the ServletUnit framework to help us develop our servlets. ServletUnit allowed us to develop our servlets in isolation without having to configure or maintain a real servlet container. I then showed you how to develop a servlet for the Football Pool application in a simple step-by-step manner using TDD.

After the main methods of the servlet were developed, we then worked on developing JSPs. Again using ServletUnit as the test framework, we developed a JSP in a simple, incremental way. This allowed us to concentrate on the design of the JSP as well as define what data needs to be exchanged between the servlet and JSP.

The final section of the chapter showed how to put the servlet and JSP together to make sure they work together and contain all the features needed to implement the required behavior. Of course, at this point the servlet and JSP are still not completely finished. We have not proven that they will work when they get deployed to a real application server, nor have we integrated the database with the servlet. These tasks can only be done once we start putting the application together. Using TDD to perform these tasks will be explained in Chapter 6. The next chapter, Chapter 5, will explain how to use TDD to develop GUIs by creating the Admin GUI for the Football Pool application.

■■■

Developing User Interfaces Using Test-Driven Development

Beauty is only skin deep, but ugly goes straight to the bone. In other words, an ugly, poorly functioning user interface can ruin an application even if it has a good core. TDD cannot help you make the user interface look better, but it can help you create a user interface that has fewer bugs and is easier to maintain. Automated testing has not been as widely used with user interfaces as it has with server-side components like servlets and EJBs, mostly due to lack of good testing tools as well as general difficulty of testing user interfaces. But there are now a number of good tools for testing both web-based and Swing-based user interfaces, so there is no reason why the principles of TDD cannot be applied to user interfaces. Developing user interfaces is a lot different from developing servlets and EJBs, so the methods of TDD must be applied in a slightly different way.

This chapter will show you how you can develop Swing-based user interfaces using TDD. We will do this by going through the steps needed to create the Swing-based user interface used by the administrator to run the football pool. As you go through these steps, you will learn how to use testing tools like JFCUnit, Jemmy, and others to automate the testing of user interfaces. You will also learn how to apply the techniques of TDD to user interfaces so you will be able to develop them in a simple, incremental way.

Problems with Automated Testing of User Interfaces

You cannot test a user interface by calling its API methods like you can with servlets and EJBs because it doesn't have any API that can be called by a testing framework. Testing of user interfaces requires a user to interact with the various forms, buttons, links, and other components of the interface. This can be a tedious and error-prone process if testing is done manually during development. Also, the quality of the tests depends heavily on the experience of the tester as well as how well the test environment is set up.

It would be nice if this testing could be automated, but simulating a user's interactions is not an easy task. For example, in order to automate the clicking of a button, a testing framework would have to have some way to start the user interface, locate the button, and then simulate a user clicking it. There are a number of ways to do all these things, but sometimes automating the testing is so time consuming and complicated that it isn't any better than doing the tests manually.

It's also important to understand that user interaction with the interface is unpredictable. Users can navigate the interface in a number of different ways, so any testing has to test all different possibilities to be effective. As the size of the web site or Swing GUI increases, it gets harder and harder to effectively test all the paths that users can take through the interface, especially if the interface is constantly changing.

Despite these difficulties, automating the testing of user interfaces is possible and worthwhile. There are now a number of good tools that can simulate user interactions with both web and Swing user interfaces. Although it may take a little while to understand and learn these tools, once you master them, creating automated user interface tests becomes fairly straightforward and worth the effort.

Approach to Testing User Interfaces

Before I explain how to develop a user interface using TDD, we should talk a little about the best type of testing to use for user interfaces. Since you can only test a user interface by simulating user input, you basically have available two approaches to take: black-box testing or white-box testing.

Black-box testing is basically functional testing. You perform some action on the user interface and then check the state of the user interface after the action is complete to make sure it performed correctly. With black-box testing, tests are written against the requirements without any knowledge of the internal structure of the code.

White-box (or glass-box) testing is very similar to black-box testing except for the fact that the tests are written with the knowledge of the internal structure of the code. So white-box testing is more complete because not only are tests written from requirements but from inspection of the internal code. With white-box testing, extra tests are written to ensure that all paths of the code are properly tested.

For the most part, the TDD process for user interfaces relies on black-box testing because the tests are written from the requirements before any code exists. This means that there is no code to inspect to create white-box tests. However, since refactoring is part of the TDD process, as the code is inspected and refactored, it is possible to use white-box testing to improve test coverage.

On the whole, the tools used to test user interfaces can be employed to do both black-box and white-box testing because they are able to simulate almost any user input and test environment. Most of them are also able to validate the state of the user interface. This is all that is required to properly test a user interface.

Developing the Admin Interface Using Test-Driven Development

As described in Chapter 2, the Admin GUI will be used to set up the games for the weekly pool as well as post the results and update the pool status. Like the web interface, besides the use cases, we also have a picture that tells us how the GUI should look and work. If you look at

Figure 5-1, you will see the main screen of the Admin GUI. The list on the left side shows all the different pools that have been set up so far. When the administrator selects an item in the list, the games associated with that week appear on the right side. Four buttons appear below the list box for the pools. The function of each of these buttons is defined as follows:

- *New Pool:* This button is used to add a new entry to the list. Clicking this button opens a dialog box (Figure 5-2) that allows the administrator to enter a name and closing date for the new pool as well as create a table of games for the week.

- *Open Pool:* This button is used to change the status of the selected pool to open.

- *Close Pool:* This button is used to change the status of the selected pool to closed.

- *Delete:* This button is used to delete the selected pool.

There are also two buttons on the right side below the list of games. These buttons are used to edit the list of games or post the results for the games.

Between the description of the GUI and the use cases, we should have enough to start developing the Admin GUI, but there is one more piece of information that we need before we can start. We need to know how the GUI is going to communicate with the server and exchange information about the pool. For the Admin GUI, we decide that it will communicate to the server through RMI using a stateless session bean. This bean should contain all the methods needed by the GUI to get pool information from the server as well as create new pools and update pool information.

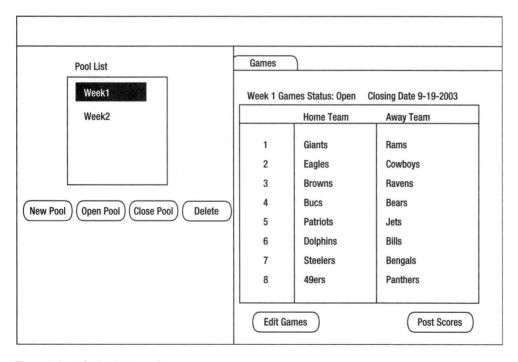

Figure 5-1. *Admin GUI mock-up*

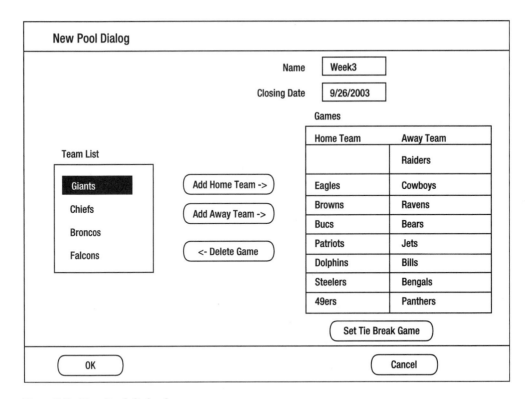

Figure 5-2. *New Pool dialog box*

The interface for this stateless session bean has not been designed yet because we hadn't yet needed it. Let's define the interface now by reviewing the behavior for the main screen of the GUI. For this screen, we need to be able to get two pieces of information in order to populate the screens. The GUI needs to be able to get the list of the weekly pools for the pool list, as well as the information about the games for the selected pool. To get the list of weekly pools, the GUI uses the getPoolList() method of the stateless session bean, which returns a vector of strings containing the pool name. To get detailed information about a particular pool, the GUI will use getPoolInfo(poolName), which will return a FootballPool class containing all the information about the games.

Creating the Stub Class

Now that we understand how the GUI should look and work and know how it will communicate to the server, we can start to develop it. The question is, as always, where to start. We could start by creating the shell of the GUI and then filling in the functionality, but before we do that we should first create a class that can be used to simulate the functionality of the stateless session bean. This will allow us to develop our GUI in isolation without having to have a J2EE server up and running. For now, to develop the main screen of the GUI, we only need to mock out the getPoolList() and getPoolInfo(poolName) methods. We start by first creating FBPoolServer, which is used to define the interface of the stateless session bean used by the GUI (see Listing 5-1). Eventually this interface will be the EJB's remote interface. For the moment this interface only has the two methods, but more will be added as we include more functionality to the GUI.

Listing 5-1. *FBPoolServer Interface*

```
public interface FBPoolServer{
    /** Get a list of the pools that are defined */
    Vector getPoolList();
    /** Get all the information about a particular pool */
    FootballPool getPoolInfo(String poolName);
}
```

Next we need to implement this interface. We could use mock objects like we did in some of the tests in Chapters 3 and 4, but the GUI development will require a more complicated representation of the stateless session bean, so we decide to develop a stub class to implement the interface. We create the stub as we do any other class, by first creating a test. The first test we need to write is the test to get the pool list. This test gets an FBPoolServer object by just creating a new FBPoolServerStub object. It then calls the getPoolList() method and gets a vector of pool names. For this test, we decide that to develop the GUI we only need a list that contains the first three weeks of games for the pool (see Listing 5-2).

Listing 5-2. *testGetPoolList() Method*

```
public void testGetPoolList()
{
        FBPoolServer fbPoolServer = new FBPoolServerStub();
        Vector poolList = fbPoolServer.getPoolList();
        assertEquals(poolList.size(), 3);
        String poolName = (String)poolList.elementAt(0);
        assertEquals("2004-09-10", poolName);
        poolName = (String)poolList.elementAt(1);
        assertEquals("2004-09-17", poolName);
        poolName = (String)poolList.elementAt(2);
        assertEquals("2004-09-24", poolName);
}
```

To get this test to work, we create the FBPoolServerStub class and implement the getPoolList() method as shown in Listing 5-3. To implement the getPoolList() method, this class just creates a dummy poolList vector at initialization and returns this vector when the getPoolList() method is called.

Listing 5-3. *FBPoolServerStub*

```
public class FBPoolServerStub implements FBPoolServer
{
    Vector m_poolList = new Vector();

    public FBPoolServerStub()
    {
```

```
            //Initialize the pool list and pool info list with dummy information
            // that will be used by the mock object
            initPoolData();
        }
        /** Get a list of the pools that are defined */
        public Vector getPoolList(){
            return(m_poolList);
        }
        /** Get all the information about a particular pool */
        public FootballPool getPoolInfo(String poolName) {
            FootballPool fbPool = null;
            return(fbPool);
        }
    private void initPoolData()
    {
        m_poolList.addElement("2004-09-10");
        m_poolList.addElement("2004-09-17");
        m_poolList.addElement("2004-09-24");
    }
}
```

The next test we need to implement is the test of the getPoolInfo() method. This method will return a FootballPool object given the name of the pool. First we create a test for the getPoolInfo() method as shown in Listing 5-4. This test just gets the football pool for date 9/17/2004 and checks to make sure all the games are correct.

Listing 5-4. *testGetPoolInfo() Method*

```
public void testGetPoolInfo() {
        FBPoolServer fbPoolServer = new FBPoolServerStub();
        FootballPool pool = fbPoolServer.getPoolInfo("2004-09-17");
        assertEquals("Kansas City",pool.getAwayTeam(0));
        assertEquals("Green Bay",pool.getHomeTeam(0));
        assertEquals("Houston",pool.getAwayTeam(1));
        assertEquals("Tennessee",pool.getHomeTeam(1));
        assertEquals("Carolina",pool.getAwayTeam(2));
        assertEquals("Indianapolis",pool.getHomeTeam(2));
        assertEquals("NY Giants",pool.getAwayTeam(3));
        assertEquals("New England",pool.getHomeTeam(3));
        assertEquals("Chicago",pool.getAwayTeam(4));
        assertEquals("New Orleans",pool.getHomeTeam(4));
        assertEquals("Oakland",pool.getAwayTeam(5));
        assertEquals("Cleveland",pool.getHomeTeam(5));
        assertEquals("Philadelphia",pool.getAwayTeam(6));
        assertEquals("Dallas",pool.getHomeTeam(6));
        assertEquals("Tampa Bay",pool.getAwayTeam(7));
        assertEquals("Washington",pool.getHomeTeam(7));
        assertEquals("Miami",pool.getAwayTeam(8));
```

```
        assertEquals("Jacksonville",pool.getHomeTeam(8));
        assertEquals("Pittsburgh",pool.getAwayTeam(9));
        assertEquals("Denver",pool.getHomeTeam(9));
        assertEquals("Buffalo",pool.getAwayTeam(10));
        assertEquals("NY Jets",pool.getHomeTeam(10));
        assertEquals("Baltimore",pool.getAwayTeam(11));
        assertEquals("Arizona",pool.getHomeTeam(11));
        assertEquals("San Francisco",pool.getAwayTeam(12));
        assertEquals("Seattle",pool.getHomeTeam(12));
        assertEquals("Atlanta",pool.getAwayTeam(13));
        assertEquals("St. Louis",pool.getHomeTeam(13));
    }
```

To get the test to work, we have to add the code in Listing 5-5 to the FBPoolServerStub class.

Listing 5-5. *getPoolInfo() Method for FBPoolServerStub*

```
public FootballPool getPoolInfo(String poolName) {
        FootballPool pool = new FootballPool("2004-09-17");
        try
        {
            pool.addGame("Kansas City", "Green Bay");
                pool.addGame("Houston", "Tennessee");
                pool.addGame("Carolina", "Indianapolis");
                pool.addGame("NY Giants", "New England");
                pool.addGame("Chicago", "New Orleans");
                pool.addGame("Oakland", "Cleveland");
                pool.addGame("Philadelphia", "Dallas");
                pool.addGame("Tampa Bay", "Washington");
                pool.addGame("Miami", "Jacksonville");
                pool.addGame("Pittsburgh", "Denver");
                pool.addGame("Buffalo", "NY Jets");
                pool.addGame("Baltimore", "Arizona");
                pool.addGame("San Francisco", "Seattle");
                pool.addGame("Atlanta", "St. Louis");
        }
        catch (Exception e)
        {
            System.out.println("Exception getting football pool info Exception is "
                                    + e);
        }
        return(pool);
    }
```

The method allows the test to pass but has a problem. It returns the same pool no matter what pool name is passed in. We will fix this problem later when we need to distinguish between the different pools, but for now we are following the TDD philosophy of doing only what is required to get the test to pass.

Creating the Shell of the GUI

We are now ready to start work on the actual Admin GUI. The first thing we will need to do is create the shell of the GUI. This shell will contain all the components of the Admin GUI as shown in the mock-up, but none of the components will contain any data or function. The code to implement the main class of the GUI is shown in Listing 5-6. Figure 5-3 shows what the empty GUI looks like.

Listing 5-6. *AdminMain Class*

```
package com.apress.tddbook.gui;

import javax.swing.*;
import javax.swing.table.TableColumn;
import java.awt.event.WindowAdapter;
import java.awt.event.WindowEvent;
import java.awt.*;
import java.util.Vector;

public class AdminMain extends JFrame
{
    JSplitPane sPane = new JSplitPane();
    JLabel listLabel = new JLabel("Pool List");
    JList poolList = new JList();
    JScrollPane listScrollPane = new JScrollPane();
    JButton newPoolButton = new JButton("New Pool");
    JButton closePoolButton = new JButton("Close Pool");
    JButton openPoolButton = new JButton("Open Pool");
    JButton deletePoolButton = new JButton("Delete");
    JLabel gameTableLabel = new JLabel("Week 1 Games");
    JLabel statusLabel = new JLabel("Status:Open");
    JLabel closeDateLabel = new JLabel("Closing Date 9-19-2003");
    JTable gameTable = new JTable(14, 3);

    public AdminMain()
    {
        initComponents();

        this.setTitle("Football Pool Administrator");
        this.setName("Football Pool Administrator");
        this.setSize(400, 500);
        this.setVisible(true);
        this.pack();
    }

    /**
     * Set up all the components
     */
```

```
public void initComponents()
{
    newPoolButton.setName("NewPoolButton");
    statusLabel.setHorizontalAlignment(JLabel.CENTER);
    //Set the table column names
    String colName = gameTable.getColumnName(0);
    TableColumn column = gameTable.getColumn(colName);
    column.setMaxWidth(50);
    column.setHeaderValue("");
    colName = gameTable.getColumnName(1);
    column = gameTable.getColumn(colName);
    column.setHeaderValue("Home Team");
    colName = gameTable.getColumnName(2);
    column = gameTable.getColumn(colName);
    column.setHeaderValue("Away Team");

    JScrollPane tableScrollPane = new JScrollPane();
    JButton editGamesButton = new JButton("Edit Games");
    JButton postScoresButton = new JButton("Post Scores");
    JPanel listPanel = new JPanel();
    JPanel tablePanel = new JPanel();
    JPanel listButtonPanel = new JPanel();
    JPanel tableButtonPanel = new JPanel();

    listPanel.setLayout(new BorderLayout());
    listPanel.add(listLabel, BorderLayout.NORTH);
    poolList.setVisibleRowCount(6);
    listScrollPane.setViewportView(poolList);
    listPanel.add(listScrollPane, BorderLayout.CENTER);

    listButtonPanel.add(newPoolButton);
    listButtonPanel.add(openPoolButton);
    listButtonPanel.add(closePoolButton);
    listButtonPanel.add(deletePoolButton);

    listPanel.add(listButtonPanel, BorderLayout.SOUTH);

    JPanel tableLabelPane = new JPanel();
    tableLabelPane.setLayout(new BorderLayout());
    tableLabelPane.add(gameTableLabel, BorderLayout.WEST);
    tableLabelPane.add(statusLabel, BorderLayout.CENTER);
    tableLabelPane.add(closeDateLabel, BorderLayout.EAST);
    tablePanel.setLayout(new BorderLayout());
    tablePanel.add(tableLabelPane, BorderLayout.NORTH);
    tableScrollPane.setViewportView(gameTable);
    tablePanel.add(tableScrollPane, BorderLayout.CENTER);
```

```
        tableButtonPanel.add(editGamesButton);
        tableButtonPanel.add(postScoresButton);

        tablePanel.add(tableButtonPanel, BorderLayout.SOUTH);

        sPane.setLeftComponent(listPanel);
        sPane.setRightComponent(tablePanel);

        addWindowListener(new WindowAdapter()
        {
            public void windowClosing(WindowEvent e)
            {
                System.exit(0);
            }
        });

        this.getContentPane().add(sPane);
    }

    public static void main(String[] args)
    {
        AdminMain fbAdmin = new AdminMain();
    }
}
```

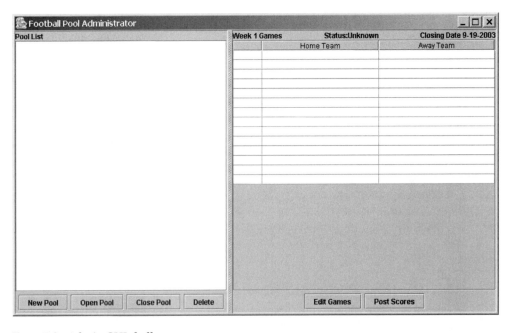

Figure 5-3. *Admin GUI shell*

You may have noticed that we actually wrote some code without having an associated test. When developing GUIs, you usually have to create the shell of the application before you can start testing it. This is because the decisions used to create the shell of the application usually have more to do with aesthetics than functionality, and as far as I know there is no way to test for aesthetics. However, now that we have the shell of the GUI, we can start the normal TDD process of creating a test to drive development and incrementally add functionality to the GUI. The first test we create, though, will not help us add any functionality to the GUI but will help us set up the GUI testing framework.

Setting Up the GUI Testing Framework

In order to set up the GUI testing framework, we have to choose one to use. There are several good ones available. To get the latest list of available GUI testing frameworks, check out the Extensions section of the JUnit site (http://www.junit.org). GUI testing frameworks come in two broad varieties: capture and replay or direct API.

A capture-and-replay testing framework allows users to record their interactions with a GUI and replay those actions back at a later time. Also, when replaying the recorded interactions, you can watch the mouse pointer moving across the frames of the target application without touching the mouse, and you will see the keyboard input performed without using the keyboard. Most capture-and-replay frameworks not only provide a way to simulate user interaction with the GUI, but also provide a way to get the values of labels, text fields, etc., in the GUI. This allows you to create tests that validate the state of the GUI after some actions are performed.

A direct API testing framework is one that uses a JUnit-like API to run tests on a GUI. These APIs usually contain methods to run the GUI, find the individual components of the GUI, get the attributes of any GUI component, and simulate a user's interaction.

Although capture-and-replay testing frameworks are useful for testing GUIs, they are not the best tools for developing GUIs using TDD. These tools usually don't require any programming knowledge and are easy to use. They are often used by Quality Assurance teams to run functional testing after the GUI is complete. However, since tests can't be created until after the GUI contains the functionality being tested, this breaks the TDD model. The other problem with capture-and-replay testing frameworks is that they may be sensitive to the layout of the components of the GUI. This means if the GUI layout changes, you may have to rerecord all the tests. With all this said, however, capture-and-reply frameworks can be useful if you want to quickly create a set of tests that can be used for regression testing.

So for our GUI testing framework, we are going to use a direct API testing framework. There are two good ones available: JFCUnit (https://sourceforge.net/projects/jfcunit/) and Jemmy (http://jemmy.netbeans.org/). Both will be used throughout the examples so you can understand the strengths and weaknesses of each.

GUI TESTING WITH JFCUNIT

Testing a Swing application is a lot different from testing other Java classes. To test a Swing application, you want to start the application and then interact with it by typing in some text and maybe clicking some buttons. If you tried to test a Swing application with the normal JUnit classes, you would run into two problems. The first problem is that your tests would start running before the Swing application is started because JUnit is run in a separate thread from the application. So what would happen is that you start the Swing application in the constructor of the JUnit test and then start running the test methods; since the Swing application would probably take some time to start, the test methods would fail.

The second problem is that even if the test methods waited for the Swing application to start, they would have a hard time interacting with the Swing application because there is no easy way to find and manipulate Swing components from outside the application. Although it is very low level and limited, Java does have the Robot class, which provides a way to automatically enter keystrokes and mouse events. If you wanted to use the Robot class to test Swing applications, you would have to create an additional API that would be used to find the location of the components that you want to test.

The JFCUnit extension solves these two problems. The first thing it provides is a class called JFCTestCase, which is an extension to JUnit's TestCase, that allows the unit test to better work with the AWT thread of the Swing application. The next thing that JFCUnit provides is the JFCTestHelper class. This class is started at the beginning of the unit test and listens to the events on the AWT thread. It keeps track of all the components that are created and has finder methods that can be used by the test methods to get a handle to any component.

The other main feature that JFCUnit provides is a way to interact with the AWT thread. During test method execution, the AWT thread is blocked, so any calls to Swing components will have no effect. In order to interact with Swing components, JFCUnit provides two methods, awtSleep() and awtSleep(long time), that can be used to wake up the AWT thread and allow it to process events. In this way, a test can interact with a Swing component by calling the component's method, doing an awtSleep(), then checking that the action was completed successfully.

For a more details on the JFCUnit API, check out https://sourceforge.net/projects/jfcunit/ or check out my article on JFCUnit at http://www.developer.com/java/other/article.php/1016841.

Creating a test using JFCUnit is not much harder than creating a JUnit test. Let's create a simple JFCUnit test that starts the Admin GUI and then checks to see that the main window is displayed properly (see Listing 5-7).

Listing 5-7. *JFCUnit Test for AdminMain Class*

```
public class AdminGUITester extends JFCTestCase
{
    private JFCTestHelper helper;
    private AdminMain adminGUI;

    public AdminGUITester(String name)
    {
        super(name);
```

```java
    }
    protected void setUp() throws Exception
    {
        super.setUp();
        //Start listening for window open events
        helper = new JFCTestHelper();
    }

    public void testMainWindow()
    {
        Window appWindow = helper.getWindow("Football Pool Administrator");
        assertNotNull("Unable to get main window", appWindow);
        JList poolList = (JList) helper.findComponent(JList.class, appWindow, 0);
        assertNotNull("Unable to find pool list", poolList);
        JTable gameTable =
                    (JTable) helper.findComponent(JTable.class, appWindow, 0);
        assertNotNull("Unable to find gameTable", gameTable);
        JButton closePoolButton =
                (JButton) helper.findComponent(JButton.class, appWindow, 2);
        assertNotNull("Unable to find Close Pool button", closePoolButton);
        assertEquals("Close Pool", closePoolButton.getText());
        JButton newPoolButton =
                            (JButton) helper.findNamedComponent(JButton.class,
                                            "NewPoolButton", appWindow, 0);
        assertNotNull("Unable to find New Pool button", poolList);
        assertEquals("New Pool", newPoolButton.getText());
    }


    protected void tearDown() throws Exception
    {
        super.tearDown();
    }

    /** Set up the suite*/
    public static Test suite()
    {
        TestSuite suite = new TestSuite(AdminGUITester.class);
        return suite;
    }

    public static final void main(String[] args)
    {
        // Start AdminGUI
        AdminMain.main(args);
        junit.textui.TestRunner.run(suite());
    }
}
```

The test extends the JFCTestCase class instead of the JUnit TestCase class. The setup method creates an instance of the JFCTestHelper class. What this class does is to keep track of all the GUI components created and has methods that allow you to find any GUI component and interact with it. The testMainWindow() method uses the JFCTestHelper class to locate the main window of the application. The JFCTestHelper class has a number of different methods that can be used to find the main window. You can use the getWindow() method to return all the currently visible windows, then search the returned set for the specific window of interest, or, as shown in the code, you can use the getWindow(String titleString) method to find a window that contains the specified title string. The JFCTestHelper class also has a number of other getWindow() methods that can be used to find the main window.

Once the main window has been found, the next thing the testMainWindow() method does is try to locate a few components of the main window and verify their presence. To find a component, the JFCTestHelper class provides a number of findComponent() and findNamedComponent() methods that can be used to find any component. In the example code, the findComponent() method is used to find the Pool List, Game Table, and Close Pool button components. The findComponent() method here takes three arguments:

- The first argument is the class of the component that you want to find.

- The second argument is the window or container that should contain the component.

- The third argument is a zero-based index that can be used to distinguish between the different components that match the find criteria.

For the Pool List and Game Table components, the third argument of the findComponent() method is zero because the main window only contains one JList and JTable. For the Close Pool button, the third argument is 2 because the Close Pool button is the third JButton component that is found by the findComponent() method. The third argument of 2 was found by trial and error, and there is no way to derive it other than to keep running the test and changing the value until the correct one is found.

When multiple components of the same class exist, it is usually better to use the findNamedComponent() method. This method takes four arguments:

- The first argument is the class of the component you want to find.

- The second argument is the component's name.

- The third argument is the window or container that should contain the component.

- The fourth argument is a zero-based index that can be used to distinguish between the different components that match the find criteria.

In order to use the findNamedComponent() method, you have to make sure that you name your components when they are created. Any Swing component can be named by using the setName(String name) method. If you look back at the code used to create the GUI, you will see that when the New Pool button is created, the setName() method is used to set the name to NewPoolButton. Finding the New Pool button is much easier than finding the Close Pool button because we can use the findNamedComponent() method, which can find the component, by using its class and name.

Of course, using the findNamedComponent() method means that you are adding extra code in the GUI that serves no other purpose than to make testing easier. Some people may object to this, but adding this extra code to make the tests easier to run means that you are more likely to write more tests and hence have a better GUI.

Adding Data to the Pool List

Now that we have the GUI testing framework set up, we can now start adding tests that will help us drive the development of the GUI. The present GUI has all the components as shown in the Admin GUI mock up; what's missing is the data. Let's start by creating a test that will determine whether or not the GUI can properly display a pool list. To do this, we add the test shown in Listing 5-8 to the AdminGUITester.

Listing 5-8. *testDisplayPoolList() Method*

```
public void testDisplayPoolList()
    {
        Window appWindow = helper.getWindow("Football Pool Administrator");
        assertNotNull("Unable to get main window", appWindow);
        JList guiPoolJList =
                    (JList) helper.findComponent(JList.class, appWindow, 0);
        assertNotNull("Unable to find pool list", guiPoolJList);
        //Determine if list is the right size and contains the correct values
        Vector serverPoolList = m_fbPoolServer.getPoolList();
        int poolSize = serverPoolList.size();
        assertEquals(poolSize, guiPoolJList.getModel().getSize());
        String guiPoolName = (String) guiPoolJList.getModel().getElementAt(0);
        String serverPoolName = (String) serverPoolList.elementAt(0);
        assertEquals(serverPoolName, guiPoolName);
        guiPoolName = (String) guiPoolJList.getModel().getElementAt(1);
        serverPoolName = (String) serverPoolList.elementAt(1);
        assertEquals(serverPoolName, guiPoolName);
        guiPoolName = (String) guiPoolJList.getModel().getElementAt(2);
        serverPoolName = (String) serverPoolList.elementAt(2);
        assertEquals(serverPoolName, guiPoolName);
    }
```

The first thing this test case does is to find the main window and then the JList component in the main window. It compares the number of elements in the JList with the number of elements in the pool list obtained from the mock server. The m_fbPoolServer variable is just an instance of the FBPoolServerStub that was initialized in the setUp() method with the following line:

```
m_fbPoolServer = new FBPoolServerStub();
```

Comparing the values from the GUI to the data obtained from the FBPoolServerStub is better than hard coding the expected values, because as the FBPoolServerStub is updated to support development of the GUI, there should be no need to go back and update the assert statements.

Besides checking the size of the JList against the expected size, the test also checks to make sure that each of the individual FootballPool elements are correct.

If we run this test now, it should fail where it compares the number of elements of the GUI pool list to the number obtained from the server list. Now that we have verified that it fails, we can now add some GUI code to get the test to pass.

To get the test to pass, we have to populate the list, but we have to do a couple things before we can actually add elements to the list. The first thing we have to do is to add a method in the GUI to get an instance of the FBPoolServer. We will use this FBPoolServer instance in the GUI to get the data needed for the list. In the final version of the GUI, this FBPoolServer object will be an instance of the stateless session bean, but for development this will be an instance of the FBPoolServerStub as shown in the method that follows. We will create a method called getFBPoolServerBean(). For now, this method will return the FBPoolServerStub, but eventually we will update this method so it will be able to return the FBPoolServerStub or the real stateless session bean, depending on an argument passed into the GUI. This way we will be able to test the GUI in isolation using the FBPoolServerStub class or run it with the real stateless session bean when we want to do some integration or functional testing.

```
public FBPoolServer getFBPoolServerBean()
    {
      return(new FBPoolServerStub());
    }
```

We add this method to the constructor of the Admin GUI as follows (**new code in bold**):

```
public AdminMain()
    {
        m_fbPoolServer = getFBPoolServerBean();
        //Initialize GUI components
        initComponents();

        this.setTitle("Football Pool Administrator");
        this.setName("Football Pool Administrator");
        this.setSize(400, 500);
        this.setVisible(true);
        this.pack();
    }
```

As you can see, in the constructor we add a call to the getFBPoolServerBean() method and store the result of the call in the m_fbPoolServer variable, which is of type FBPoolServer. This is a private variable that can be used by any method in the Admin GUI to call any of the methods of the FBPoolServer interface.

Now that we have a way to call the methods of the FBPoolServer interface, we can add a method to populate the pool list as follows:

```
private void populatePoolList()
    {
        Vector gameList = m_fbPoolServer.getPoolList();
        poolList.setListData(gameList);
    }
```

We can then add a call to this method in the constructor (**new code in bold**):

```
public AdminMain()
{
    m_fbPoolServer = getFBPoolServerBean();
    //Initialize GUI components
    initComponents();
    //Populate pool list
    populatePoolList();

    this.setTitle("Football Pool Administrator");
    this.setName("Football Pool Administrator");
    this.setSize(400, 500);
    this.setVisible(true);
    this.pack();
}
```

With this code added, we can now run the test and see that it passes.

Adding Data to the Game Table

Now that the pool list is populated, the next step is to add the ability to select an entry in the Pool List component and have the Game Table component populated with the correct games. As always, we start by adding a test for the new behavior, as shown in Listing 5-9.

Listing 5-9. *testDisplayGames() Method*

```
public void testDisplayGames()
{
    //Get pool list and game table
    Window appWindow = helper.getWindow("Football Pool Administrator");
    JList guiPoolJList =
                (JList) helper.findComponent(JList.class, appWindow, 0);
    JTable gameTable =
            (JTable) helper.findComponent(JTable.class, appWindow, 0);
    //Select the second entry in the pool list
    JListMouseEventData listEvent =
                            new JListMouseEventData(this, guiPoolJList, 1, 1);
    helper.enterClickAndLeave(listEvent);
    String gameNum = (String) gameTable.getValueAt(0, 0);
    String homeTeam = (String) gameTable.getValueAt(0, 1);
    String awayTeam = (String) gameTable.getValueAt(0, 2);

    FootballPool fbPool = m_fbPoolServer.getPoolInfo("2004-09-17");
    assertEquals("1", gameNum);
    assertEquals(fbPool.getHomeTeam(0), homeTeam);
    assertEquals(fbPool.getAwayTeam(0), awayTeam);

}
```

This test is very similar to the other tests we created. It starts out by getting the main window, the pool list, and the game table. The next thing the test has to do is to select the second entry in the pool list. To do this, JFCUnit provides a number of different mouse event data classes. These classes can be used to fire mouse events in lists, trees, tables, etc. For our test, we create a new JListMouseEventData instance and then use the helper.enterClickAndLeave() method to fire the event. The JListMouseEventData takes four arguments:

- The first argument is the JFCUnit test case.

- The second argument is the list to execute the mouse event on.

- The third argument is the element to select in the list.

- The forth argument is the number of clicks of the mouse to fire.

Once this mouse event has been fired, the only thing left to do for the test is to check the values of the table to make sure they are the correct values. In the test shown, we are only checking the first row of the table to make the test easier to read, but in the real world you would check all the rows of the table.

The new test fails, so we add the code necessary to get it to work. To get this test to work, we need to add a ListSelectionListener to the pool list, so we add the following code to the initComponent method of the AdminMain class:

```
poolList.addListSelectionListener(
        new ListSelectionListener()
        {
            public void valueChanged(ListSelectionEvent e)
            {
                updateGameTable();
            }
        });
```

We then add the updateGameTable() method, shown in Listing 5-10. This method will be called to update the game table every time an item is selected in the pool list.

Listing 5-10. *updateGameTable() Method for the AdminMain Class*

```
    private void updateGameTable()
    {
        String poolName = (String) poolList.getSelectedValue();
        if ((poolName != null) && (poolName.length() > 0))
        {
            FootballPool poolData = m_fbPoolServer.getPoolInfo(poolName);
            //Use selectedPool to create a table model that will be used
            // to populate the table
            TableModel model = new FBGamesTableModel(poolData);
            gameTable.setModel(model);
            String colName = gameTable.getColumnName(0);
            TableColumn column = gameTable.getColumn(colName);
            column.setMaxWidth(50);
```

```
        String poolStatus = m_fbPoolServer.getStatus(poolName);
        statusLabel.setText("Status:" + poolStatus);
    }
}
```

The updateGameTable() method gets the selected pool name from the pool list, then gets the pool data for the selected pool and uses it to create a table model. This table model is then used by the game table to display the games. The code for the table model is not shown here but can be found in the downloadable source code for this chapter.

The creation of the table model class brings up an interesting question. The FBGamesTableModel class was created as a result of trying to get the testDisplayGames() test to pass. The question is how the FBGamesTableModel class should be created. The FBGamesTableModel class is a simple implementation of the AbstractTableModel class that will contain a known set of methods. From a pure TDD perspective, each of the methods of the FBGamesTableModel class should be created by making tests for each of the methods required by the AbstractTableModel's interface, but most experienced Swing developers are very familiar with developing table models and don't need the tests to help them develop the table model, especially if the implementation is trivial. Whether or not tests are used to develop these types of classes should depend on how complex these classes are to implement. If the implementation is trivial, then no tests are needed, but if the implementation has any complexity, then tests should be created to guide the development.

At this point, the Admin GUI now correctly displays data and all its components correctly, or does it? The testDisplayGames() only tests to make sure the games of week 9/17/2004 are correctly displayed; we should also make sure the games of week 9/10/2004 and 9/24/2004 are displayed correctly. Let's update the testDisplayGames() test to test all three weeks as shown in Listing 5-11 (**updated lines are in bold**).

Listing 5-11. *Updated testDisplayGames() Method*

```
public void testDisplayGames()
{
    //Get pool list and game table
    Window appWindow = helper.getWindow("Football Pool Administrator");
    JList guiPoolJList =
                    (JList) helper.findComponent(JList.class, appWindow, 0);
    JTable gameTable =
                  (JTable) helper.findComponent(JTable.class, appWindow, 0);
    //Select the second entry in the pool list
    JListMouseEventData listEvent =
                        new JListMouseEventData(this, guiPoolJList, 1, 1);
    helper.enterClickAndLeave(listEvent);
    String gameNum = (String) gameTable.getValueAt(0, 0);
    String homeTeam = (String) gameTable.getValueAt(0, 1);
    String awayTeam = (String) gameTable.getValueAt(0, 2);

    FootballPool fbPool = m_fbPoolServer.getPoolInfo("2004-09-17");
    assertEquals("1", gameNum);
    assertEquals(fbPool.getHomeTeam(0), homeTeam);
```

```
        assertEquals(fbPool.getAwayTeam(0), awayTeam);

        listEvent = new JListMouseEventData(this, guiPoolJList, 0, 1);
        helper.enterClickAndLeave(listEvent);
        gameNum = (String) gameTable.getValueAt(0, 0);
        homeTeam = (String) gameTable.getValueAt(0, 1);
        awayTeam = (String) gameTable.getValueAt(0, 2);

        fbPool = m_fbPoolServer.getPoolInfo("2004-09-10");
        assertEquals("1", gameNum);
        assertEquals(fbPool.getHomeTeam(0), homeTeam);
        assertEquals(fbPool.getAwayTeam(0), awayTeam);

        listEvent = new JListMouseEventData(this, guiPoolJList, 2, 1);
        helper.enterClickAndLeave(listEvent);
        gameNum = (String) gameTable.getValueAt(0, 0);
        homeTeam = (String) gameTable.getValueAt(0, 1);
        awayTeam = (String) gameTable.getValueAt(0, 2);

        fbPool = m_fbPoolServer.getPoolInfo("2004-09-24");
        assertEquals("1", gameNum);
        assertEquals(fbPool.getHomeTeam(0), homeTeam);
        assertEquals(fbPool.getAwayTeam(0), awayTeam);
    }
```

If you run this test, it passes; however, if you actually run the Admin GUI manually, you will see that the games for each of the weeks are the same. This is not a problem with the Admin GUI but with the FBPoolServerStub class's getPoolInfo() method. No matter what argument you pass into this method, it always returns the same set of games. We need to fix this to make our tests better reflect real-world conditions, but it also reminds us of the point that in order to develop using tests, those tests should accurately test the condition the GUI will see when used by a real user. Therefore, it is important that you run the GUI manually before or after each new test is created to make sure the test accurately reflects the way the user will use the GUI.

So let's fix the FBPoolServerStub class. The first thing we need to do is to update the FBPoolServerTest to test all three weeks of the football pool, as shown in Listing 5-12 (**new code in bold**).

Listing 5-12. *Updated testGetPoolInfo() Method*

```
public void testGetPoolInfo()
{
    FBPoolServer fbPoolServer = new FBPoolServerStub();
    FootballPool pool = fbPoolServer.getPoolInfo("2004-09-17");
    assertEquals("Kansas City",pool.getAwayTeam(0));
    assertEquals("Green Bay",pool.getHomeTeam(0));
    assertEquals("Houston",pool.getAwayTeam(1));
    assertEquals("Tennessee",pool.getHomeTeam(1));
```

```
assertEquals("Carolina",pool.getAwayTeam(2));
assertEquals("Indianapolis",pool.getHomeTeam(2));
assertEquals("NY Giants",pool.getAwayTeam(3));
assertEquals("New England",pool.getHomeTeam(3));
assertEquals("Chicago",pool.getAwayTeam(4));
assertEquals("New Orleans",pool.getHomeTeam(4));
assertEquals("Oakland",pool.getAwayTeam(5));
assertEquals("Cleveland",pool.getHomeTeam(5));
assertEquals("Philadelphia",pool.getAwayTeam(6));
assertEquals("Dallas",pool.getHomeTeam(6));
assertEquals("Tampa Bay",pool.getAwayTeam(7));
assertEquals("Washington",pool.getHomeTeam(7));
assertEquals("Miami",pool.getAwayTeam(8));
assertEquals("Jacksonville",pool.getHomeTeam(8));
assertEquals("Pittsburgh",pool.getAwayTeam(9));
assertEquals("Denver",pool.getHomeTeam(9));
assertEquals("Buffalo",pool.getAwayTeam(10));
assertEquals("NY Jets",pool.getHomeTeam(10));
assertEquals("Baltimore",pool.getAwayTeam(11));
assertEquals("Arizona",pool.getHomeTeam(11));
assertEquals("San Francisco",pool.getAwayTeam(12));
assertEquals("Seattle",pool.getHomeTeam(12));
assertEquals("Atlanta",pool.getAwayTeam(13));
assertEquals("St. Louis",pool.getHomeTeam(13));

pool = fbPoolServer.getPoolInfo("2004-09-10");
assertEquals("Kansas City",pool.getAwayTeam(7));
assertEquals("Green Bay",pool.getHomeTeam(1));
assertEquals("Houston",pool.getAwayTeam(6));
assertEquals("Tennessee",pool.getHomeTeam(0));
assertEquals("Carolina",pool.getAwayTeam(5));
assertEquals("Indianapolis",pool.getHomeTeam(3));
assertEquals("NY Giants",pool.getAwayTeam(4));
assertEquals("New England",pool.getHomeTeam(2));
assertEquals("Chicago",pool.getAwayTeam(3));
assertEquals("New Orleans",pool.getHomeTeam(5));
assertEquals("Oakland",pool.getAwayTeam(2));
assertEquals("Cleveland",pool.getHomeTeam(4));
assertEquals("Philadelphia",pool.getAwayTeam(1));
assertEquals("Dallas",pool.getHomeTeam(7));
assertEquals("Tampa Bay",pool.getAwayTeam(0));
assertEquals("Washington",pool.getHomeTeam(6));
assertEquals("Miami",pool.getAwayTeam(13));
assertEquals("Jacksonville",pool.getHomeTeam(9));
assertEquals("Pittsburgh",pool.getAwayTeam(12));
assertEquals("Denver",pool.getHomeTeam(8));
assertEquals("Buffalo",pool.getAwayTeam(11));
```

```
    assertEquals("NY Jets",pool.getHomeTeam(11));
    assertEquals("Baltimore",pool.getAwayTeam(10));
    assertEquals("Arizona",pool.getHomeTeam(10));
    assertEquals("San Francisco",pool.getAwayTeam(9));
    assertEquals("Seattle",pool.getHomeTeam(13));
    assertEquals("Atlanta",pool.getAwayTeam(8));
    assertEquals("St. Louis",pool.getHomeTeam(12));

    pool = fbPoolServer.getPoolInfo("2004-09-24");
    assertEquals("Kansas City",pool.getAwayTeam(3));
    assertEquals("Green Bay",pool.getHomeTeam(13));
    assertEquals("Houston",pool.getAwayTeam(4));
    assertEquals("Tennessee",pool.getHomeTeam(12));
    assertEquals("Carolina",pool.getAwayTeam(5));
    assertEquals("Indianapolis",pool.getHomeTeam(11));
    assertEquals("NY Giants",pool.getAwayTeam(6));
    assertEquals("New England",pool.getHomeTeam(10));
    assertEquals("Chicago",pool.getAwayTeam(7));
    assertEquals("New Orleans",pool.getHomeTeam(9));
    assertEquals("Oakland",pool.getAwayTeam(8));
    assertEquals("Cleveland",pool.getHomeTeam(8));
    assertEquals("Philadelphia",pool.getAwayTeam(9));
    assertEquals("Dallas",pool.getHomeTeam(7));
    assertEquals("Tampa Bay",pool.getAwayTeam(10));
    assertEquals("Washington",pool.getHomeTeam(6));
    assertEquals("Miami",pool.getAwayTeam(11));
    assertEquals("Jacksonville",pool.getHomeTeam(5));
    assertEquals("Pittsburgh",pool.getAwayTeam(12));
    assertEquals("Denver",pool.getHomeTeam(4));
    assertEquals("Buffalo",pool.getAwayTeam(13));
    assertEquals("NY Jets",pool.getHomeTeam(3));
    assertEquals("Baltimore",pool.getAwayTeam(0));
    assertEquals("Arizona",pool.getHomeTeam(2));
    assertEquals("San Francisco",pool.getAwayTeam(1));
    assertEquals("Seattle",pool.getHomeTeam(1));
    assertEquals("Atlanta",pool.getAwayTeam(2));
    assertEquals("St. Louis",pool.getHomeTeam(0));
}
```

Next we update FBPoolServerStub to get the test to pass (see Listing 5-13).

Listing 5-13. *Updated getPoolInfo() Method*

```
public FootballPool getPoolInfo(String poolName)
{
    FootballPool pool = new FootballPool(poolDate);
    try
    {
```

```
if (poolDate.equals("2004-09-17"))
{
    pool.addGame("Kansas City", "Green Bay");
    pool.addGame("Houston", "Tennessee");
    pool.addGame("Carolina", "Indianapolis");
    pool.addGame("NY Giants", "New England");
    pool.addGame("Chicago", "New Orleans");
    pool.addGame("Oakland", "Cleveland");
    pool.addGame("Philadelphia", "Dallas");
    pool.addGame("Tampa Bay", "Washington");
    pool.addGame("Miami", "Jacksonville");
    pool.addGame("Pittsburgh", "Denver");
    pool.addGame("Buffalo", "NY Jets");
    pool.addGame("Baltimore", "Arizona");
    pool.addGame("San Francisco", "Seattle");
    pool.addGame("Atlanta", "St. Louis");
}
else if (poolDate.equals("2004-09-10"))
{

    pool.addGame("Tampa Bay","Tennessee");
    pool.addGame("Philadelphia","Green Bay");
    pool.addGame("Oakland","New England");
    pool.addGame("Chicago","Indianapolis");
    pool.addGame("NY Giants","Cleveland");
    pool.addGame("Carolina","New Orleans");
    pool.addGame("Houston","Washington");
    pool.addGame("Kansas City","Dallas");
    pool.addGame("Atlanta","Denver");
    pool.addGame("San Francisco","Jacksonville");
    pool.addGame("Baltimore","Arizona");
    pool.addGame("Buffalo","NY Jets");
    pool.addGame("Pittsburgh","St. Louis");
    pool.addGame("Miami","Seattle");
}
else if (poolDate.equals("2004-09-24"))
{
    pool.addGame( "Baltimore","St. Louis");
    pool.addGame("San Francisco","Seattle");
    pool.addGame("Atlanta","Arizona");
    pool.addGame("Kansas City","NY Jets");
    pool.addGame("Houston","Denver");
    pool.addGame("Carolina","Jacksonville");
    pool.addGame("NY Giants","Washington");
    pool.addGame("Chicago","Dallas");
    pool.addGame("Oakland","Cleveland");
    pool.addGame("Philadelphia","New Orleans");
```

```
                    pool.addGame("Tampa Bay","New England");
                    pool.addGame("Miami","Indianapolis");
                    pool.addGame("Pittsburgh","Tennessee");
                    pool.addGame("Buffalo","Green Bay");
                }
            }
            catch (Exception e)
            {
                System.out.println("Exception getting football pool info Exception is "
                            + e);
            }
            return (pool);
    }
```

Now the FBPoolServerStub works for all three weeks of the football pool, and the data in the GUI is more interesting and will make for better tests. Of course, there is no reason to update the testDisplayGames() method because we were smart enough not to hard code the assert conditions in the test but drove the assert conditions off the FBPoolServerStub.

Using Jemmy to Drive GUI Development

Now that the Admin GUI can display the pool list and games correctly, we need to work on getting the buttons to function. To do that, we are going to switch to using Jemmy as our testing framework so you can see the difference between Jemmy and JFCUnit. The first thing we are going to do is rewrite the current tests written in JFCUnit using Jemmy so we can highlight the differences, as shown in Listing 5-14. (**The new Jemmy-specific code is highlighted in bold.**)

GUI TESTING WITH JEMMY

Jemmy is a Java library that you can use to reproduce all user actions that can be performed on Swing/AWT components. Jemmy was created as an IDE extension of the NetBeans IDE. Fortunately, the designer of Jemmy designed it in such a way that it functions as a stand-alone library that can be used, by itself, outside of the NetBeans IDE. This means you can use Jemmy with any IDE or testing framework.

Jemmy finds and interacts with Swing components using *operators*. There are operators that correspond to almost every Swing component. Jemmy operators follow a naming convention whereby the operator name exactly corresponds to the AWT or Swing component counterpart, which takes the form of the AWT or Swing component class name without the packages prefix, but with the suffix. For example, JDialogOperator is the Jemmy operator corresponding to javax.swing.JDialog. To find a component, you create an instance of an operator that corresponds to the component you are trying to find. The arguments of the operator's constructor are used to specify some parameters for finding the component. Once an instance of an operator is created, it can be used to interact with the component.

Unlike JFCUnit, Jemmy is not an extension of the JUnit framework and does not contain any classes that can be used to organize or run tests or keep track of test results. This means if you want to automate GUI tests using Jemmy, you have to run the tests inside a testing framework.

For a more details on the Jemmy API, check out the NetBeans web site at http://jemmy.netbeans.org/.

Listing 5-14. *AdminMain Tests Rewritten to Use Jemmy*

```
public class AdminGUIJemmyTester extends TestCase
{
    private FBPoolServer m_fbPoolServer;
     private static boolean guiStarted = false;

    public AdminGUIJemmyTester(String name)
    {
        super(name);
    }

    protected void setUp() throws Exception
    {
        super.setUp();
        if (!guiStarted)
        {
            // Start AdminGUI
            new
ClassReference("com.apress.tddbook.gui.AdminMain").startApplication();
            guiStarted = true;
        }
        m_fbPoolServer = new FBPoolServerStub();
    }

    /**
     * Test that the main window was displayed
     */
    public void testMainWindow()
    {
        JFrameOperator appWindow =
                        new JFrameOperator("Football PoolAdministrator");
        JListOperator poolList = new JListOperator(appWindow);
        JTableOperator gameTable = new JTableOperator(appWindow);
        JButtonOperator closePoolButton =
                        new JButtonOperator(appWindow, "Close Pool");
        assertEquals("Close Pool", closePoolButton.getText());
        JButtonOperator newPoolButton =
         new JButtonOperator(appWindow, new NameCompChooser("NewPoolButton"));
        assertEquals("New Pool", newPoolButton.getText());
    }

    /**
     * Test that the GUI can correctly display a pool List
     */
    public void testDisplayPoolList()
    {
        //Get pool list
```

```
    JFrameOperator appWindow =
                    new JFrameOperator("Football Pool Administrator");
    JListOperator guiPoolJList = new JListOperator(appWindow);
    //Determine if list is the right size and contains the correct values
    Vector serverPoolList = m_fbPoolServer.getPoolList();
    int poolSize = serverPoolList.size();
    assertEquals(poolSize,guiPoolJList.getModel().getSize());
    String guiPoolName = (String)guiPoolJList.getModel().getElementAt(0);
    String serverPoolName = (String)serverPoolList.elementAt(0);
    assertEquals(serverPoolName, guiPoolName);
    guiPoolName = (String)guiPoolJList.getModel().getElementAt(1);
    serverPoolName = (String)serverPoolList.elementAt(1);
    assertEquals(serverPoolName, guiPoolName);
    guiPoolName = (String)guiPoolJList.getModel().getElementAt(2);
    serverPoolName = (String)serverPoolList.elementAt(2);
    assertEquals(serverPoolName, guiPoolName);

}
/**
 * Select Week 2 in the pool list and check to make sure that
 *   the correct games are displayed
 */
public void testDisplayGames()
{
    //Get pool list and game table
    JFrameOperator appWindow =
                    new JFrameOperator("Football Pool Administrator");
    JListOperator guiPoolJList = new JListOperator(appWindow);
    JTableOperator gameTable = new JTableOperator(appWindow);
    //Select the second entry in the pool list
    guiPoolJList.selectItem(1);
    String gameNum = (String)gameTable.getValueAt(0,0);
    String homeTeam = (String)gameTable.getValueAt(0,1);
    String awayTeam = (String)gameTable.getValueAt(0,2);

    FootballPool fbPool = m_fbPoolServer.getPoolInfo("2004-09-17");
    assertEquals("1", gameNum);
    assertEquals(fbPool.getHomeTeam(0), homeTeam);
    assertEquals(fbPool.getAwayTeam(0), awayTeam);

    guiPoolJList.selectItem(0);
    gameNum = (String)gameTable.getValueAt(0,0);
    homeTeam = (String)gameTable.getValueAt(0,1);
    awayTeam = (String)gameTable.getValueAt(0,2);

    fbPool = m_fbPoolServer.getPoolInfo("2004-09-10");
    assertEquals("1", gameNum);
```

```java
        assertEquals(fbPool.getHomeTeam(0), homeTeam);
        assertEquals(fbPool.getAwayTeam(0), awayTeam);

        guiPoolJList.selectItem(2);
        gameNum = (String)gameTable.getValueAt(0,0);
        homeTeam = (String)gameTable.getValueAt(0,1);
        awayTeam = (String)gameTable.getValueAt(0,2);

        fbPool = m_fbPoolServer.getPoolInfo("2004-09-24");
        assertEquals("1", gameNum);
        assertEquals(fbPool.getHomeTeam(0), homeTeam);
        assertEquals(fbPool.getAwayTeam(0), awayTeam);
    }

    protected void tearDown() throws Exception
    {
        super.tearDown();
    }

    /** Set up the suite*/
    public static Test suite()
    {
        TestSuite suite = new TestSuite(AdminGUIJemmyTester.class);
        return suite;
    }

    public static final void main(String[] args)
    {
        junit.textui.TestRunner.run(suite());
    }
}
```

The first difference you will notice is that unlike JFCUnit, Jemmy is not an extension of JUnit. In fact, Jemmy does not have a base class but is just a set of methods for finding the components of a GUI and interacting with them. This means that you can run Jemmy inside a regular JUnit test as the code shows. Of course, you don't have to use Jemmy inside a JUnit test, but doing so allows you to use the regular JUnit assert methods to check the contents of the GUI.

The next difference you may notice is the way the application is started. Like JFCUnit, Jemmy requires the Swing application to run in the same JVM as the test. In our JFCUnit test, we start the application by calling its main method in the setUp() method. This approach would also work with Jemmy, but Jemmy also provides a class called ClassReference that can be used to start the application. The startApplication method simply calls the main method of the specified class with no arguments.

The main difference between JFCUnit and Jemmy is the way Jemmy finds and manipulates GUI components. Jemmy uses *operator* methods to find components and interact with them. Jemmy contains an operator for almost every type of Swing component. In our testMainWindow() method, we use the JFrameOperator to find the main window by supplying

the title of the main window as the argument to the constructor. Likewise, we use the
`JListOperator` and `JTableOperator` to find the pool list and game table by supplying the
`appWindow` as the argument to the constructor. Most operator methods have several different
constructors that can be used to find a component. In the `testMainWindow()` method, you can
see two of the many `JButtonOperators` that can be used to find a button. To find the Close Pool
button, we use the `JButtonOperator` and pass in the `appWindow` and text of the button. We could
have used the same constructor for the New Pool button, but I wanted to demonstrate the use
of the `ComponentChooser` interface.

If you remember our JFCUnit code, you know that we got the New Pool button by searching for the button component using its name. Jemmy doesn't have a way to find components
by their name, but it has an interface called `ComponentChooser` through which you can create
custom finder methods that allow an operator to find a component. Since we named the New
Pool button, we are going create a `ComponentChooser` that will be able to find a component by
its name. The `ComponentChooser` interface specifies two methods that need to be implemented:
`checkComponent()` and `getDescription()`. The `checkComponent()` method is used to find the
actual component based on the criteria specified in the method. If the component passed in
matches the criteria, then true is returned; otherwise false is returned. The `getDescription()`
method just returns a description of the `ComponentChooser`. The code to implement a
`ComponentChooser` to find a named component is as shown in Listing 5-15.

Listing 5-15. *NameCompChooser Class*

```
public class NameCompChooser implements ComponentChooser
{
    String m_compName;
    public NameCompChooser(String name)
    {
        m_compName = name;
    }
    public boolean checkComponent(Component component)
    {
        String compName = component.getName();
        if((compName != null) && (compName.equals(m_compName)))
        {
            return true;
        }
        else
        {
            return false;
        }
    }
    public String getDescription()
    {
        return "Finds components based on components name";
    }
}
```

The method constructor simply stores the name of the component that you are looking for. The checkComponent() method just checks the name of the component passed in. If the component has a name and the name matches the component we are looking for, then true is returned.

If you look at the testMainWindow() method of the Jemmy test, you will see how the NameCompChooser class is used to find the New Pool button.

One nice thing about the operator methods is that they throw a TimeoutExpiredException if the component can't be found. This means that there is no need to use the assertNotNull method to check whether the component is found. This makes the test code a little cleaner.

Once a component is found, the operator provides methods that can be used to interact with the components. These methods are very similar to the methods found in the actual Swing components. In the testDisaplyGames() method of the test, you can see how the JListOperator provides a method to select an item in the list.

Now that we have an understanding of how Jemmy works, we can now use it to add some more functionality to the Admin GUI.

Implementing the Open Pool Button Behavior

The next functionality that we are going to add to the GUI is the ability to update the state of the pool. Let's review the life cycle of the football pool so we understand its behavior. A football pool can have four states: created, open, closed, and completed. A football pool starts out with a status of created after it has been created and before it is opened. The status is then changed to open when the administrator opens the pool to the players to make their picks. The status is then changed to closed at a certain date. At this point the players can no longer make or change their picks. After all the games have been played and the results posted, the status of the pool is changed to completed. The administrator changes the status of the pool using the buttons at the bottom of the GUI. The New Pool button is used to bring up a dialog box that will allow the administrator to create the pool and populate it with games. The Open Pool button changes the state of the pool to open. The Close Pool button is used to change the state of the pool to closed. The Post Results button will bring up a dialog box that will allow the administrator to post the game scores and post the winner of the pool. Once the results are posted, the status of the pool is changed to completed.

Let's start off implementing the Open Pool button behavior. In order for the administrator to open a pool, he or she will have to first select a pool in the pool list and then click the Open Pool button. At this point the status of the pool should change from created to open. Now that we understand the behavior, let's write the test (see Listing 5-16).

Listing 5-16. *testOpenPoolButton() Method*

```
public void testOpenPoolButton()
{
    //Get pool list and game table
    JFrameOperator appWindow =
                    new JFrameOperator("Football Pool Administrator");
    JListOperator guiPoolJList = new JListOperator(appWindow);
    JTableOperator gameTable = new JTableOperator(appWindow);
    JLabelOperator statusLabel =
            new JLabelOperator(appWindow,new NameCompChooser("StatusLabel"));
```

```
JButtonOperator openButton =
 new JButtonOperator(appWindow,new NameCompChooser("OpenPoolButton"));
//Select the second entry in the pool list
guiPoolJList.selectItem(1);
//Check the current status of the selected pool
assertEquals("Status:Created", statusLabel.getText());
//Click the open button
openButton.push();
//Check to make sure the status was updated correctly
assertEquals("Status:Open", statusLabel.getText());
}
```

The test is very simple; it just selects the second entry in the pool list, and then clicks the Open Pool button. If the status changes from created to open, then the test passes. If you run this test it fails, but not where it should. The test fails where the current status of the pool is checked. It expects the current status to be created, but the status is unknown. This is because the status of the pool was set to unknown in the initComponents() method and never updated. The correct behavior is to update the status of the pool every time an item is selected in the pool list. This is a condition we forgot to check in our testDisplayPoolList() test. We should go back and update the test, but for now let's just add the code needed to get the first assert of the testOpenPoolButton() method to work. To do this we have to add the code shown in Listing 5-17 to the updateGameTableMethod() of the AdminGUI class (**updated lines are in bold**).

Listing 5-17. *Updated updateGameTable() Method*

```
private void updateGameTable()
{
    String poolName = (String)poolList.getSelectedValue();
    FootballPool poolData = m_fbPoolServer.getPoolInfo(poolName);
    //Use selectedPool to create a table model that will be used
    // to populate the table
    TableModel model = new FBGamesTableModel(poolData);
    gameTable.setModel(model);
    String colName = gameTable.getColumnName(0);
    TableColumn column = gameTable.getColumn(colName);
    column.setMaxWidth(50);
    String poolStatus = m_fbPoolServer.getPoolStatus(poolName);
    statusLabel.setText("Status:" + poolStatus);
}
```

The code added to the updateGameTable() method just gets the status of the pool from the FBPoolServer and updates the status label. The only problem with this is that we did not know we needed the getPoolStatus() method until now, so neither the FBPoolServer interface nor the FBPoolServerStub class contain the required method. Before we can go any further, we have to add this method to the FBPoolServer interface. We do this by first adding the test shown in Listing 5-18 to FBPoolServerTest.

Listing 5-18. *testGetPoolStatus() Method*

```
public void testGetPoolStatus()
{
    FBPoolServer fbPoolServer = new FBPoolServerStub();
    String poolStatus = fbPoolServer.getStatus("2004-09-10");
    assertEquals("Closed", poolStatus);
    poolStatus = fbPoolServer.getStatus("2004-09-17");
    assertEquals("Open", poolStatus);
    poolStatus = fbPoolServer.getStatus("2004-09-24");
    assertEquals("Created", poolStatus);
}
```

If you look at the test, you will see that we make the three different pools have different status. This will allow us to better test all the conditions in the AdminGUI.

We then add the getStatus() method to the FBPoolServer interface and the code in Listing 5-19 to the FBPoolServerStub.

Listing 5-19. *getStatus() Method*

```
public String getStatus(String poolName)
{
    if (poolName.equals("2004-09-10"))
    {
        return(week1Status);
    }
    else if (poolName.equals("2004-09-17"))
    {
        return(week2Status);
    }
    else if (poolName.equals("2004-09-24"))
    {
        return(week3Status);
    }
    else
    {
        return("Unknown");
    }
}
```

The week1Status, week2Status, and week3Status variables are just private String values that are initially set to "Closed", "Open", and "Created", respectively. Once we add this code, the test still fails; but the failure occurs at the assert after the Open Pool button is pushed, which is expected, since we have not yet added the code for the Open Pool button.

The first thing we have to do is to add some code to the initComponents method to add an ActionListener to the button. The ActionListener just calls the openPool() method, which does all the work.

```
openPoolButton.addActionListener(new java.awt.event.ActionListener()
    {
        public void actionPerformed(ActionEvent e)
        {
            openPool();
        }
    });
```

The next thing we have to do is to implement the openPool() method (see Listing 5-20). The first thing this method does is to get the currently selected pool. The next thing it does is to call the FBPoolServer to update the status of the selected pool. The last thing it does is to reselect the list item so the status field gets updated. Of course, to get the test to pass, we could simply set the status label to open, but this would be wrong since the status of the pool needs to be sent back to the FBPoolServer so that the status of the pool can be maintained in a central location.

Listing 5-20. *openPool() Method*

```
private void openPool()
{
    String poolName = (String)poolList.getSelectedValue();
    m_fbPoolServer.openPool(poolName);
    poolList.clearSelection();
    poolList.setSelectedValue(poolName, true);
}
```

If you look at the updated openPool() method in the AdminGUI class, you will see we need to add the openPool() method to the FBPoolServer interface and FBPoolServerStub. So we add the test in Listing 5-21 to the FBPoolServerTest class.

Listing 5-21. *testOpenPool() Method*

```
public void testOpenPool()
{
    FBPoolServer fbPoolServer = new FBPoolServerStub();
    String poolStatus = fbPoolServer.getStatus("2004-09-24");
    assertEquals("Created", poolStatus);
    fbPoolServer.openPool("2004-09-24");
    poolStatus = fbPoolServer.getStatus("2004-09-24");
    assertEquals("Open", poolStatus);
}
```

Then we add the openPool() method to the FBPoolServer interface and the code in Listing 5-22 to the FBPoolServerStub to get the test to pass.

Listing 5-22. *openPool() Method for the FBPoolServerStub*

```
public void openPool(String poolName)
{
    if (poolName.equals("2004-09-10"))
    {
        week1Status = "Open";
    }
    else if (poolName.equals("2004-09-17"))
    {
        week2Status = "Open";
    }
    else if (poolName.equals("2004-09-24"))
    {
        week3Status = "Open";
    }
}
```

If you run the testOpenPoolButton() method now, the test finally passes. As you can see, writing a test and then getting it to pass can take a number of different steps. This is because as we add GUI tests, we are also updating the FBPoolServer class and FBPoolServerStub to allow us to properly test the GUI. This may seem like a lot of work, but the overhead is worth it because when the GUI development is done, not only will we have a well-tested GUI, but the FBPoolServer class can now serve as the interface for the stateless session bean with all its methods well defined. Also, the FBPoolServerTest will provide a good baseline of tests for the stateless session bean.

Adding Tests for User Errors

Now that we have the Open Pool button working correctly, we can start to add functionality for the other buttons; but before we do that, we should think about adding some error checking to the Open Pool button. As you add functionality to the GUI, you need to test not only the normal user behavior, but also bad user behavior. For example, with the Open Pool button there are two obvious user errors that need to be addressed. What happens if the user does not select a pool before clicking the Open Pool button, and what happens if the user tries to open a pool that is already open? For both these cases, a warning dialog box should be display informing the user of his or her error.

Now that we understand the possible errors and what the GUI should do when these errors are encountered, let's add this functionality to the GUI. First we need to add two tests, one for each error condition (see Listing 5-23).

Listing 5-23. *testOpenPoolButtonSelectError() and testOpenPoolButtonAlreadyOpenError()*
Methods

```
public void testOpenPoolButtonSelectError()
{
    //Get pool list and game table
    JFrameOperator appWindow =
                new JFrameOperator("Football Pool Administrator");
    JListOperator guiPoolJList = new JListOperator(appWindow);
    JButtonOperator openButton =
                            new JButtonOperator(appWindow,
                                new NameCompChooser("OpenPoolButton"));
    //Clear the pool list selection
    guiPoolJList.clearSelection();
    //Click the open button
    openButton.pushNoBlock();
    //Get error dialog and check to make sure it contains the correct message
    JDialogOperator dialogBox = new JDialogOperator("Error");
    JLabelOperator messageLabel = new JLabelOperator(dialogBox);
    String message = messageLabel.getText();
    assertEquals("No Pool Selected", message);
}

public void testOpenPoolButtonAlreadyOpenError()
{
    //Get pool list and game table
    JFrameOperator appWindow =
                new JFrameOperator("Football Pool Administrator");
    JListOperator guiPoolJList = new JListOperator(appWindow);
    JLabelOperator statusLabel =
            new JLabelOperator(appWindow,new NameCompChooser("StatusLabel"));
    JButtonOperator openButton =
     new JButtonOperator(appWindow,new NameCompChooser("OpenPoolButton"));
    //Select the third entry in the pool list
    guiPoolJList.selectItem(1);
    //Check the current status of the selected pool
    assertEquals("Status:Open", statusLabel.getText());
    //Click the open button
    openButton.push();
    //Get error dialog and check to make sure it contains the correct message
    JDialogOperator dialogBox = new JDialogOperator(appWindow);
    String title = dialogBox.getTitle();
    assertEquals("Error", title);
    JLabelOperator dialogText = new JLabelOperator(dialogBox);
    System.out.println(dialogText);
}
```

Both tests first set up the condition needed for the error condition and then push the
Open Pool button and check to see that the correct dialog box is shown. To get these tests to
work, we have to change some existing code. To get the testOpenPoolButtonSelectError()
test to pass, we have to add the code in Listing 5-24 to the openPool() method (**updated lines
in bold**).

Listing 5-24. *Updated openPool() Method for Select Error*

```
private void openPool()
{
    String poolName = (String) poolList.getSelectedValue();
    if(poolName != null)
    {
        m_fbPoolServer.openPool(poolName);
        poolList.clearSelection();
        poolList.setSelectedValue(poolName, true);
    }
    else //Nothing selected, show error
    {
        JOptionPane.showMessageDialog(this, "No Pool Selected","Error",
                                JOptionPane.ERROR_MESSAGE);
    }
}
```

To get the testOpenPoolButtonAlreadyOpenError() test to pass, we have to add the code
shown in Listing 5-25 to the openPool() method (**updated lines in bold**).

Listing 5-25. *Updated openPool() Method for Already Open Error*

```
private void openPool()
{
    String poolName = (String) poolList.getSelectedValue();
    if (poolName != null)
    {
        String poolStatus = m_fbPoolServer.getStatus(poolName);
          // Can't open a pool that is already opened
        if (poolStatus.equals("Open"))
        {
            JOptionPane.showMessageDialog(this, "Pool Already Opened",
                                    "Error", JOptionPane.ERROR_MESSAGE);
        }
        else
        {
            m_fbPoolServer.openPool(poolName);
            poolList.clearSelection();
            poolList.setSelectedValue(poolName, true);
        }
    }
}
```

```
        else //Nothing selected, show error
        {
            JOptionPane.showMessageDialog(this,
                    "No Pool Selected", "Error", JOptionPane.ERROR_MESSAGE);
        }
    }
}
```

There is a lot more functionality that needs to be added to the GUI, but at this point you should now have a good understanding of how to create a GUI using TDD. The process of developing a GUI using TDD is really not much different from developing other code. Let's review what we have done so far:

- Use a mock object or stub to develop in isolation.

- Create the shell of the GUI first before adding any functionality.

- Create the test using a GUI testing framework such as JFCUnit or Jemmy.

- Update the GUI to get the test to pass.

- Run the GUI manually from time to time to verify it has the correct behavior.

- Update the mock object or stub as needed when the GUI requires more functionality.

- Test not only normal user behavior but also bad user behavior.

The main difference in developing a GUI using TDD is the tools that are used. It is important that you take the time to learn the GUI testing framework you are using so that it becomes second nature to take a desired GUI behavior and create a test for it. Once you are comfortable with the testing framework, it becomes easy to develop a GUI in a simple, incremental manner.

Hands-On Exercises

You're on your own now. It's time to test your knowledge of GUI development using TDD to add some more functionality to the application on your own. Your assignment is to add the functionality needed to allow the Admin GUI to add a new pool to the list of available football pools. This means that you will have to develop the tests and code needed to get the New Pool button working on the main GUI as well as develop the tests and code needed to get the New Pool dialog box shown in Figure 5-2 working. This may require adding more methods to the FBPoolServer and FBPoolServerStub classes as well as adding other classes to the project.

Techniques for Optimizing GUI Development

The last section showed you how to use a GUI testing framework to develop a Swing-based GUI using TDD. Now it's time to take a step back and reexamine the tests that we developed so far and see how we can refactor them to be more efficient and easier to use.

Removing Duplicate Code

The number one reason to refactor is because of duplicate code. Let's take a look at a couple of the tests that we created and see if we can find any duplication (see Listing 5-26).

Listing 5-26. *Two Test Methods for the AdminGUI*

```
public void testMainWindow()
{
    JFrameOperator appWindow =
                        new JFrameOperator("Football Pool Administrator");
    JListOperator poolList = new JListOperator(appWindow);
    JTableOperator gameTable = new JTableOperator(appWindow);
    JButtonOperator closePoolButton =
                            new JButtonOperator(appWindow, "Close Pool");
    assertEquals("Close Pool", closePoolButton.getText());
    JButtonOperator newPoolButton =
    new JButtonOperator(appWindow, new NameCompChooser("NewPoolButton"));
    assertEquals("New Pool", newPoolButton.getText());
}


public void testDisplayPoolList()
{
    //Get pool list
    JFrameOperator appWindow =
                        new JFrameOperator("Football Pool Administrator");
    JListOperator guiPoolJList = new JListOperator(appWindow);
    //Determine if list is the right size and contains the correct values
    Vector serverPoolList = m_fbPoolServer.getPoolList();
    int poolSize = serverPoolList.size();
    assertEquals(poolSize,guiPoolJList.getModel().getSize());
    String guiPoolName = (String)guiPoolJList.getModel().getElementAt(0);
    String serverPoolName = (String)serverPoolList.elementAt(0);
    assertEquals(serverPoolName, guiPoolName);
    guiPoolName = (String)guiPoolJList.getModel().getElementAt(1);
    serverPoolName = (String)serverPoolList.elementAt(1);
    assertEquals(serverPoolName, guiPoolName);
    guiPoolName = (String)guiPoolJList.getModel().getElementAt(2);
    serverPoolName = (String)serverPoolList.elementAt(2);
    assertEquals(serverPoolName, guiPoolName);
}
```

If you look at these two test methods, you see that both use the Jemmy operator methods to find the main window and pool list. Although this duplication may not seem like a problem, it is. The problem is if you ever change the way any of these components are found, you will have to make changes to all the test methods. For example, if you change the name of the main window, you have to change the argument to all the JFrameOperator() methods in all the tests. It would be better if we could centralize the finding of components so that if we have to make a change to the way we find them, then all we have to do is to change one centralized method. Let's do this for the main window of the Admin GUI. The first thing we need to do is to create a private method to find the main window.

```
private JFrameOperator getMainWindow()
{
    return(new JFrameOperator("Football Pool Administrator"));
}
```

Then we have to change our tests to use this new method.

```
public void testMainWindow()
{
    JFrameOperator appWindow = getMainWindow();
    JListOperator poolList = new JListOperator(appWindow);
    JTableOperator gameTable = new JTableOperator(appWindow);
    JButtonOperator closePoolButton =
                           new JButtonOperator(appWindow, "Close Pool");
    assertEquals("Close Pool", closePoolButton.getText());
    JButtonOperator newPoolButton =
     new JButtonOperator(appWindow, new NameCompChooser("NewPoolButton"));
    assertEquals("New Pool", newPoolButton.getText());
}
```

Once we do this, it becomes easier to update the test if the parameters of the main window change. Of course, we should do this for all the other components of the GUI for the same reason. This way, as the components of the GUI change or are updated, the way the tests find each component is centralized and can be easily updated.

The Model View Controller Pattern

A chapter about GUI development would not be complete without discussion of the Model View Controller (MVC) pattern. The MVC pattern is a common pattern that is used by applications that have to maintain multiple views of the same data. The main idea behind the MVC pattern is to have a clean separation between the data being displayed (model) and the way it is displayed (view). In our example, the FBPoolServer is the model that represents the data of the football pool, and the Admin GUI is the view of the data. As you can see, if you look back at the code for the Admin GUI, you will notice that the method contains two types of calls, calls to FBPoolServer and calls to other GUI components. The Admin GUI does not contain any business logic and therefore conforms to the MVC pattern for two reasons. The main reason is that the J2EE platform architecture, which is based on interfaces, helps promote the separation of the logical functions of a system. The other reason is that when you develop using TDD, this tends to create classes that are well encapsulated because of the small incremental steps of the TDD process. This encapsulation also promotes separation of logical functions of the system.

One thing you can do to help keep the GUI as isolated from the model as possible is to always call the model methods through an interface. There should only be two types of calls in any GUI code: calls to other Swing components and calls to the model through an interface. The main advantage of using an interface is that it makes it easy to switch how the model is implemented. For example, in the Admin GUI we used, the model is represented by the FBPoolServer interface. The interface is implemented by the FBPoolServerStub but can easily be switch to the stateless session bean once it is implemented. The other advantage of using an interface is that it allows you to create one set of tests that can be used to test multiple implementations.

Conforming to the MVC pattern is important because having a clean separation between the model and the view makes testing the GUI easier. Using the MVC pattern, testing the GUI only involves making sure it properly calls the methods in the model.

Some people question the need to use TDD to develop GUIs since they are merely a way to make calls to the model. They argue that the overhead of developing a GUI through testing is not worth the result since the model can be more easily developed outside the GUI tests. This may be true for a small, trivial GUI that does simple sets and gets, but developing a GUI of any complexity requires a lot more than putting a pretty interface on a model. Most of the use cases or requirements of the system are written from the user interface point of view, so it makes sense to drive the design of the system from the user interface. As the examples in this chapter showed, developing a GUI using tests helps not only to create a well-designed GUI, but also to discover the design of the model. It would be very hard to define all the methods needed in the model before writing the GUI. Using tests to develop the GUI also helps keep the developer focused on the user experience and how best to implement the required functionality. The side benefit of developing the GUI using tests is that when you are done you will have a good baseline of tests that can be used for regression testing. Although you can test a GUI manually, there is no substitute for a good set of automated tests.

The Limitations of GUI Testing

A GUI can only be tested at a functional level; there is no way to create unit tests for a GUI since it is only a view of a model. It is important that the GUI tests be structured to test the functionality of the display, not the validity of the data being displayed. The data behind the GUI needs to have its own set of tests separate from the GUI tests. A GUI is made of a lot of different components such as data models, table models, list models, etc. All these models can be created and tested outside the GUI using normal unit tests. It's important that as the GUI is developed the separation between the tests for the models of the GUI's display be maintained, because there is a strong tendency to use the functional tests of the GUI's display to test the data behind the GUI.

The process of learning to use the GUI test tools and creating the actual GUI tests is time consuming, so it is only worth doing if the GUI being developed is going to be around for a while, because the benefits of developing a GUI using tests may not be realized until several versions of it have been released.

Another thing that has to be pointed out is that GUI testing is mostly black-box testing, so the tests created do not completely test the internal GUI code. GUI testing is only part of the solution and does not replace good software development practices. It's also important to remember that GUI testing only ensures that the GUI functions properly. Using tests won't prevent you from creating an ugly, hard-to-use GUI. Therefore, it's always important to get some feedback from real users when possible to help improve the usability of the GUI.

Summary

In this chapter I have tried to explain the tools and techniques that can be used to develop a Swing-based GUI using TDD. This has involved learning how to use tools like JFCUnit and Jemmy to simulate the user input that is required to test GUIs in an automated way. We then used these tools to build the GUI in a simple, incremental way using the normal process of TDD in a slightly different fashion. Creating GUIs using TDD is different from creating other types of code using TDD because a GUI is just a view of some data model and can only be tested using functional tests. Despite the difficulties and limitations of GUI testing, using tests to develop GUIs has a number of advantages. These advantages include the normal TDD benefits like automated regression testing as well as the ability to use the GUI tests to help define some of the interfaces needed for the data models. The advantages of having automated regression tests for the GUI cannot be overemphasized because they really help reduce the overall development cycle time as well as reduce the tedious, error-prone process of manual testing. Also, since a lot of the requirements for an application are written from the user interface point of view, driving the development of some of the data models from the needs of the GUI makes a lot of sense.

So the next time you need to develop a GUI, take the time to learn how to use a GUI testing framework and start to use TDD to develop the GUI. Once you are experienced with the testing framework, using TDD for a GUI will become second nature, and you will realize the advantages of it.

This chapter finishes the development of the individual pieces of the application. In the next chapter, we will put the pieces together and show how to use TDD to finish the application.

CHAPTER 6

■■■

Putting the Application Together

So far, we have concentrated on using TDD to develop the individual pieces of the application in isolation, but there comes a time when you have to put the pieces together to create the finished application. Ideally, if you have developed the individual pieces correctly, then putting them together should be easy, but in the real world this never happens.

The integration phase of software is kind of like the story of the blind men and the elephant. The story goes like this: four blind men are asked to describe what an elephant looks like by touching it. The first blind man touches the elephant's leg and reports that it "looks" like a pillar. The second blind man touches the elephant's tummy and says that an elephant is a wall. The third blind man touches the elephant's ear and says that it is a piece of cloth. The fourth blind man holds onto the tail and describes the elephant as a piece of rope. One of the things this story shows us is that different people can view the same object in different ways. None of these views are right or wrong, but all the views are incomplete and do not entirely describe the object.

The same idea is true in software development. Each developer has a different view of the application. The JSP developer sees the application from the end user's point of view and only worries about what the final web pages will look like. He or she doesn't care about how the data the application needs is stored or organized. On the other hand, the database developer sees the application as a set of tables and indexes that are used to store and retrieve the data needed by the application. He or she has no idea how the data will be displayed to the user. Each developer's view of the application is correct, but incomplete. Neither understands the entire application. It's only when the application is integrated that they start to understand it as a whole.

As the application is developed, each developer makes decisions about the best way to implement his or her piece of the application based on his or her view of the application. Because these views are different, when the pieces of an application are put together for the first time, a lot of problems will be discovered not only in the interface between the different pieces of the application but also in the design of some of the pieces.

Although TDD helps to create better software with well-designed interfaces, it does not eliminate the problems encountered during the integration phase of development. During the integration phase, it's possible that you'll discover some of the assumptions made about the architecture or individual pieces were wrong and parts of the application will need to be rewritten. That is why it's important to continue to use TDD during integration to help identify and solve the problems encountered.

Finishing the Last Few Pieces

Before we can integrate the various sections of our example code to make a complete application, there are a few individual pieces we still have to finish. For our development so far, we have been using a mock object in place of the database. The use of the mock object has made developing the tests a lot easier and has also helped us discover the interface for the database. Now that most of the pieces of the application have been developed, the interface to the database is well defined, and we can now create a real database and implement the actual class needed to communicate with it. The other piece of the application that we need to develop is the EJB that will allow the Admin GUI to talk to the application server. In Chapter 5, we stubbed out the EJB to make development easier. This allowed us to develop the GUI in isolation and also helped us define what methods the EJB needs. Now that we are ready to put the application together, we need to develop the real EJB so that we can connect the Admin GUI to the application server.

The Database

Until now, we have used stubs and mock objects to simulate access to the database. This has helped us develop the different parts of the application in isolation and define the type of data that we need to retrieve and store for the Football Pool application. It's now time to take all this information and create a real database, and then create the classes needed to communicate with the database.

The benefit of using stubs and mock objects to develop the code so far has been to totally separate the database from the rest of the application. This means that it doesn't matter how we implement the database access or the persistence mechanism; as long as we implement the interfaces used by the stubs and mock objects incorporated into our testing, the application should work.

For the football application, we have a number of ways to provide access to the database: we could use JDBC or Entity Beans or a Java Data Objects (JDOs) or something else. The correct one to use depends on a number of factors including size of the application, scalability, and error recovery. For purposes of keeping the examples simple, we are going to use JDBC.

Creating the Database Tables

In order to create the database schema, we have to understand what type of data needs to be stored and retrieved. For our purposes, we are not going to design the entire database at this time, but instead concentrate on the data needed for the players to make their picks.

From the tests that we have developed so far, we have a good understanding of what type of data needs to be stored. Basically, we need to store both the FootballPool object and the PlayerPicks object. These are pretty simple objects, so it's easy to convert each of these objects into a database table. For a more detailed discussion on mapping objects to relation databases, see Scott Ambler's article "The Fundamentals of Mapping Objects to Relational Databases" at http://www.agiledata.org/essays/mappingObjects.html.

Converting the data from the FootballPool object to a set of tables can be done in a couple different ways. After some thought, we decide to break the data into two tables. The first table, called the Pool table, contains information on the date, status, and winner of the pool. The table also contains a field called the PoolID, which is a unique ID used to link this table with other tables. The schema for this table is shown in Table 6-1.

Table 6-1. *Database Schema for Pool Table*

Field Name	Type	Comments
Date	Date	Date of the pool
Status	String	Status of the pool
Winner	String	Name of the winner of the pool
PoolID	Integer	Unique ID used to identify the pool

The second table, the Game table, contains information about each of the games in a pool. The PoolID field is used to link each entry back to the Pool table. The Game table schema is shown in Table 6-2.

Table 6-2. *Database Schema for Game Table*

Field Name	Type	Comments
PoolID	Integer	PoolID that this game belongs to
GameNum	Integer	Order of a game in the pool
HomeTeam	String	Name of the home team
AwayTeam	String	Name of the away team

If you look at the two tables, you will see they contain all the information needed to reconstruct the FootballPool object given the appropriate query.

Converting the PlayerPicks object into a set of tables requires us to add one more table to the database. The table will be called the Picks table, and it will contain all the information needed to retrieve and store each player's pick information. The schema is shown in Table 6-3.

Table 6-3. *Database Schema for Picks Table*

Field Name	Type	Comments
PoolID	Integer	PoolID that this game pick belongs to
UserName	String	User who made this pick
GameNum	Integer	Order of a game in the pool
PickedTeam	String	Name of the team that the user picked for this game number

The PlayerPicks object will be a little harder to create because it will require information from three different tables, but we now have a set of tables that we can use to start doing some integration testing. All we have to do now is create the database and add some data to it, and then we can start writing some tests. These tests will be used to help us create an implementation of the PoolDatabase interface that will let us communicate with the real database.

Communicating with the Database

Now that we have a real database, we need to hook the database into the application by implementing the PoolDatabase class. Up to this point, we have used a mock object to simulate access to a database, but we now need to create a class that can communicate with a real database in order to complete the application. We can create this class just like any other Java class by first creating a test. Testing database code, however, is a little different from anything we have tested before. The main difference is, because the test has to be run against a real database, the developer has to have a database setup that contains the correct schema, and the database also has to be populated with the correct data. Although this may seem like a lot of work, there is actually a framework called DBUnit that can be used to test database-dependent code. The DBUnit framework will help you develop tests for classes that depend on the state of a real database. For a brief primer on DBUnit, see the sidebar "DBUnit Overview."

DBUNIT OVERVIEW

DBUnit is a JUnit extension that allows you to test code that relies on interactions with a database. DBUnit provides methods to set the state of the database to a know state before each test and to check the state of the database at any time during a test. The DBUnit API can be used as part of a normal JUnit test, but using DBUnit this way requires you to provide a setUp() method to set the database up for each test.

The preferred way to use DBUnit is to have your test extend the DatabaseTestCase class. This will require you to implement two template methods: getConnection(), to return a connection to your database, and getDataSet(), to return a dataset that will be used to set up the database. A dataset is usually an XML file with a set of data in it for each table that is needed for the tests. If your tests extend the DatabaseTestCase, then before each test all the tables in the dataset are emptied and reset with the values in the dataset. DBUnit also provides methods to manipulate the data after it has been loaded in the database so that the data can be tailored for each test.

During your tests, DBUnit provides methods that can be used to compare database tables to the expected results. For example, to get the data for a table called PERSONNEL_DATA, you would write the following code:

```
IDataSet databaseDataSet = getConnection().createDataSet();
ITable actualTable = databaseDataSet.getTable("PERSONNEL_DATA");
```

You would then get the expected results from a dataset file as follows:

```
IDataSet expectedDataSet = new FlatXmlDataSet("expectedDataSet.xml");
ITable expectedTable = expectedDataSet.getTable("TABLE_NAME");
```

And then compare the expected results with the actual table data as follows:

```
Assertion.assertEquals(expectedTable, databaseTable);
```

Besides using the normal JUnit test framework to run DBUnit tests, it's also possible to run the DBUnit tests using the included dbunit ant task. This allows the setup and execution of the tests from within a build file. Using DBUnit makes it easy to test database-dependent code; you simply create a dataset, write a test that exercises the database code, and then use the method of the DBUnit API to make sure the database tables are in the expected state. For more information on DBUnit, check out the DBUnit web site at http://www.dbunit.org.

To create our first DBUnit test, we need to begin by setting up a database with the correct schema for our tests. Although the finished application may use an industrial-strength database such as Oracle or DB2, it isn't necessary for each developer to set up an exact copy of the production database, since the developer is only testing the functionality of the database code and doesn't care about performance. Therefore, for testing purposes the developer can use a database like HSQL or MySQL to run the tests. For our tests, we are going to use the HSQL database (http://hsqldb.sourceforge.net/) because of its small footprint and ease of use.

Once we install the database, the next thing we need to do is to create the schema. We can do this manually by issuing some SQL commands, but the best thing to do is to create a script that we can run anytime to produce the schema. That way all we have to do is run the script, and the database is ready for use. This script should be put into the Configuration Management system so that it can be shared by all the developers on the project. This way, if the database schema changes, the script is updated, and all the developers see the changes.

To create the database schema on our database, we run the following script:

```
create table pool (
pool_id int primary key,
date date,
winner varchar,
status varchar);

create table game (
pool_id int,
game_num int,
home_team varchar,
away_team varchar);

create table picks (
pool_id int,
user_name varchar,
game_num int,
picked_team varchar);
```

Now that the database and schema are set up, we can start writing tests. These tests will test a class that implements the PoolDatabase interface. This interface has three methods:

- getPoolWithStatus(): Gets a list of FootballPools given a status

- savePlayersPicks(): Saves a set of player picks for a particular pool

- getPlayersPicks(): Retrieves a set of player picks for a particular pool

Let's start by writing a test for the first method, getPoolWithStatus(). The behavior for this method is pretty simple for a given status (open, closed, etc.)—the method returns a list of FootballPools. To create a test for this behavior, we write the code shown in Listing 6-1.

Listing 6-1. *PoolDataDBTester*

```
public class PoolDataDBTester extends DatabaseTestCase
{
    public PoolDataDBTester(String name)
    {
        super(name);
    }
    protected IDatabaseConnection getConnection() throws Exception
    {
        Class driverClass = Class.forName("org.hsqldb.jdbcDriver");
        Connection jdbcConnection =
        DriverManager.getConnection("jdbc:hsqldb:hsql://localhost", "sa", "");
        return new DatabaseConnection(jdbcConnection);
    }

    protected IDataSet getDataSet() throws Exception
    {
        return new FlatXmlDataSet(new FileInputStream("dataset1.xml"));
    }

    public void testGetFBPoolFromDB() throws Exception
    {
        PoolDatabase poolDB =
            new PoolDatabaseImpl("jdbc:hsqldb:hsql://localhost", "sa", "");
        Vector openPoolList = poolDB.getPoolWithStatus("Open");
        //DB should only have one open pool
        assertEquals(1, openPoolList.size());
        //Get pool and check to make sure it has the correct games
        FootballPool openPool = (FootballPool) openPoolList.elementAt(0);
        assertEquals("Kansas City", openPool.getAwayTeam(0));
        assertEquals("Green Bay", openPool.getHomeTeam(0));
        assertEquals("Houston", openPool.getAwayTeam(1));
        assertEquals("Tennessee", openPool.getHomeTeam(1));
        assertEquals("Carolina", openPool.getAwayTeam(2));
        assertEquals("Indianapolis", openPool.getHomeTeam(2));
        assertEquals("NY Giants", openPool.getAwayTeam(3));
        assertEquals("New England", openPool.getHomeTeam(3));
        assertEquals("Chicago", openPool.getAwayTeam(4));
        assertEquals("New Orleans", openPool.getHomeTeam(4));
        assertEquals("Oakland", openPool.getAwayTeam(5));
        assertEquals("Cleveland", openPool.getHomeTeam(5));
        assertEquals("Philadelphia", openPool.getAwayTeam(6));
        assertEquals("Dallas", openPool.getHomeTeam(6));
        assertEquals("Tampa Bay", openPool.getAwayTeam(7));
        assertEquals("Washington", openPool.getHomeTeam(7));
        assertEquals("Miami", openPool.getAwayTeam(8));
        assertEquals("Jacksonville", openPool.getHomeTeam(8));
```

```
        assertEquals("Pittsburgh", openPool.getAwayTeam(9));
        assertEquals("Denver", openPool.getHomeTeam(9));
        assertEquals("Buffalo", openPool.getAwayTeam(10));
        assertEquals("NY Jets", openPool.getHomeTeam(10));
        assertEquals("Baltimore", openPool.getAwayTeam(11));
        assertEquals("Arizona", openPool.getHomeTeam(11));
        assertEquals("San Francisco", openPool.getAwayTeam(12));
        assertEquals("Seattle", openPool.getHomeTeam(12));
        assertEquals("Atlanta", openPool.getAwayTeam(13));
        assertEquals("St. Louis", openPool.getHomeTeam(13));
    }
}
```

If you look at the test, you will see it is a DBUnit test because this class extends the
DatabaseTestCase. Because of this, we have to implement the getConnection() and
getDataSet() methods. The getConnection() method connects the test to the database
and just involves setting up the driver and connection to the database being tested. The
getDataSet() method populates the database with a set of data before each test. This method
returns an IDataSet, which is a set of table data for the database. This data is usually created
from an XML file, as is done in this case. Once you understand DBUnit, implementing these
methods is very straightforward. The testGetFBPoolFromDB() method is also very simple: all it
does is get a list of the open pools from the database, of which there should only be one, and
make sure the pool has the correct data.

Of course, when you run the test, it fails, because we have not created the dataset or the
PoolDatabaseImpl class yet.

Let's start by first creating the PoolDatabaseImpl class to implement the PoolDatabase
interface. We will just stub out the savePlayersPicks() and getPlayersPicks() methods
for now and concentrate on implementing the getPoolWithStatus() method. Creating a
FootballPool object from the tables is going to take a couple of queries. We first have to query
the Pool table to get a list of pools that have the correct status. Then for each row returned, we
have to take the pool_id of each returned row and query the Game table to get a list of the
games associated with each pool. Of course, in order to talk to the database, we need to be
able to create a connection to the database, which means we have to pass in some information to the PoolDatabaseImpl class in order to make this connection. Since we decided to use a
JDBC connection to communicate to the database, we implement the PoolDatabaseImpl class
as shown in Listing 6-2.

Listing 6-2. *PoolDatabaseImpl Class*

```
public class PoolDatabaseImpl implements PoolDatabase
{
    private Connection m_Conn;

    public PoolDatabaseImpl(String dbPath, String userName,
                String passwd) throws SQLException, ClassNotFoundException
    {
        Class driverClass = Class.forName("org.hsqldb.jdbcDriver");
        m_Conn = DriverManager.getConnection(dbPath, userName, passwd);
```

```java
        }
    public Vector getPoolWithStatus(String status)
    {
        int poolID;
        Date poolDate;
        String poolWinner;
        String poolStatus;
        int gameNum;
        String homeTeam;
        String awayTeam;

        FootballPool fbPool = null;
        Vector poolList = new Vector();
        //Query pool table to get open pool
        String sqlQuery =
    "Select pool_id, date, winner, status from pool where status = '" + status + "'";
        try
        {
            PreparedStatement poolTBStmt = m_Conn.prepareStatement(sqlQuery);
            ResultSet poolTBResults = poolTBStmt.executeQuery();
            boolean morePoolResults = poolTBResults.next();
            while(morePoolResults)
            {
                poolID = poolTBResults.getInt(1);
                poolDate = poolTBResults.getDate(2);
                poolWinner = poolTBResults.getString(3);
                poolStatus = poolTBResults.getString(4);
                fbPool = new FootballPool(poolDate.toString());
                //Query game table to get games for this poolID
                sqlQuery =
                "Select game_num, home_team, away_team from game where pool_id =
                                " + poolID + "order by game_num";
                PreparedStatement gameTBStmt = m_Conn.prepareStatement(sqlQuery);
                ResultSet gameTBResults = gameTBStmt.executeQuery();
                boolean moreGameResults = gameTBResults.next();
                while(moreGameResults)
                {
                    gameNum = gameTBResults.getInt(1);
                    homeTeam = gameTBResults.getString(2);
                    awayTeam = gameTBResults.getString(3);
                    fbPool.addGame(awayTeam, homeTeam);
                    moreGameResults = gameTBResults.next();
                }
                poolList.addElement(fbPool);
                morePoolResults = poolTBResults.next();
            }
        }
```

```
        catch (SQLException e)
        {
            System.out.println("Error getting getting Pool.  Exception is " + e);
            e.printStackTrace();
        }

        return poolList;
    }

    public void savePlayersPicks(PlayersPicks picks)
    {
    }

    public PlayersPicks getPlayersPicks(String name, String poolDate)
    {
        return null;
    }
}
```

As you can see, we pass in the information needed to connect to the database in the constructor. This connection is then used in the getPoolWithStatus() method to execute a set of nested queries for creating a FootballPool object from the tables of the database.

Now that we have the PoolDatabaseImpl class written, we have a better understanding of how the data in the database relates to the FootballPool object. We can now use this knowledge to create a dataset that can be employed to set up the database to allow our test to pass. In order to get our test to pass, we need one entry in the Pool table with the status set to open and a set of games in the Game table that correspond to the pool_id of the entry in the Pool table. This set of games in the Game table must correspond with the expectations of the test. So with these requirements, we create the dataset shown in Listing 6-3.

Listing 6-3. *Dataset for Database Test*

```
<dataset>
    <POOL    POOL_ID="1"
                 DATE="2003-09-17"
                 WINNER=""
                 STATUS="Open"/>
    <GAME POOL_ID="1"
                GAME_NUM ="1"
                HOME_TEAM ="Green Bay"
                AWAY_TEAM="Kansas City"/>
    <GAME POOL_ID="1"
                GAME_NUM ="2"
                HOME_TEAM ="Tennessee"
                AWAY_TEAM="Houston"/>
    <GAME POOL_ID="1"
                GAME_NUM ="3"
                HOME_TEAM ="Indianapolis"
```

```xml
                        AWAY_TEAM="Carolina"/>
        <GAME POOL_ID="1"
                        GAME_NUM ="4"
                        HOME_TEAM ="New England"
                        AWAY_TEAM="NY Giants"/>
         <GAME POOL_ID="1"
                        GAME_NUM ="5"
                        HOME_TEAM ="New Orleans"
                        AWAY_TEAM="Chicago"/>
        <GAME POOL_ID="1"
                        GAME_NUM ="6"
                        HOME_TEAM ="Cleveland"
                        AWAY_TEAM="Oakland"/>
        <GAME POOL_ID="1"
                        GAME_NUM ="7"
                        HOME_TEAM ="Dallas"
                        AWAY_TEAM="Philadelphia"/>
        <GAME POOL_ID="1"
                        GAME_NUM ="8"
                        HOME_TEAM ="Washington"
                        AWAY_TEAM="Tampa Bay"/>
        <GAME POOL_ID="1"
                        GAME_NUM ="9"
                        HOME_TEAM ="Jacksonville"
                        AWAY_TEAM="Miami"/>
        <GAME POOL_ID="1"
                        GAME_NUM ="10"
                        HOME_TEAM ="Denver"
                        AWAY_TEAM="Pittsburgh"/>
        <GAME POOL_ID="1"
                        GAME_NUM ="11"
                        HOME_TEAM ="NY Jets"
                        AWAY_TEAM="Buffalo"/>
        <GAME POOL_ID="1"
                        GAME_NUM ="12"
                        HOME_TEAM ="Arizona"
                        AWAY_TEAM="Baltimore"/>
        <GAME POOL_ID="1"
                        GAME_NUM ="13"
                        HOME_TEAM ="Seattle"
                        AWAY_TEAM="San Francisco"/>
        <GAME POOL_ID="1"
                        GAME_NUM ="14"
                        HOME_TEAM ="St. Louis"
                        AWAY_TEAM="Atlanta"/>
    <PICKS />
</dataset>
```

As you can see, this is an XML file. This file has one entry for each row of each table that needs to be inserted into the database. Before each test, DBUnit will empty every table that is referenced in the dataset and repopulate it with the data in the dataset. This ensures that each test starts out with the database in a known state.

Now that we have created our dataset and `PoolDatabaseImpl` class, the test now passes. Although this test took a little more work than some of the other tests we have created, this test has helped us take our first step toward integration of the application by helping us connect the code to a real database.

The next method we have to implement is `savePlayersPicks()`. The behavior of this method is pretty simple: it just takes the player picks and stores them in the database. All the test has to do is pass the player picks to the `savePlayersPicks()` method and then check the database to make sure the new picks were added to the Picks table. With that in mind, we write the test shown in Listing 6-4.

Listing 6-4. *testSavePlayerPicksToDB Method*

```
public void testSavePlayerPicksToDB() throws Exception, ClassNotFoundException
{
    PoolDatabase poolDB =
                new PoolDatabaseImpl("jdbc:hsqldb:hsql://localhost", "sa", "");
    Vector openPoolList = poolDB.getPoolWithStatus("Open");
    FootballPool openPool = (FootballPool) openPoolList.elementAt(0);
    PlayersPicks playPicks = createPlayersPicks(openPool);
    //Save the player picks to the database
    poolDB.savePlayersPicks (playPicks);

    //Verify that the database contains the correct data
    IDataSet databaseDataSet = getConnection().createDataSet();
    ITable actualTable = databaseDataSet.getTable("Picks");

    // Load expected data from an XML dataset
    IDataSet expectedDataSet =
        new FlatXmlDataSet(new FileInputStream("expectedDataset1.xml"));
    ITable expectedTable = expectedDataSet.getTable("Picks");

    // Assert actual database table matches expected table
    Assertion.assertEquals(expectedTable, actualTable);

}
```

The way this test works is that it creates a set of player picks using the first open pool. It then calls the `savePlayersPicks()` method to save the picks to the database. In order to check to see whether the picks were saved correctly, we need to retrieve the values from the Picks table and compare them to a set of expected values. DBUnit provides an easy way to get a set of data from the table with the `IDataSet.getTable()` method. In order to see whether the data in the table is correct, you need to create a dataset that has the expected values for the table. The easiest way to do this is to create an XML dataset file similar to the one that is used to load the database before each test. Once the file is created, it can be loaded by the test and used to compare the contents of the real table. For our test, we create the file expectedDataset1.xml, which has the contents shown in Listing 6-5.

Listing 6-5. *Expected Database Set for Test*

```
<dataset>
    <PICKS POOL_ID="1"
            GAME_NUM ="1"
            PICKED_TEAM ="Green Bay"
            USER_NAME="EDDYC"/>
    <PICKS POOL_ID="1"
            GAME_NUM ="2"
            PICKED_TEAM ="Tennessee"
            USER_NAME="EDDYC"/>
    <PICKS POOL_ID="1"
            GAME_NUM ="3"
            PICKED_TEAM ="Indianapolis"
            USER_NAME="EDDYC"/>
    <PICKS POOL_ID="1"
            GAME_NUM ="4"
            PICKED_TEAM ="New England"
            USER_NAME="EDDYC"/>
    <PICKS POOL_ID="1"
            GAME_NUM ="5"
            PICKED_TEAM ="New Orleans"
            USER_NAME="EDDYC"/>
    <PICKS POOL_ID="1"
            GAME_NUM ="6"
            PICKED_TEAM ="Cleveland"
            USER_NAME="EDDYC"/>
    <PICKS POOL_ID="1"
            GAME_NUM ="7"
            PICKED_TEAM ="Dallas"
            USER_NAME="EDDYC"/>
    <PICKS POOL_ID="1"
            GAME_NUM ="8"
            PICKED_TEAM ="Washington"
            USER_NAME="EDDYC"/>
    <PICKS POOL_ID="1"
            GAME_NUM ="9"
            PICKED_TEAM ="Jacksonville"
            USER_NAME="EDDYC"/>
    <PICKS POOL_ID="1"
            GAME_NUM ="10"
            PICKED_TEAM ="Denver"
            USER_NAME="EDDYC"/>
```

```
<PICKS POOL_ID="1"
            GAME_NUM ="11"
            PICKED_TEAM ="NY Jets"
            USER_NAME="EDDYC"/>
<PICKS POOL_ID="1"
            GAME_NUM ="12"
            PICKED_TEAM ="Arizona"
            USER_NAME="EDDYC"/>
<PICKS POOL_ID="1"
            GAME_NUM ="13"
            PICKED_TEAM ="Seattle"
            USER_NAME="EDDYC"/>
<PICKS POOL_ID="1"
            GAME_NUM ="14"
            PICKED_TEAM ="St. Louis"
            USER_NAME="EDDYC"/>
</dataset>
```

This is the expected result of the Picks table after the savePlayersPicks() method has been called. Of course, when we run the test, it fails because we have not implemented the savePlayersPicks() method, so we add the code shown in Listing 6-6 to the PoolDatabaseImpl class to get the test to pass.

Listing 6-6. *savePlayersPicks Method*

```
public void savePlayersPicks (PlayersPicks picks)
{
    int poolID;
    String playersName = picks.getPlayersName();
    String poolDate = picks.getPoolDate();
    //Get pool_id for given pool date
  String sqlQuery = "Select pool_id from pool where date = '" + poolDate + "'";
    try
    {
        PreparedStatement poolTBStmt = m_Conn.prepareStatement(sqlQuery);
        ResultSet poolTBResults = poolTBStmt.executeQuery();
        boolean morePoolResults = poolTBResults.next();
        if(morePoolResults)
        {
            poolID = poolTBResults.getInt(1);
            //insert a row into the Picks table for each game
            String insertStr;
            for(int i = 0; i < 14; i++)
            {
                insertStr =
                "Insert into picks (pool_id, user_name, game_num, picked_team)
                " + "Values(" + poolID + ",'" + playersName + "'," + (i+1)
```

```
                                + ",'" + picks.getPickedTeam(i) + "'" + ")";
                     PreparedStatement pickTBStmt =
                                          m_Conn.prepareStatement(insertStr);
                     pickTBStmt.execute();
               }
           }
       }
       catch (SQLException e)
       {
           System.out.println("Error saving picks.  Exception is " + e);
           e.printStackTrace();
       }
   }
}
```

The `PlayerPicks` passed into the method do not contain the `pool_id` for the pool that the picks belong to, so the first thing the method has to do is query the Pool table to get the `pool_id` for the pool the picks belong to. Once this is done, the method then inserts a row into the Picks table for each game.

With this added code, the test now passes, and we can move on to implementing the final method of the `PoolDatabase` interface, which is the `getPlayersPicks()` method.

The `getPlayersPicks()` method is used to get a set of `PlayersPicks` from the database given a pool date and player's name. To implement this method, we first write the test shown in Listing 6-7.

Listing 6-7. *testGetPlayerPicksFromDB Method*

```
public void testGetPlayerPicksFromDB() throws Exception, ClassNotFoundException
{
    // Reset the database contents with the data needed for the test to pass
    IDataSet dataSet =
                   new FlatXmlDataSet(new FileInputStream("dataset2.xml"));
    DatabaseOperation.CLEAN_INSERT.execute(getConnection(), dataSet);
    String playerName = "BOBG";
    String poolDate = "2003-09-17";
    PoolDatabase poolDB =
                   new PoolDatabaseImpl("jdbc:hsqldb:hsql://localhost", "sa", "");
    //Get picks from Database
    PlayersPicks picks = poolDB.getPlayersPicks(playerName, poolDate);
    //Verify that the picks are correct
    assertEquals("Green Bay", picks.getPickedTeam(0));
    assertEquals("Tennessee", picks.getPickedTeam(1));
    assertEquals("Indianapolis", picks.getPickedTeam(2));
    assertEquals("New England", picks.getPickedTeam(3));
    assertEquals("New Orleans", picks.getPickedTeam(4));
    assertEquals("Cleveland", picks.getPickedTeam(5));
    assertEquals("Dallas", picks.getPickedTeam(6));
    assertEquals("Washington", picks.getPickedTeam(7));
    assertEquals("Jacksonville", picks.getPickedTeam(8));
```

```
        assertEquals("Denver", picks.getPickedTeam(9));
        assertEquals("NY Jets", picks.getPickedTeam(10));
        assertEquals("Arizona", picks.getPickedTeam(11));
        assertEquals("Seattle", picks.getPickedTeam(12));
        assertEquals("St. Louis", picks.getPickedTeam(13));
    }
```

If you look at the test, you will see that the first thing that is done is the database is reset with a new dataset (dataset2.xml). This is because dataset1.xml, which is loaded by default, does not contain any entries for the Picks table, so we need to reset the database so that it has the correct entries in the Picks table. Its possible that we could refactor dataset1.xml so that it will work for all tests, but there will be times when it will be impossible to come up with one set of data that will work for all tests.

In general, you should try to minimize the number of datasets that you need to create for database testing, since the datasets need to be maintained; so the fewer datasets that you have, the easier they will be to maintain. It's not important to optimize the datasets while you are developing tests, but after the tests are developed, it is probably worth the time to take a hard look at all the data developed for the tests and optimize it if possible (i.e., refactor the data).

Now that we have the test written, all that is left to do is implement the getPlayersPicks() method to get the test to pass. The data for the players' picks is spread through the three different tables. You have to query the Pool table to get the pool_id for a given pool date. You have to get the list of games for a given pool from the Game table, and you have the get the actual picks for each player from the Picks table. Since the query that will be used in this method will be complicated, before you implement the method you will probably need to run some test queries against the database to figure out the best query to use to get the data from the database. Of course, you will have to load the database with some data to run the queries, but this is easy. All you have to do is to run the test. It will fail, but before it fails it will set up the database with the data you need to run the queries. After a few queries, we decide to implement the getPlayersPicks() method as shown in Listing 6-8.

Listing 6-8. *getPlayersPicks Method*

```
public PlayersPicks getPlayersPicks(String name, String poolDate)
{
    int poolID;
    int gameNum;
    String pickedTeam;
    String homeTeam;
    String awayTeam;
    Game game;
    Vector gameList = new Vector();
    PlayersPicks picks = null;
    //Get pool_id for given pool date
    String sqlQuery = "Select pool_id from pool where date = '" + poolDate + "'";
    try
    {
        PreparedStatement poolTBStmt = m_Conn.prepareStatement(sqlQuery);
```

```
                ResultSet poolTBResults = poolTBStmt.executeQuery();
                boolean morePoolResults = poolTBResults.next();
                if (morePoolResults)
                {
                    poolID = poolTBResults.getInt(1);
                    //Get the rows from the Picks table that match the pool_id
                    //  and name
                    String SelecttStr;
                    for (int i = 0; i < 14; i++)
                    {
                        SelecttStr =
                            "select g.game_num, g.home_team, g.away_team,p.picked_team"
                            + " from picks p, game g  " + "where g.pool_id =
                            p.pool_id and g.pool_id=" +
                            poolID + " and user_name = '" + name + "'" +
                            " and p.game_num = g.game_num order by game_num";

                        PreparedStatement pickTBStmt =
                                        m_Conn.prepareStatement(SelecttStr);
                        ResultSet pickResults = pickTBStmt.executeQuery();
                        boolean morePickResults = pickResults.next();
                        while (morePickResults)
                        {
                            gameNum = pickResults.getInt(1);
                            homeTeam = pickResults.getString(2);
                            awayTeam = pickResults.getString(3);
                            pickedTeam = pickResults.getString(4);
                            game = new Game(awayTeam, homeTeam);
                            game.set_pickedGame(pickedTeam);
                            gameList.addElement(game);
                            morePickResults = pickResults.next();
                        }
                        picks = new PlayersPicks(name, poolDate, gameList);
                    }
                }
            }
            catch (SQLException e)
            {
                System.out.println("Error saving picks.  Exception is " + e);
                e.printStackTrace();
            }
            return(picks);
        }
```

This method uses two queries to create the PlayersPicks for the given pool data and player name. With this code written, the test passes, and we have the basic implementation of the PoolDatabase interface. There are still a lot more tests that have to be written to make sure the methods of the `PoolDatabaseImpl` class work in all conditions, but I've shown that developing database code is not much different from developing any other code with TDD. Different tools may be used for different types of code, but the process is the same.

Hands-On Exercises

So far, the tests have helped us to implement the three methods of the `PoolDatabase` interface, but there is still a lot more work to do. The tests developed have only tested the simple default case wherein the database is set up correctly and there are no error conditions. Create a set of tests that will test the following error conditions:

- Try to get a list of open pools from a database with no pools that are open.

- Try to save a set of player picks for a pool date that doesn't exist.

- Try to get a set of player picks for a player who doesn't exist.

Use the tests developed to improve the `PoolDatabaseImpl` class so it can handle these error conditions.

The EJB

In Chapter 5, we created a stub class, `FBPoolServerStub`, to take the place of the EJB that helped us create the Admin GUI and define the interface for the EJB. We now need to take the interface and create the rest of the classes for the EJB. The advantage of creating `FBPoolServerStub` first before the creating the real EJB is that we now know exactly what methods we need to create for the EJB. `FBPoolServerStub` also has an associated set of tests that can be adapted to help us develop the EJB. Although it may have seemed like overkill to use tests to develop a stub class, these tests will come in handy as we develop the EJB.

The first question we need to answer before we start development is how we are going to create tests to help us develop the EJB. Unfortunately, testing an EJB is not easy because, like a servlet, it requires a container to run. To test the EJB, we could use mock objects to simulate the EJB container or use in-container testing. The best approach to use for testing depends on the type of EJB being tested and the architecture of the application. In the case of the Football Pool application, the EJB that needs to be developed will be pretty simple because of our decision to use JDBC to persist the data. This means that most of the logic needed to implement the required methods of the EJB will be implemented by the `PoolDatabase` class. As a result, the EJB won't be much more than a façade that allows the client to access the `PoolDatabase` methods.

A *façade* is a common pattern used when building EJBs that allows you to use regular Java classes to develop most of the code needed for the EJB. This makes the application more testable because most of the code needed to implement the EJB can be developed and tested in isolation. The EJB is only used to connect the pieces together. In the Football Pool application, most of the work of the EJB will be done by the `PoolDatabase` class. As you will see, this will make it easy to develop the EJB in isolation.

Although the façade strategy is used a lot, it cannot be used in some situations, such as when EJBs have to call other EJBs or when an EJB uses Container Managed Persistence (CMP) or some other service provided by the container. In these cases, using mock objects to test

these EJBs in isolation can be difficult, and the best choice for testing will be in-container testing. Later in the chapter, in the section "Integrating the Servlet with the Application Server,"
I will demonstrate how to test the EJB in-container.

Developing the FBPoolServer EJB

The EJB we need to develop for the Football Pool application is a simple façade, so we are
going to develop it in two steps. In the first step, we are going to take the FBPoolServerStub
class we created in Chapter 5 and make it a real class that gets its data from the database.
Once this is done, we will then assemble an EJB using this class and deploy it to a real server
so we can implement the EJB-specific code we need to make the class work on the application
server.

We will call the EJB we need to develop FBPoolServerEJB, and as always use tests to
develop it. The good news is that we don't have to develop the tests from scratch because we
already have a set of tests from Chapter 5 that we can adapt. Let's go through the tests from
Chapter 5 and see how they need to be changed to help us develop our EJB.

If we look at the first test from our FBPoolServerTest class, as shown in Listing 6-9, you
will see that very few changes are needed to adapt it to test an EJB.

Listing 6-9. *testGetPoolList Method*

```
public void testGetPoolList()
{
        FBPoolServer fbPoolServer = new FBPoolServerStub();
        Vector poolList = fbPoolServer.getPoolList();
        assertEquals(poolList.size(), 3);
        String poolDate = (String)poolList.elementAt(0);
        assertEquals("2004-09-11", poolDate);
        poolDate = (String)poolList.elementAt(1);
        assertEquals("2004-09-18", poolDate);
        poolDate = (String)poolList.elementAt(2);
        assertEquals("2004-09-25", poolDate);
}
```

The main thing we have to do is change the way the test gets the FBPoolServer class;
instead of using the FBPoolServerStub class, we need to use the FBPoolServerEJB class, so we
change the first line of the test to

```
        FBPoolServerEJB fbPoolServer = new FBPoolServerEJB();
```

Making this change means that we can't use this test to test the stub class anymore. It
would be nice if we could write the test in such a way that it could be used to test both classes.
If we wanted to do this, we could by adding a little extra code. We won't bother doing it now,
but I will show a couple of ways to do this in Chapter 7.

Now that we have the test written, we have to add some code to the FBPoolServerEJB to
get this test to pass. This should be easy because all we have to do is to use the PoolDatabase
class to get the information we need. Knowing this, we write the code shown in Listing 6-10.

Listing 6-10. *getPoolList Method*

```
public Vector getPoolList() throws RemoteException
{
    Vector poolList = m_poolDB.getAllPoolDates();
    return (poolList);
}
```

There are a couple of problems here. The first problem is that if we want the
FBPoolServerEJB class to use the PoolDatabase class, we need to initialize it. So we do this in
the constructor by adding the following line:

```
m_poolDB = new PoolDatabaseImpl(m_dbLocation, m_userName, m_passwd);
```

For now, we initialize the m_dbLocation, m_userName, and m_passwd variables with some
default values that allow us to connect to our test database. When we turn this class into an
EJB, we will determine the better way to initialize these variables.

The second problem is that the PoolDatabase interface does not have the
getAllPoolDates() method. In the stub class, we just created a list of pool date strings to
return, but in the real EJB we have to get the list from the database. Thus we have to add
the method shown in Listing 6-11 to the PoolDatabase interface and the code shown in
Listing 6-11 to the PoolDatabaseImpl class.

Listing 6-11. *getAllPoolDates Method*

```
public Vector getAllPoolDates()
{
    Date poolDate;
    String homeTeam;
    String awayTeam;

    Vector poolList = new Vector();
    //Query pool table to get all pools
    String sqlQuery = "Select date from pool";
    try
    {
        PreparedStatement poolTBStmt = m_Conn.prepareStatement(sqlQuery);
        ResultSet poolTBResults = poolTBStmt.executeQuery();
        boolean morePoolResults = poolTBResults.next();
        while (morePoolResults)
        {
            poolDate = poolTBResults.getDate(1);
            poolList.addElement(poolDate.toString());
            morePoolResults = poolTBResults.next();
        }
    }
    catch (SQLException e)
```

```
        {
            System.out.println("Error getting getting Pool.  Exception is " + e);
            e.printStackTrace();
        }

        return poolList;
    }
```

Once we add this code and go back to the test, we find a couple of problems that we have to fix before we can run the test. Because we are using the PoolDatabaseImpl class in our EJB, the test will not work unless we initialize the database properly. In order to do this, we update our test so that it extends the DatabaseTestCase class as in our database tests. We also add the required methods to set up the database and also create a dataset file with the data needed for our tests to pass.

Another problem with the test is that after adding PoolDatabase to FBPoolServerEJB some of the methods of the class now throw some new exceptions that weren't thrown by the stub class. This means that the test now has to catch these exceptions. After we make all these changes, the new test looks as shown in Listing 6-12.

Listing 6-12. *testGetPoolList Method*

```
public void testGetPoolList()
{
    try
    {
        FBPoolServerEJB fbPoolServer = new FBPoolServerEJB();
        Vector poolList = fbPoolServer.getPoolList();
        assertEquals(poolList.size(), 3);
        String poolDate = (String) poolList.elementAt(0);
        assertEquals("2004-09-11", poolDate);
        poolDate = (String) poolList.elementAt(1);
        assertEquals("2004-09-18", poolDate);
        poolDate = (String) poolList.elementAt(2);
        assertEquals("2004-09-25", poolDate);
    }
    catch (Exception e)
    {
        System.out.println("Error getting getting Pool List.  Exception is
                                      " + e);
        e.printStackTrace();
    }
}
```

With this code added, the test now passes. We then repeat this process for the rest of the tests in the FBPoolServerTest class and add the methods shown in Listing 6-13 to FBPoolServerEJB.

Listing 6-13. *getPoolInfo Method*

```
public FootballPool getPoolInfo(String poolDate) throws RemoteException
{
    FootballPool pool = m_poolDB.getPoolWithDate(poolDate);
    return (pool);
}
public String getStatus(String poolDate) throws RemoteException
{
    FootballPool pool = m_poolDB.getPoolWithDate(poolDate);
    if(pool == null)
    {
        return ("Unknown");
    }
    else
    {
        return(pool.getStatus());
    }
}


public void openPool(String poolDate) throws RemoteException
{
    m_poolDB.setPoolStatus(poolDate, "Open");
}
```

We also have to add the methods shown in Listing 6-14 to the PoolDatabaseImpl class.

Listing 6-14. *getPoolWithDate and setPoolStatus Methods*

```
public FootballPool getPoolWithDate(String poolDateStr)
{
    int poolID;
    Date poolDate;
    String poolWinner;
    String poolStatus;
    int gameNum;
    String homeTeam;
    String awayTeam;

    FootballPool fbPool = null;
    //Query pool table to get pool with specified date
    String sqlQuery = "Select pool_id, date, winner, status from pool
                            where date = '" + poolDateStr + "'";
    try
    {
        PreparedStatement poolTBStmt = m_Conn.prepareStatement(sqlQuery);
        ResultSet poolTBResults = poolTBStmt.executeQuery();
        boolean morePoolResults = poolTBResults.next();
        if (morePoolResults)
```

```java
            {
                poolID = poolTBResults.getInt(1);
                poolDate = poolTBResults.getDate(2);
                poolWinner = poolTBResults.getString(3);
                poolStatus = poolTBResults.getString(4);
                fbPool = new FootballPool(poolDate.toString());
                fbPool.setStatus(poolStatus);
                fbPool.setWinner(poolWinner);
                //Query game table to get games for this poolID
                sqlQuery = "Select game_num, home_team, away_team from
                        game where pool_id = " + poolID + "order by game_num";
                PreparedStatement gameTBStmt = m_Conn.prepareStatement(sqlQuery);
                ResultSet gameTBResults = gameTBStmt.executeQuery();
                boolean moreGameResults = gameTBResults.next();
                while (moreGameResults)
                {
                    gameNum = gameTBResults.getInt(1);
                    homeTeam = gameTBResults.getString(2);
                    awayTeam = gameTBResults.getString(3);
                    fbPool.addGame(awayTeam, homeTeam);
                    moreGameResults = gameTBResults.next();
                }
            }
        }
        catch (SQLException e)
        {
            System.out.println("Error getting getting Pool.  Exception is " + e);
            e.printStackTrace();
        }

        return (fbPool);
    }
    public void setPoolStatus(String poolDate, String status)
    {
        String sqlQuery = "Update pool set status = '"
        + status + "' where pool_id = " +
                    "select pool_id from pool where date = '" + poolDate + "'";
        try
        {
            PreparedStatement poolTBStmt = m_Conn.prepareStatement(sqlQuery);
            poolTBStmt.execute();
        }
        catch (SQLException e)
        {
            System.out.println("Error updating pool status.  Exception is " + e);
            e.printStackTrace();
        }
    }
}
```

We now have finished the development of the main class of the EJB. There is no more we can do with it until we test it on a real application server. To do this, we first have to create the supporting remote and home interfaces for the EJB, create a deployment descriptor, and package all the files up so that they can be deployed to the application server. These tasks are best left to your favorite IDE. IDEs such as Eclipse, JBuilder, and IDEA all have the ability to create the classes and deployment descriptor needed for an EJB, as well as package the EJB and deploy it to the application server.

Once you understand how to package the EJB, you should add a task to the main build file so that the EJB can be integrated into the project. This will allow you to work out any build issues or deployment issues that may occur because of the addition of the new EJB. To see the classes and deployment descriptor needed for the EJB as well as the build script used to package and deploy the EJB, check out the source code for this chapter.

Finishing the FBPoolServer EJB

Once the packaging and deployment issues are resolved, we can continue the development of the EJB. Although the tests we have created for the EJB have given us confidence that it should work, we know that our test environment is different from the environment of the application server. Testing in isolation is a good way to start the development of an EJB, but these tests have limitations because they cannot simulate the real environment of the EJB container. The only way you can tell that you are finished developing an EJB is to deploy it and run tests against a real application server. To run these tests, it's important to have the EJB build and deploy operation be as automated as possible because you will be continually redeploying the EJB as tests are run and changes are made. In our case, the way we automate this process is to add an Ant task to the build that automatically deploys the EJB jar file to our application server and another task that runs the EJB test. This lets us quickly deploy the EJB after a change is made and also easily run the test. The goal is to make the build ➤ deploy ➤ test cycle as simple as possible so that you can get feedback about a change as quickly as possible. These tasks are included with the build file provided with the source code of this chapter.

Using the deploy task in the build file, we deploy the EJB jar to the application server. In our case, we are using JBoss. (For information on setting up and using JBoss, check out http://www.jboss.com). Once the EJB is deployed, we can use the FBPoolServerTest class to test the EJB, but before we can use it we need to make one minor change. We have to change the way we get the EJB. The last time we used this test we just called the EJB constructor directly, but now that the EJB is deployed, we have to get the reference to the EJB in a different way. What we do is write the method shown in Listing 6-15 to get a reference to the EJB.

Listing 6-15. *getEJB Method*

```
private FBPoolServer getEJB() throws NamingException,
                          RemoteException, CreateException
{
    FBPoolServerHome fbPoolHome = null;
    Hashtable env = new Hashtable();

    env.put(Context.INITIAL_CONTEXT_FACTORY,
            "org.jnp.interfaces.NamingContextFactory");
    env.put(Context.PROVIDER_URL, "localhost:1099");
```

```
            env.put("java.naming.factory.url.pkgs",
                    "org.jboss.naming:org.jnp.interfaces");
            Context ctx = new InitialContext(env);
            System.out.println("Before lookup of FBPoolHome");
            fbPoolHome = (FBPoolServerHome)
            javax.rmi.PortableRemoteObject.narrow
                            (ctx.lookup("FBPoolServerEJB"), FBPoolServerHome.class);
            System.out.println("Before create on FBPoolServerHome");
            return(fbPoolHome.create());
        }
```

Then we update the test methods to use this method to get a reference to the EJB.

```
FBPoolServer fbPoolServer = getEJB();
```

We can now run the tests, which we do, and they fail. There are a couple of problems that we discover. The first issue is that the database we used for our initial tests is different from the one that we are using when the EJB is deployed. We hard coded the information needed to connect to the database when we created the EJB; now we need to make it more dynamic so the EJB will work with any database we choose. To do this, we add a resource reference to the deployment descriptor as follows:

```
<resource-ref>
                <res-ref-name>jdbc/PoolDB</res-ref-name>
                <res-type>java.sql.DataSource</res-type>
                <res-auth> Container</res-auth>
</resource-ref>
```

We then add the code in Listing 6-16 to the EJB.

Listing 6-16. *getConnection Method*

```
private Connection getConnection() throws SQLException NamingException
{
    Context initial = new InitialContext();
    DataSource dataSource = (DataSource) initial.lookup("jdbc/PoolDB");
    return(dataSource.getConnection());
}
```

The last thing that needs to be done is to add the data source for the database that is going to be used to the application server so that the JNDI lookup works. Once this is done, we run the test again and we get a little further, but all the tests still fail. From the log file and exceptions thrown by the application server, we see that the EJB connects to the database but then has trouble returning the FootballPool class to the tests. The problem is that since the FootballPool object is being returned through RMI, the FootballPool object needs to be serialized in order to be returned. Since the FootballPool does not implement the Serializable interface, the return causes an exception. This is easy to fix: all we have to do is add the Serializable interface to both the FootballPool class and the Game class.

Once this is done, we redeploy the EJB, and the tests should work, but they probably won't. There is actually nothing wrong with the code at this point, but there is probably a problem with the application server configuration. While preparing code for this book, I ran into a number of problems getting the EJB to work on JBoss because of configuration issues. These are normal problems that occur during the integration phase of the project. To solve these issues usually takes a lot of trial-and-error work. The tests developed so far and the automation of the build ➤ deploy ➤ test cycle really help developers quickly try different configuration options until the problems are solved.

With the configuration issues solved, the tests run and we are finished with the EJB development. There may still be some issues when we integrate the EJB with the Admin GUI, but since the EJB was developed from FBPoolServerStub, any problems found should be small ones.

As you can see, developing EJBs using TDD is not that much different from developing other types of classes. If possible, EJBs should be developed in isolation as much as possible using mock objects and normal JUnit tests. When necessary, the EJB should be deployed to the application server and tested in a real container so that any code developed in isolation can be validated. Testing against a real application server also helps you create and verify all the configuration and deployment descriptors associated with EJBs.

Some EJBs such as entity beans that use CMP cannot be developed in isolation because of their dependence on the EJB container. In these cases, your only choice is to use in-container testing. If your EJB does not provide an RMI interface like the football pool's EJB, then your best choice for accessing it is to write a servlet that calls the EJB. This way you can write tests against the servlet to test out the functionality of the EJB and help drive its development.[1]

The Role of TDD During Application Integration

TDD can be used not only to develop the individual pieces of the application, but also throughout the different stages of the project. As the EJB example shows, developing in isolation has its limitations. It wasn't until we deployed the EJB to the application server that we really finished the development. The pieces of a J2EE application such as servlets and EJBs are more than just a set of Java classes that interact with each other. There are databases, security constraints, deployment descriptors, configuration files, etc. that all must be set up correctly in order for the application to work. Getting all these pieces working together can be a tough job, but with the right testing framework and a series of tests, a J2EE application can be assembled step by step until the whole application is fully integrated.

To demonstrate how to take the pieces of the application and put them together, we are going to take the servlets and JSPs developed in Chapter 4, connect them to the database, and then deploy them to a real application server. All these tasks will be driven using tests that will measure our progress and let us know when the application is fully integrated.

To start the integration, we first need to develop a test. We could start by taking the servlet tests developed in Chapter 4 and remove the mock objects from those tests. This would allow us to verify that the servlets work with a real database. In order to do this, we would have to change the servlet tests like we did with the FBPoolServerTest so that they use DBUnit to set up a database and verify the results. Although this would make sure that the servlet can get data from a real database, it really would not help us finish the development of the servlet.

---

1. For a more detailed discussion of all the different ways to test the different types of EJBs, I recommend *JUnit in Action* by Vincent Massol and Ted Husted (Manning Publications, 2003).

We have already tested the PoolData and PoolDatabase classes, and we know that they work with a real database. We also have tested the servlet using mock objects for the PoolData and PoolDatabase classes in a simulated servlet container. We are also confident that if the implementation of the PoolData and PoolDatabase classes works, then the servlet should have no problem using a real database. In order to start the integration of the servlet into a real

CACTUS OVERVIEW

Cactus is an extension of JUnit that can be used to test server-side code (EJBs, servlets, TagLibs, etc). In order to test server-side code, Cactus tests have both a client-side test component and a server-side test component. These components are connected through a redirector (see Figure 6-1). Cactus has test-case classes and redirectors for servlets, JSPs, and filters. (No classes exist for testing EJBs directly.)

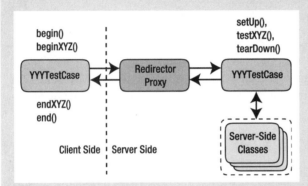

Figure 6-1. *Cactus architecture*

Cactus tests look similar to JUnit tests but contain a few new methods and operate a little differently. JUnit tests run in the same JVM as the code being tested. Cactus tests run in two different JVMs: the JVM where the test is executed and the application server's JVM. Cactus uses a redirector class to coordinate the test between the two JVMs. The additional test methods that Cactus provides allow you to create a custom setup and teardown method for each individual test. For example, if you are writing a test called testMyJSP(), you could write a beginMyJSP() method to set up the parameters needed by the MyJSP test and an endMyJSP() method that would check the return values of the JSP. Cactus also provides a general begin() method that will be called before every test. When you run a Cactus test, the first thing that happens is that an instance of the test class is created on the client. It then executes any beginXYZ(), testXYZ(), and endXYZ() methods (where XYZ is the name of the test). When these methods are executed on the client side, they send commands to the redirector, which is running on the server. The redirector creates a server instance of the test class and executes the beginXYZ(), testXYZ(), and endXYZ() methods on the sever side and passes the results back to the client.

Cactus was written to work on any application server and has been tested on JBoss, Tomcat, WebLogic, and a few others. Cactus provides a couple of Ant tasks that can be used to set up and run Cactus tests automatically. For more information on how to download and configure Cactus, check out the Cactus web site at http://jakarta.apache.org/cactus/.

application server, what we need to do is deploy the servlets to the application server and then create some in-container tests to help us verify that the servlets we have developed will work on a real application server. To create these tests, we are going to use the Cactus testing framework. For a brief primer of Cactus, see the sidebar "Cactus Overview."

Integrating the Servlet with the Application Server

So you can see just how Cactus works, we are going to use it to help us integrate the servlet with the application server. As always, we start by creating tests. What we are going to do is to take the tests we developed in Chapter 4 and rewrite them as Cactus tests. One thing you have to keep in mind while writing these Cactus tests is that they are distributed tests and require a properly configured application server. They may also require some setting up of the system where the tests are being run from to ensure they can communicate with the application server properly. The distributed nature of the tests can cause some frustration until you fully understand how to set up the environment and write the tests, but this work will be worth the time because it will allow us to test the PlayerPickServlet on a real application server and finish its development. The first test we are going to rewrite is from the end of Chapter 4 where we tested the integrated servlet and JSP. That test was called testDisplayPlayerPicksWithRealJSP() (see Listing 4-17). If we rewrite the test as a Cactus test, we get the code shown in Listing 6-17.

Listing 6-17. *PlayerPickIntTester Class*

```
public class PlayerPickIntTester extends ServletTestCase
{
    public PlayerPickIntTester(String s)
    {
        super(s);
    }
    public void beginGetOpenPool(WebRequest webRequest)
    {
        webRequest.addParameter("username", "TimmyC");
    }

    public void testGetOpenPool() throws Exception
    {
        System.out.println("Starting Test");
        PlayerPickServlet servlet = new PlayerPickServlet();
        servlet.init(config);
        servlet.doPost(request, response);
    }

    public void endGetOpenPool(WebResponse response) throws Exception
    {
        assertTrue(response.isHTML());
        assertEquals("tables", 1, response.getTables().length);
        assertEquals("columns", 3,
                    response.getTables()[0].getColumnCount());
        assertEquals("rows", 15,
```

```
        response.getTables()[0].getRowCount());
    }
}
```

As you can see from the code, the format of the Cactus test is slightly different from a normal JUnit test. It takes three methods to run the test. The beginGetOpenPool() method is used to set up the user name that will be passed to the servlet. The testGetOpenPool() method executes the actual servlet. The endGetOpenPool() method checks the return of the servlet to make sure the results are as expected. In our tests we are executing the doPost() method of the servlet, so we are checking the HTML output of the JSP to make sure it is what we expect, but with Cactus it is also possible to call the internal methods of the servlet. So we could call the servlet's getOpenPool() method if we wanted to do finer-grain testing. Another thing to keep in mind as you build Cactus tests is that the redirector provides access to the container objects only on the application server. Because the container objects are not available until the test is running on the server side, you cannot use container objects in the methods that are executed on the client side.

Running a Cactus test is a little harder than running normal unit tests. In order to run the Cactus test, not only do you have to deploy the application to the server, but you also have to package the application so that it contains the dependent Cactus jar files and the associated changes in the deployment descriptors that are needed for the Cactus redirectors. Doing this packing manually would be difficult and would make the tests hard to run.

Luckily, Cactus provides an Ant task, cactifywar, that automatically updates a war file with all the information necessary to run the Cactus test. Cactus also provides another Ant task called cactus that can be used to automatically run the tests. The cactus task performs a number of different operations that you need to run the tests. It first deploys a war file to the application server, and then starts the application server and runs the tests. After the tests are run, the cactus task stops the application server. The cactus task has built-in support for the JBoss, Tomcat, Orion, Resin, and WebLogic application servers and also has a Generic subtask that can be used to support any other application server. These two tasks are real time savers and take the hassle out of running tests on an actual application server. Although it may take some time to understand how to use the tasks in your environment, once you have them set up, running the tests is pretty painless, which means you can concentrate on the test ➤ code ➤ debug cycle. Following is the Ant task that can be used to run our Cactus test:

```
<target name="runPlayerPickTests" depends="dist">
    <taskdef resource="cactus.tasks">
        <classpath>
            <pathelement location="${jars.dir}/cactus-1.6.1.jar"/>
            <pathelement location="${jars.dir}/cactus-ant-1.6.1.jar"/>
            <pathelement location="${jars.dir}/commons-httpclient-2.0.jar"/>
            <pathelement location="${jars.dir}/commons-logging-1.0.3.jar"/>
            <pathelement location="${jars.dir}/aspectjrt-1.1.1.jar"/>
            <pathelement location="${jars.dir}/dbunit-2.0.jar"/>
        </classpath>
    </taskdef>
<cactifywar srcfile="${dist.dir}/lib/${war.name}.war"
            destfile="${dist.dir}/lib/${war.name}-cf.war">
</cactifywar>
```

```
        <cactus warfile="${dist.dir}/lib/${war.name}-cf.war"
            printsummary="yes" failureproperty="tests.failed">
            <classpath>
                <path refid="compile.path"/>
                <pathelement location="${build-classes.dir}"/>
            </classpath>
            <containerset>
                <tomcat4x dir="${tomcat.dir}" port="8080"
                    todir="${testdata.dir}"/>
            </containerset>
            <formatter type="xml"/>
            <batchtest>
                <fileset dir="${test-int.dir}">
                    <include name="**/PlayerPickIntTest*.java"/>
                </fileset>
            </batchtest>
        </cactus>
    </target>
```

Although an Ant task is the easiest way to run Cactus tests, you can also run the tests from the Java command line, an IDE, or even a browser. (See the Cactus documentation for the details on the different ways Cactus can be run.) Now that we have written our test and have an easy way to run it, we execute the test and it fails. The main reason it fails is because the servlet is not able to get data from the database, as the PoolData class has not been initialized. In our previous servlet tests, we passed in the PoolData class as a mock object to simulate access to the database, so we never worried about how the servlet was actually going to initialize it. Now that we are integrating the servlet with the actual application server and database, we have to decide how to create a valid instance of the **PoolData** class. After some thought, we decide to add an init() method to the servlet that will create the PoolData class that contains a connection to the real database. The PoolData class can then be used by all the other methods of the servlet to communicate to the database. So we add the init method as shown in Listing 6-18 and then change all the servlet methods that depend on the PoolData class to use the instance of the class created in the init method.

Listing 6-18. *PlayerPickServlet init Method*

```
PoolData poolData;
public void init(ServletConfig config) throws ServletException
{

    try
    {
        super.init(config);
        String dbLocation = config.getInitParameter("dbLocation");
        String dbUser = config.getInitParameter("dbUser");
        String dbPass = config.getInitParameter("dbPass");
        PoolDatabase poolDB = new PoolDatabaseImpl(dbLocation, dbUser, dbPass);
        poolData = new PoolDataImpl();
```

```
                poolData.set_poolDB(poolDB);
        }
        catch (Exception ex)
        {
            System.out.println("Error initializing servlet Exception is " + ex);
            ex.printStackTrace();
        }


    }
```

Because the servlet now requires some init parameters, we have to update the test to supply these parameters. In the finished application, these parameters will be provided in the web.xml file. We also have to update the test so that it initializes the database with the correct data needed for the test to pass. With these changes added, the test code looks as shown in Listing 6-19 (**updates in bold**).

Listing 6-19. *PlayerPickIntTester Class Updated*

```
public class PlayerPickIntTester extends ServletTestCase
{
    public PlayerPickIntTester(String s)
    {
        super(s);
    }

    //Set up the database with default values for the test
    public void setUp() throws ClassNotFoundException, SQLException,
            IOException, DatabaseUnitException
    {
        Class driverClass = Class.forName("org.hsqldb.jdbcDriver");
        Connection jdbcConnection =
            DriverManager.getConnection("jdbc:hsqldb:hsql://localhost", "sa", "");
        IDatabaseConnection dbConn = new DatabaseConnection(jdbcConnection);
        IDataSet dataSet = new FlatXmlDataSet(new
          FileInputStream("C:\\Java\\Projects\\TddBook\\DB_Scripts\\dataset1.xml"));
        DatabaseOperation.CLEAN_INSERT.execute(dbConn, dataSet);
    }

    public void beginGetOpenPool(WebRequest webRequest)
    {
        webRequest.addParameter("username", "TimmyC");
    }

    public void testGetOpenPool() throws Exception
    {
        System.out.println("Starting Test");
```

```
    PlayerPickServlet servlet = new PlayerPickServlet();
    //Set up the init params needed to initialize the database
    config.setInitParameter("dbLocation", "jdbc:hsqldb:hsql://localhost");
    config.setInitParameter("dbUser", "sa");
    config.setInitParameter("dbPass", "");
    servlet.init(config);
    servlet.doPost(request, response);
}

public void endGetOpenPool(WebResponse response) throws Exception
{
    assertTrue(response.isHTML());

    assertEquals("tables", 1, response.getTables().length);
    assertEquals("columns", 3,
            response.getTables()[0].getColumnCount());
    assertEquals("rows", 15,
            response.getTables()[0].getRowCount());
}
}
```

The test now has a setUp() method that is used to initialize the database, and we have added three calls to the setInitParameter() method in the testGetOpenPool() method to supply the init parameters needed by the servlet. With these changes, the test passes, and we can now continue to write additional Cactus tests to verify that the rest of the servlet works as desired.

Hands-On Exercises

It's now your turn to work on finishing the integration of the PlayerPickServlet by writing an additional Cactus test to test out one of the other behaviors of the servlet. Write a Cactus test to verify that a player can create a set of picks from a set of games for the currently open pool.

EJB and Servlet Integration Summary

As we have seen with the EJB and servlet example presented in this chapter, TDD can be used during integration testing to drive the development of an application and help work out problems that are encountered during the integration phase of a project. The tests that are developed during integration are harder to set up and run than normal unit tests. But the process of writing and automating these tests help ensure the application meets its required functionality and has fewer bugs. Although the tests developed during the integration phase will not be run as often as the normal suite of unit tests, they will prove extremely useful as bugs are found and requirements change. The integration tests will allow developers to monitor any changes to the code or configuration and ensure they will work in the deployed environment.

The Finishing Touches

Now that we have all the pieces of the application finished, the last step in the process is to put them together and ensure the finished application works as desired. To do this, we are going to use functional tests to ensure that the sum of the parts do indeed create a finished application. We will need to create two sets of functional tests: one to test the Admin GUI that will be used to administer the application, and another set to test web pages used by players to manage their picks.

Finishing the Admin GUI

When we initially developed the Admin GUI, we developed it in isolation using the FBPoolServerStub class. This allowed us to concentrate on the development of the GUI without having to worry about how our GUI was going to talk to the server. The tests we created to help us develop the GUI were functional tests because you cannot create unit tests for GUI code. These tests can now be used to help us make sure that the GUI works correctly when it's integrated with the EJB on the application server. The tests we created for the GUI used the FBPoolServerStub class, so in order to use them to test the GUI on the real application server, we are going to have to make some changes to the tests. We are going to have to change the tests so that they use the real FBPoolServerEJB class, and we need to set up the database before each test so that it is in the correct state for each test to pass.

To do this, we take the tests we created in Chapter 5 and add the method shown in Listing 6-20 to get the EJB from the application server instead of using the FBPoolServerStub class.

Listing 6-20. *getEJB Method*

```
private FBPoolServer getEJB() throws NamingException,
                             RemoteException, CreateException
{
    FBPoolServerHome fbPoolHome = null;
    Hashtable env = new Hashtable();

    env.put(Context.INITIAL_CONTEXT_FACTORY,
            "org.jnp.interfaces.NamingContextFactory");
    env.put(Context.PROVIDER_URL, "localhost:1099");
    env.put("java.naming.factory.url.pkgs",
            "org.jboss.naming:org.jnp.interfaces");
    Context ctx = new InitialContext(env);
    System.out.println("Before lookup of FBPoolHome");
    fbPoolHome = (FBPoolServerHome)
      javax.rmi.PortableRemoteObject.narrow(ctx.lookup("FBPoolServerEJB"),
                                            FBPoolServerHome.class);
    System.out.println("Before create on FBPoolServerHome");
    return(fbPoolHome.create());
}
```

We then change the setUp() method of the testCase, as shown in Listing 6-21, so that it initializes the database and also starts up the Admin GUI with the parameters it needs to get the EJB from the application server (**changes in bold**).

Listing 6-21. *setUp() Method for Admin GUI Tests*

```
protected void setUp() throws Exception
{
    super.setUp();
    if(!useStub)
    {
        //Load Database with test data
        Class driverClass = Class.forName("org.hsqldb.jdbcDriver");
        Connection jdbcConnection =
            DriverManager.getConnection("jdbc:hsqldb:hsql://localhost:1701",
                                                             "sa", "");
        IDatabaseConnection dbConn = new DatabaseConnection(jdbcConnection);
        IDataSet dataSet = new FlatXmlDataSet(new
        FileInputStream("C:\\Java\\Projects\\TddBook\\DB_Scripts
                                        \\datasetEJB1.xml"));
        DatabaseOperation.CLEAN_INSERT.execute(dbConn, dataSet);
    }

    //Start GUI
    if (!guiStarted)
    {
        // Start AdminGUI
        String[] args = new String[3];
        if (useStub)
        {
            args = null;
        }
        else
        {
            args[0] = "org.jnp.interfaces.NamingContextFactory";
            args[1] = "localhost:1099";
            args[2] =  "org.jboss.naming:org.jnp.interfaces";
        }

        AdminMain.main(args);
        guiStarted = true;
    }
    //Start listening for window open events
    helper = new JFCTestHelper();
    if (useStub)
    {
        m_fbPoolServer = new FBPoolServerStub();
```

```
    }
    else
    {
        m_fbPoolServer = getEJB();
    }
}
```

If you look at the changed code in the setUp() method, you will see that we have introduced a useStub variable. The useStub variable is a boolean that tells the test whether or not to use the real EJB class or the FBPoolServerStub class. This will allow us to run the test either way depending on whether we want to test against a server or not. If the useStub variable is set to true, then the test executes as it did before. If the useStub variable is set to false, then the test will set up the real database and tell the Admin GUI to use the real EJB. The way the test tells the Admin GUI to use the real EJB is to pass in three arguments. These arguments are the ones needed to perform the lookup of the EJB. The way the test is designed, if the arguments are null, the Admin GUI uses the FBPoolServerStub class. If there are arguments present, then the Admin GUI will use the real EJB.

Now that we have changed the test, we have to update the Admin GUI so that it will work with the new arguments being passed in. To do this, we update the main method as shown in Listing 6-22.

Listing 6-22. *Main Method for Admin GUI*

```
public static void main(String[] args)
{
    Hashtable env = null;

    if ((args != null) && (args.length == 3))
    {
        env = new Hashtable();
        env.put(Context.INITIAL_CONTEXT_FACTORY, args[0]);
        env.put(Context.PROVIDER_URL, args[1]);
        env.put("java.naming.factory.url.pkgs", args[2]);
    }
    try
    {
        AdminMain fbAdmin = new AdminMain(env);
    }
    catch (Exception e)
    {
        System.out.println("Unable to start Admin GUI Exception is " + e);
        e.printStackTrace();
    }
}
```

The main method of the Admin GUI now uses any arguments passed in to create a hashtable of environmental variables that it passes to the constructor. We then update the constructor as shown in Listing 6-23 (**changes in bold**).

Listing 6-23. *Constructor for Admin GUI*

```
public AdminMain(Hashtable env) throws NamingException,
                                       RemoteException, CreateException
{
    m_fbPoolServer = getFBPoolServerBean(env);
    //Initialize GUI components
    initComponents();
    //Populate Pool List
    populatePoolList();

    this.setTitle("Football Pool Administrator");
    this.setName("Football Pool Administrator");
    this.setSize(400, 500);
    this.setVisible(true);
    this.pack();
}
```

We also update the getFBPoolServerBean() method, as shown in Listing 6-24, so it can get either the FBPoolServerStub class or the real EJB depending on the value of the env object.

Listing 6-24. *getFBPoolServerBean Method*

```
public FBPoolServer getFBPoolServerBean(Hashtable env) throws
               RemoteException, CreateException, NamingException
{
    FBPoolServerHome fbPoolHome = null;

    if (env == null)
    {
        return (new FBPoolServerStub());
    }
    else
    {
        Context ctx = new InitialContext(env);
        System.out.println("Before lookup of FBPoolHome");
        fbPoolHome = (FBPoolServerHome)
            javax.rmi.PortableRemoteObject.narrow(ctx.lookup("FBPoolServerEJB"),
                                                  FBPoolServerHome.class);
        System.out.println("Before create on FBPoolServerHome");
        return (FBPoolServer) (fbPoolHome.create());
    }

}
```

With these changes made, we can now run the Admin GUI tests, and as long as we have created a good dataset for the tests, they pass. This means that we are finished with the Admin

GUI for now, until some user finds a bug or requests a new feature. Of course, since the GUI tests only test the functionality of a GUI, it is always a good idea to run a few GUI tests manually to verify the look and feel are correct.

Finishing the Web Client

We have done a lot of testing to make sure the servlets and JSPs that make up the web client work as desired. We have tested the pieces individually in isolation and together on a real application server. What we haven't done is to do an end-to-end test using the real server and a browser.

In Chapter 4, you learned how to develop the servlets and JSPs in isolation using TDD. In this chapter, you learned how to use Cactus to perform integration tests to ensure the servlets and JSPs work on a real application server and produce valid output. Now we are going to put those pieces together along with some HTML pages to create the actual web site by using tests.

In order to write the tests, there are two prerequisites. The first prerequisite is to make sure that the application server that the application will be deployed on is set up and configured correctly. There is nothing worse than finding problems in tests that are related to configuration issues. This includes setting up security constraints, database configuration, etc. Prerequisite two is to make sure that you have automated the build ➤ deploy ➤ test process as much as possible. Again, Ant is a great tool for automation because it can do almost any task required.

In order to start our testing, we will need to use an index.html page. For the moment, this is just a simple HTML page with a single H1 header in it that says, "Welcome to the Football Pool". This page will eventually be replaced with a more sophisticated page, but for now it serves as a starting point.

We also need to modify the web.xml file. We need to add an entry for the home page and an entry that specifies how users are authenticated. The entries that need to be added to the web.xml file are shown here:

```
<welcome-file-list>
    <welcome-file>index.html</welcome-file>
</welcome-file-list>
<login-config>
    <auth-method>BASIC</auth-method>
</login-config>
```

Since we need to know the identity of the user for our application, we will require some type of login, so let's choose basic authentication. This means that you will have to configure the application server to request user authentication.

Now that we have the environment set up, we can finish the development of the web site. As always, our first step is to create a test. Let's start by writing a test that verifies that we can log in to the web site and bring up the home page, as shown in Listing 6-25. To do this, we have to write some functional (i.e., black-box) tests that emulate the behavior of a web browser accessing the home page. Although there are a couple of ways to do this, the best way is to use the HttpUnit test framework. HttpUnit is a popular, well-supported, easy-to-use framework that will allow us to emulate the actions of a browser (see the sidebar "HttpUnit" for a quick explanation of HttpUnit).

Listing 6-25. *testHomePage Method*

```
public void testHomePage() throws Exception {
        WebConversation conversation = new WebConversation();
        conversation.setAuthorization("tom", "tom");
        WebRequest request = new
            GetMethodWebRequest("http://localhost:8080/FootBallPool");

        //Get response should be initial page
        WebResponse response = conversation.getResponse(request);
        Document welcomeDoc = response.getDOM();
        NodeList h1NodeList = welcomeDoc.getElementsByTagName("h1");

        if (h1NodeList.getLength() > 0) {
            Node h1Node = h1NodeList.item(0);
            Node textNode = h1Node.getFirstChild();
            String h1NodeStr = textNode.getNodeValue();
            assertEquals("Welcome to the Football Pool", h1NodeStr);
        } else {
            fail("Error getting home page");
        }
    }
```

HTTPUNIT

HttpUnit is an API that provides a set of methods that can be used to emulate web browser behavior, including form submission, basic HTTP authentication, cookies, and automatic page redirection. The main focus of HttpUnit is the `WebConversation` class. The idea is that this class provides a way for JUnit test methods to have a conversation with a web site. The `WebConversion` class basically provides access to the objects that are needed by a browser like HTTP response, cookies, session context, etc. The other main classes are `WebRequest`, which is used to create an HTTP request to be sent to the server, and `WebResponse`, which is used to represent the response returned by the server for a particular request. HttpUnit also provides classes that allow test methods to view the `WebResponse` in a number of ways:

- Getting the actual input stream of the response and parsing through it

- Converting the returned HTML into an XML DOM and then parsing and searching it as an XML document

In addition, the HTML forms, tables, and links can be viewed as a collection of HttpUnit web forms, web tables, and web links.

Using these classes, you can create simple JUnit tests that can be used to verify that a web site is working properly. For more details on HttpUnit, check out the HttpUnit web site at `http://www.httpunit.org`.

Using HttpUnit, we are able to simulate a user using a browser to interact with a web site. Our testHomePage() test creates a WebConversation, sets the user name and password needed to log in, makes a request to get the home page, and finally checks the contents of the response to make sure the home page is correct. At this point, the home page just has a single H1 tag that needs to be checked, but this will change as the home page contents get more sophisticated. The important thing this test proves is that the web server and authentication mechanism are set up correctly.

Now it's time to add more content to the home page. In Chapter 2, the requirements of the web application were described in Use Cases 5 through 8. These use cases define the following requirements for the web interface:

- The player must log in to the web interface.

- There will be a page that players can use to enter their weekly picks.

- A page will allow players to view the pick summary for all players.

- A page will allow players to view the results of the weekly pool.

- A page will allow players to view the standings of all the players in the pool as well as records for the football teams.

Although these requirements define what information should be on the web site, they don't define how this information should be organized or how it should be presented. With server-side components, you can usually start writing tests once you have some requirements defined, but with user interfaces there is an additional step that must be performed before any test can be written. This step is the design of the look and feel and organization of the web site, and it's usually done by either creating some simple drawings of the pages of a web site or creating some static HTML mock-ups of the site. These web site mock-ups are then usually shown to someone familiar with the end user so that he or she can provide feedback on the design. Once the design is approved, then it can be implemented.

The first thing we need to decide for our web site is how to organize the data. We basically have four types of information that need to be displayed: the weekly pick sheet, which players will use to make their picks; the pick summary, which will show a summary of all the player picks; the pick results, which show player standings once all the games have been played; and a page that will show the player stats for the pool. Each of these pieces of information that needs to be displayed will have its own page. We also need a home page that will provide users with a starting point and allow them to get to all the other pages. So basically the web site will have five pages that will be linked together as shown in Figure 6-2.

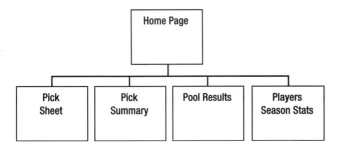

Figure 6-2. *Web site hierarchy*

The links shown in Figure 6-2 are not static but rather conditional. For example, users will not be allowed to go from the home page to the pick summary until the pool is closed. These conditions were identified in Chapter 2, but let's review them again here:

- The player can only go to the pick sheet page if the pool status is open.

- The player can only get to the pick summary page from the home page if the pool status is closed.

- The player can only see the pool results page after the pool is closed and the results posted.

Now that we have an understanding of the behavior and layout of the site, we can start to write some tests to put together and improve the different parts of the web site. So far, we have only been concerned with developing the servlets and JSPs to produce the individual pages, and the tests developed so far only tested that the individual pages were created correctly. It's now time to start writing tests that will help us implement the interaction between the web pages.

At this point in the development, we would already have some tests for the home page. The tests would have checked the home page for a couple of different users to verify that user-specific information is rendered correctly. These tests as well as an implementation of the HomePageServlet are included in the source code for this chapter. A picture of what the home page will look like for a typical player is shown in Figure 6-3.

Basically, the home page contains three tables of data. It shows the list of games for the upcoming week, the results for the players from last week's pool, and each player's pick history. The page also needs to contain links to the other pages. The links that are present will depend on the pool status. Although we may have verified that the correct links are present during our initial testing, we need to add some tests to ensure not only that the correct links are shown but also that the links lead to the correct pages. These tests will help us ensure the web site flows correctly and is not missing anything.

To test to make sure the links are shown correctly, we are going to write a test to determine the presence or absence of the links depending on the status of the pool. These tests will, of course, fail, but they will help us create the code needed to add links.

As shown in Figure 6-3, the home page can contain links to the pick page, pick summary page, and team stats. The team stats link will always be present, but the pick page link and pick summary link will only be shown when the pool is in a certain state as outlined previously, so let's write a test to reflect these rules (see Listing 6-26).

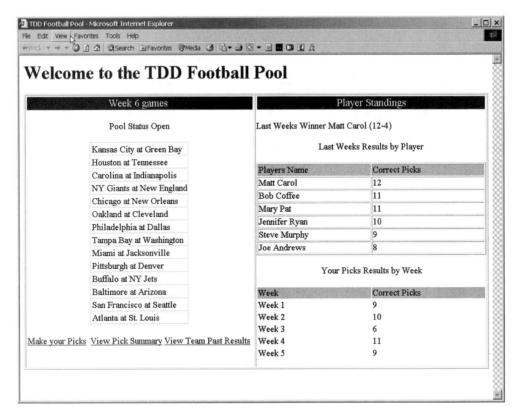

Figure 6-3. *Football Pool home page*

Listing 6-26. *testHomePageLinks Method*

```
public void testHomePageLinks() throws Exception {
        WebConversation conversation = new WebConversation();
        conversation.setAuthorization("tom", "tom");
        WebRequest request = new WebRequest request = new
                GetMethodWebRequest("http://localhost:8080/FootBallPool
                    /HomePageServlet?playersName=Tom&poolDate=2004-09-18");
        //Get response
        WebResponse response = conversation.getResponse(request);
        Document welcomeDoc = response.getDOM();
        //Check to make sure the correct links are shown based on the pool status
        String responseStr = response.getText();
        int index = responseStr.indexOf("Pool Status");
        if (index < 0) {
            fail("Unable to find Pool Status");
        }
        String poolStatus = responseStr.substring(index + 12, index + 16);
        System.out.println("Pool Status is " + poolStatus);
```

```
//This link should always be present
WebLink teamResultsLink = response.getLinkWith("View Team");
if (teamResultsLink == null) {
    fail("View Past Team Results Link not present");
}
// These links may or may not be present based on the pool status
WebLink makePickLink = response.getLinkWith("Make your Picks");
WebLink pickSummaryLink = response.getLinkWith("View Pick Summary");
if (poolStatus.equalsIgnoreCase("Open")) {
    //If pool is open then make pick link should be present
    // but not the pick summary link
    assertEquals((pickSummaryLink == null), true);
    assertEquals((makePickLink != null), true);
} else if (poolStatus.equalsIgnoreCase("Closed")) {
    // If pool is closed then make pick link
    // should not be present but the pick
    //  summary link should be
    assertEquals((pickSummaryLink != null), true);
    assertEquals((makePickLink == null), true);
}
```

If you look at the test, you will see that it brings up the home page, checks for the three different links, and based on the state of the pool determines whether the correct links are present. It then follows the links and verifies that each link brings the user to the correct page. There is a test for each of the pool states to verify that the links only appear when the pool is in the correct state and not present all the other times. Of course, when this test is first run, it fails miserably because there are no links on the page yet. The next step is to add code in the servlet and JSP to add the links to the home page. As we add each link, we use the test to verify that the link works correctly. Of course, where you add the link is not important to the test, since HttpUnit will find the link no matter where it is. The location of the link is only important to the visual aspect of the web page. In our case, we have decided to add the links below the Game table, since all the links are related to weekly games. The updated servlet and JSP code for the HomePageServlet is included in the source code for this chapter.

It's Not Over Until It's Over

At this point, now that we have both the Admin GUI and the web client working, you might think that our work is done, but that is not really true. In most development environments, there is never enough time to test every single condition or configuration that the application may encounter. Also, even though the development of the application is over, it doesn't mean that all the use cases were implemented correctly or that somebody may not want to change some of the requirements. Software development is an iterative process, so as soon as it is finished, bugs will be found and users will request changes and enhancements. For each new bug or enhancement, tests need to be developed to help improve the application.

Even if there are no bugs, the best thing you can do at this point in the project is to keep writing tests to try and expand the current set of tests to increase the test coverage and improve the robustness of the application. These tests will help you find hidden faults and continue to improve the application. Of course, the question is how do you know when you have written enough tests. The best answer to this question is that you should stop writing tests when the tests no longer provide you with additional information. If you write a test and the test does not help you find a bug, improve the code, or help you understand the application, then the test is meaningless. When you start writing meaningless tests, it's time to stop writing tests. Of course, on most projects you will probably run out of time before you run out of tests to create. It's important, however, to take the time to ensure all the tests that you have for a project are working and are easy to run before moving on.

Summary

In this chapter, I have tried to explain how to use TDD to take the pieces of an application that were developed in isolation and put them together into a finished application by using tests to drive the process. We first started with some tests to help us develop and integrate the database into the application. We then moved on and developed the EJB using the interface we created when we developed the Admin GUI. Once these pieces were finished, we started integrating the application by testing the EJB and the servlets and JSPs on a real application server. With this done, we then added the rest of the pieces of the application and put the finishing touches on it. Each step in the process was driven with a test that helped us make the correct decisions and ensured the application worked as desired.

At this point, we have demonstrated the basic tools and techniques needed to develop an application using TDD. There are still a couple more topics that need to be discussed. The first is how to make the process more efficient. Chapter 7 will present a series of discussions that explain how to organize your tests and make them easier to run. It will also explain some of the finer details of how to use TDD to improve the design of an application. The second topic that needs to be discussed is how to transition a team to using TDD from their current development methodology. We'll tackle this topic in Chapter 8.

■ ■ ■

Improving the Process

Even though we finished developing the Football Pool application in the last chapter, there are still a number of TDD topics that need to be addressed. Although I explained the details of how to apply the ideas of TDD to a J2EE application, I have not talked about how to make the process more efficient. Just as refactoring is an important part of the TDD process, it is also important to constantly refine the TDD process to fit your environment and make it as efficient as possible. In the previous chapters, I have kept the examples simple and focused so I could explain the techniques for applying TDD to the different parts of the application that we were developing. It's now time to talk about some project- and process-related topics such as the following:

- Organizing all the tests that are developed

- Making all the test suites easier to run

- Separating test data from test code

- Making sure you have adequate test coverage

- Using tests to quickly find defects

- Refactoring the tests as the application changes

Now I plan to take a step back and look at the overall TDD process again to show you how the parts of the process work together as a whole and how it can be made more efficient.

Organizing and Running Tests and Test Suites

In Chapter 3, we briefly discussed how to group tests together using JUnit's `TestSuite` class and how to automate running of the tests using Ant's JUnit task. Let's review these tools from a project-level perspective and try to understand the best way to use them to organize our tests and make them easy to run.

Test Location

The first thing we need to discuss is the location of the test classes. You basically have two choices: you can put the test classes in the same directory and package as your source code, or you can put all your test classes in a separate directory or package.

Putting your test classes in the same package as your code allows your tests to access package-scoped members, but it clutters up the source code package and can lead to a small loss in performance. It also makes it harder to distinguish what classes are source code and what classes are test code, which is important if you want to deliver only the source code.

Putting your test classes in a separate directory or package is usually a better idea than mixing source and test code. This does limit the tests to only accessing public members of the classes being tested, but it provides a clean separation between test and source code. This makes it easier to build and organize the code. Whether you decide to use a directory or package to separate the tests from the code is a matter of personal preference. In the code for this book, we have separated the tests from the source code by using a separate directory. The top-level directory of our project has an src directory that contains all the source code for the project and a test directory that contains all the test code. These directories both have the same package structure; for example, the source code for the `PlayerPickServlet` is located in the /src/com/apress/tddbook/servlets directory, and the corresponding tests are located in the /test/com/apress/tddbook/servlets directory.

If you didn't want to use separate directories for source and test code, then you could put the test code in a subpackage. If we used subpackages for our tests, then each source code package would have a subpackage called test. For example, the source code for the `PlayerPickServlet` would be located in the /src/com/apress/tddbook/servlets directory, and the corresponding tests would be located in the /src/com/apress/tddbook/servlets/tests directory.

Test Grouping

Once you decide where to locate your source and test code, the next thing you need to decide is how to group your tests together. In a small project, you could simply create one big test suite that would just run all the tests; but in a large project, running all the tests all the time is inefficient. In a large project, you usually want to create a number of small test suites based on functionality. This way, when you're developing in one area of the code, you only have to run the test suite associated with that area. These small test suites are usually based on packages of the project. For example, in the Football Pool application that we developed in this book, you should have a test suite for each of the major subpackages; for instance, you would have a test suite for each of the following: the servlets, JSPs, GUI, and EJB package. If any of these subdirectories had a lot of subpackages, then you would further divide up the test suites.

In a similar fashion, you would probably want to create Ant tasks for each of the test suites to make them easier to run. Of course, depending on how the build is done, these tasks can be in different files. For large applications, there are usually separate build files for each major part of the application. For example, in a J2EE application you might have a build file for the EJBs, another one for the servlets, another one for the common utility classes, etc. In each of these build files, there should be a task to run the test suite for this part of the application as well as a task for each of the individual test cases that make up the test suite. Each of these tasks should be self-contained and require no setup. So, for example, if a test requires a certain set of data files be present in a known location, then the test should copy the required data files to the required location. Adding these tasks to the build file and making them self-contained will take some time, but it is well worth it because these tasks will make it easy to run the test suite or any individual test. This means that the tests will be run more often. The more often you run the tests, the more bugs you will find and fix, and the more confidence you will have in your code.

Separating Data from Tests

One of the problems with the unit tests that we have created so far is that the data is hard coded into each test. This makes it harder to maintain the tests as the data structures change and new pass/fail criteria are added to the tests. If possible, it is usually better to separate the test data from the test code. There are many advantages to separating the data from the tests, some of which are as follows:

- Makes test data easy to edit

- Makes it easier to add new test cases

- Helps reduce false failures caused by invalid data

- Gives you the ability to easily replace test data with real data

Most tests have three parts:

1. Create the classes and data needed to run the test.

2. Execute some methods of the class being tested.

3. Verify the methods executed left the software in the correct state.

To run a test, you usually need two types of data. You need setup data for part 1 of the test (i.e., input data), and you need verification data for part 3 of the test for the assert conditions. There are some APIs available such as JTestCase (http://jtestcase.sourceforge.net/) that can be used to separate the test logic and test data, but none of these APIs have been widely accepted. It's possible that one of these APIs may work for your application, so they are worth investigating, but most of the time you will have to develop a custom solution. Because of this, let's look at some simple ways to separate data from the tests.

Let's start with one of the tests we already created for the Football Pool application and see how we can modify it to remove the hard-coded data from the test. For this example, we are going to use the testPoolCreate() method from the FootBallPoolTester class.

```
public void testPoolCreate() throws Exception
{
    FootballPool pool = new FootballPool("2004-09-11");
    pool.addGame("NY Jets", "Miami");
    pool.addGame("San Francisco", "NY Giants");
    assertEquals(2, pool.size());
    assertEquals( "Game 1 away team", "Miami", pool.getHomeTeam(0) );
    assertEquals( "Game 2 away team", "NY Giants", pool.getHomeTeam(1) );
    assertEquals( "Game 1 home team", "NY Jets", pool.getAwayTeam(0) );
    assertEquals( "Game 2 home team", "San Francisco", pool.getAwayTeam(1) );
}
```

If you look at the test, you can see that it is pretty simple; all it does is create a FootballPool, add a few games, and then verify that the FootballPool contains the correct data. As you can see, the test contains a lot of hard-coded data. Let's refactor the test to try and find a simple way to remove the data for the test. The first thing we need to do is to simplify the creation and population of the FootballPool class. The creation of a football pool is done in a number of the tests; it should be pulled out of the tests and put into a utility class so that all the tests can use a common method. You may have noticed that all the instances of the FootballPool class we have created for our tests contain mostly the same data; there are only two or three variations, so centralizing the creation of the FootballPool instances will remove a lot of duplication.

To do so, we create a class called FBPoolTestData that contains the method shown in Listing 7-1.

Listing 7-1. *createFbPool() Method of FBPoolTestData Class*

```java
public FootballPool createFbPool(String date)
{
    if (date.equals("2004-09-11"))
    {
        FootballPool pool = new FootballPool("2004-09-11");
        pool.addGame("NY Jets", "Miami");
        pool.addGame("San Francisco", "NY Giants");
        return (pool);
    }
    else if (date.equals("2004-09-18"))
    {
        FootballPool pool = new FootballPool("2004-09-18");
        pool.addGame("Kansas City", "Green Bay");
        pool.addGame("Houston", "Tennessee");

        .
        .
        .

        return (pool);
    }
    else if (date.equals("2004-09-25"))
    {
        FootballPool pool = new FootballPool("2004-09-25");
        pool.addGame("St. Louis", "Green Bay");
        pool.addGame("Tampa Bay", "NY Jets");

        .
        .
        .

        return (pool);
    }
    return (null);
}
```

As you can see, the createFBPool() method can be used to create a FootballPool instance. The method takes one argument, which is the date. This allows you to create a FootballPool instance based on the date so you can have a number of different sets of data for your tests.

With this new method, we can now update the test as follows (**changes in bold**):

```
public void testPoolCreate() throws Exception
{
    FBPoolTestData testData = new FBPoolTestData();
    FootballPool pool = testData.createFbPool("2004-09-11");
    assertEquals(2, pool.size());
    assertEquals( "Game 1 away team", "Miami", pool.getHomeTeam(0) );
    assertEquals( "Game 2 away team", "NY Giants", pool.getHomeTeam(1) );
    assertEquals( "Game 1 home team", "NY Jets", pool.getAwayTeam(0) );
    assertEquals( "Game 2 home team", "San Francisco", pool.getAwayTeam(1) );
}
```

Now that we have removed the FootballPool creation data from the test, the next thing we have to do is to remove the verification data from the test. To do this, we add a method, as shown in Listing 7-2, to the FBPoolTestData class that can verify that a given FootballPool instance contains the correct data.

Listing 7-2. *verifyPool() Method of FBPoolTestData Class*

```
public boolean verifyPool(FootballPool fbPool)
{
    boolean isPoolValid = false;
    if (fbPool.getPoolDate().equals("2004-09-11"))
    {
        assertEquals(2, fbPool.size());
        assertEquals("Game 1 away team", "Miami", fbPool.getHomeTeam(0));
        assertEquals("Game 2 away team", "NY Giants", fbPool.getHomeTeam(1));
        assertEquals("Game 1 home team", "NY Jets", fbPool.getAwayTeam(0));
        assertEquals("Game 2 home team", "San Francisco",
                        fbPool.getAwayTeam(1));
        isPoolValid = true;
    }
    else if (fbPool.getPoolDate().equals("2004-09-18"))
    {
        assertEquals("Kansas City", fbPool.getAwayTeam(0));
        assertEquals("Green Bay", fbPool.getHomeTeam(0));
        assertEquals("Houston", fbPool.getAwayTeam(7));

            .

            .

            .

        isPoolValid = true;

    }
    else if (fbPool.getPoolDate().equals("2004-09-25"))
    {
        assertEquals("Kansas City", fbPool.getAwayTeam(0));
        assertEquals("Green Bay", fbPool.getHomeTeam(0));
```

```
            assertEquals("Houston", fbPool.getAwayTeam(7));
            .

            .

            .
            isPoolValid = true;
        }
        return (isPoolValid);
    }
```

What this `verifyPool()` method does is to take the `FootballPool` that was passed in and compare it to a set of expected pools. If the pool passed in matches one of the expected pools and contains the correct set of data, then the method returns true; otherwise, it returns false. We now update the test to use this method by making the following changes (**changes in bold**):

```
public void testPoolCreate() throws Exception
{
    FBPoolTestData testData = new FBPoolTestData();
    FootballPool pool = testData.createFbPool("2004-09-11");
    assertEquals(true, testData.verifyPool(pool));
}
```

So now all the assert methods in the test have been replaced with one simple assert that just calls the `verifyPool()` method. This simplifies the test, and now all the logic needed to check the data in the pool has been removed from the actual test and moved to a centralized class that can be used by all tests.

Although the example that I have shown here is a simple one, it does illustrate the advantage of separating the data from the tests and creating a centralized location for all your tests to get and verify data. In the example shown here, we put the data in a centralized location by hard coding the data into a class. This will work for small datasets, but for larger datasets this would be harder to do. One alternative is to store the data in some kind of data file and then create a class that can use such data files to generate and verify the test data. The format of the file will depend on the type of data needed for the tests, but one of the best choices is probably some kind of XML file. Of course, converting objects to/from an XML file can be a lot of work, but there are a number of Java XML Binding (JAXB) APIs out there that can be used to simplify the process.

Two of the more well-known JAXB APIs available are Sun's Reference Implementation (https://jaxb.dev.java.net/) and Castor (http://www.castor.org/), the latter being one of the best. Castor is a data-binding framework that provides a simple API that can be used to transform Java objects to/from an XML file or bind Java objects to database tables.[1] Using Castor it would be fairly easy to create a generic class that could be used to generate and verify the test data. This class would be very similar to our `FBPoolTestData` class, but instead of hard coding the test data, it could be read from an XML file using Castor.

---

1. For an introduction to Castor, see my article on it at http://www.developer.com/db/article.php/ 1730911.

Creating a Master TestCase Class

Most projects are unique and require certain environment settings to work properly. In order to test a project, you have to use tests that have some knowledge of how the project works. For example, a test might need to know the location of the home page of the project or maybe how to connect to the database. Also, as you start to write a lot of tests, you will realize that there are certain methods common to a number of tests that should be centralized. The best way to collect these common methods and properties that are shared by the tests is to create a master TestCase class. A master TestCase class is just a class that extends the JUnit TestCase class and is used as the base class for all tests. This allows you to put all the properties and common test methods in one central class.

What you put in the master TestCase depends on the project. In the case of our Football Pool application, the master TestCase would probably contain properties like the location of the database, the database driver class, URL for the pool home page, etc. The methods might include some of the database setup methods for the different tests, and maybe a couple of methods to create and verify test data. In any case, the properties and methods of the master TestCase will become apparent as the project progresses. The important point to remember is that as the number of tests grows, you should take the time to refactor the tests by moving the common properties and methods of the tests to a common class.

Making the Tests Configurable

As you develop tests, you may find a number of situations in which you want to run a particular test in a number of different ways. For example, you may want to run a test in a couple of different environments or run it using a different set of parameters, or you may need to change the test parameters for each run. To do this, you need to make the test configurable. For example, consider the tests we created for the Admin GUI. Originally we developed the tests using a stub that allowed us to develop the Admin GUI in isolation. Later on during the integration phase of the project, we used the same tests with the real EJB and a real application server to test the GUI end to end. In order to get the tests to work with the real EJB and application server, we had to manually change the tests. We added some logic to be able to switch between the stub and real EJB, but to change between the two requires updating the test class. If you look at the setUp() method of the test, you can see the logic we put in to switch between the stub and real EJB (see Listing 7-3).

Listing 7-3. *setUp() Method for Admin GUI Tests*

```
protected void setUp() throws Exception
{
    super.setUp();
    if (!useStub)
    {
        //Load Database with test data
        Class driverClass = Class.forName("org.hsqldb.jdbcDriver");
        Connection jdbcConnection = DriverManager.getConnection
                        ("jdbc:hsqldb:hsql://localhost:1701", "sa", "");
        IDatabaseConnection dbConn = new DatabaseConnection(jdbcConnection);
```

```
        IDataSet dataSet = new FlatXmlDataSet(new FileInputStream
            ("C:\\Java\\Projects\\TddBook\\DB_Scripts\\datasetEJB1.xml"));
        DatabaseOperation.CLEAN_INSERT.execute(dbConn, dataSet);
    }

    //Start GUI
    if (!guiStarted)
    {
        //Start AdminGUI
        String[] args = new String[3];
        if (useStub)
        {
            args = null;
        }
        else
        {
            args[0] = "org.jnp.interfaces.NamingContextFactory";
            args[1] = "localhost:1099";
            args[2] = "org.jboss.naming:org.jnp.interfaces";
        }

        AdminMain.main(args);
        guiStarted = true;
    }
    //Start listening for window open events
    helper = new JFCTestHelper();
    if (useStub)
    {
        m_fbPoolServer = new FBPoolServerStub();
    }
    else
    {
        m_fbPoolServer = getEJB();
    }
}
```

If you look at the code, you can see that there is a boolean useStub that determines whether to use the stub or real EJB to run the test. The only problem with this is that the value of useStub is hard coded, so to change it you have to edit the test and then recompile it. It would be better if we could set the value of useStub at run time because this would make it easier to change between the stub and real EJB. We can do this in a couple ways, but one of the easier ways is to use a property file. We have the test set the value of the useStub based on the value in a specific property file. For a complete example of how to do this, see the code that is associated with this chapter.

Of course, the Admin GUI test is not the only test that might need to be configurable, so the property file may contain a number of properties for all the tests in the project that need to be configurable. This way, the entire test suite can be made to run in different environments by changing the values in a common, centralized property file. If your project has a property file for each environment, then it is easy to create an Ant task to run the test suite in each of these environments. So if you want to run the Admin GUI using the stub, you run one Ant task, and if you want to use the real EJB, you run another.

How you make each test configurable will depend on the test and the parameters it needs to run. You could use a simple `boolean` like we did in the Admin GUI test, but you can get more sophisticated and use a property to drive a factory method to set up the objects needed for a particular test environment. No matter how you decide to make your tests configurable, you need to centralize the parameters needed to configure the tests. This will make it easy to run the same tests in a number of different ways.

Test Coverage Strategies

In order to develop software using TDD, it's important that the tests developed to drive the code cover all the conditions that will be seen when the software is released. Of course, it is an impossible task to provide 100% test coverage for any moderately complex piece of software, but there are some basic philosophies that you can follow to ensure that most of the conditions the software will encounter will be tested. Although the tests developed using TDD come from the requirements of the project, these requirements are usually incomplete and/or don't adequately specify all the conditions that the software will encounter. That's why it's important to use these simple philosophies to help improve the test coverage.

To improve test coverage, you need some way to measure it. One simple measure of test coverage is to determine the number of methods tested versus the total number of methods in the code. You could do this manually, which would be tedious, or you could use one of the many test coverage tools available like JCover (http://www.codework.com/JCover/product.html) or Clover (http://www.thecortex.net/clover/). For a list of test coverage tools for Java, see http://c2.com/cgi/wiki?CodeCoverageTools.

Test Every Path

The code developed for your project will have many different paths of execution. One philosophy to improve test coverage is to provide enough tests so that every path through the code is executed at least once. For example, let's say you have an `if-else` statement of the following form:

```
if (status.equals("created"))
{
    // Do something
}
else if (status.equals("opened"))
{
    // Do something else
}
    .
    .
    .
else
{
```

```
        // Display error?
    }
```

To test it properly, you should have a test that executes the code of each of the `if-else` statements. Now, in theory, if you developed this code using TDD, then this should not be hard, since with TDD you only add the code you need to pass a test. So then every line of code written has a corresponding test. In reality, however, there may be some pieces of code that don't have a corresponding test. For example, in the `if-else` statements shown previously, it's possible that during development the last `else` statement was added as a force of habit as opposed to being added because of a test. In this case, there is no corresponding test for this section of the code, so a test should be added to improve test coverage.

The other thing to look out for when trying to determine whether a piece of code has enough tests is to make sure you not only test every code path, but also test every data path. For example, in the `if-else` statements of the preceding example, you need to not only make sure there is a test for each `if-else` statement, but also make sure there is a test for each value that the status variable can have. It's always possible that the requirements are incomplete and don't specify the complete behavior of all the possible branches. If you make sure you have a branch for each possible value of the data being used, you will improve your test coverage and fill in some of the gaps in the requirements.

Having a test for each code path and data path does not provide complete coverage since you have not tested all the combinations of code and data paths. It is, however, a good start to improving the test coverage.

Test Boundary Conditions

Most methods work for a limited range of data. Any test suite that is used to drive the development of code should include a set of tests that determine the boundary conditions of each of the methods developed. Although the requirements of the application may not be detailed enough to define the boundary conditions for each behavior, most of the time they can be derived by doing some simple analysis.

For example, Use Case 2 in our Football Pool application defines the actions needed for an administrator to create a football pool. From this use case, we created a test that led us to develop the `FootballPool` class. The constructor for this class takes one argument, which is a string representing the date of the pool. Although the use case said nothing about limitations when creating a football pool, we know that we should not be allowed to create a `FootballPool` class with an invalid date. This means that we need to add some tests that try to create a `FootballPool` with invalid dates to make sure that the creation fails.

So even if boundary conditions are not explicitly stated in the requirements, it's important to analyze the code as it's being developed to identify derived limitations of each method developed and then add the appropriate test. This will help ensure that your application can handle error conditions caused by data being out of bounds. When you do create boundary condition tests, it's important that you test with data that is not only outside the boundary conditions, but also *at* the actual boundary conditions.

Test with Bad Data

Most requirements do not define what should happen when the application encounters bad data. For example, none of the use cases for the Football Pool application define what should happen if a player does not enter his or her picks properly. Most decisions about how to validate user input and report errors is usually left to the development team. For this reason, it is important to add tests that use bad data to the code as it is being developed.

Bad data can take on a couple different forms. It can be data that is out of range. For example, you can enter 32 for the number of days in a month. It can be the wrong type of data. For example, you can pass a method a string as an argument when it is expecting an integer. It can also be empty or null data. For example, if a method is expecting a vector for an argument, you should create a test that passes in a vector that has no data elements and null to make sure the method can handle both cases of bad data.

The type of bad data and number of test cases you need to add will depend on the application, but the more cases you add, the more confidence you will have in the error handling capabilities of the application.

Test with Random Good Data

When code is initially developed, the range of data that is used is usually limited to a few middle-of-the-road test cases. As the application matures, more test cases with good data should be created. Since it is impossible to test the entire range of data, each test added should try to use a dataset that is uniquely different in some way from the tests added so far. These tests will expand the range of data being tested and help find some hidden errors that may be data related.

Using Tests to Debug Code

No matter how much care you put into developing a piece of software, bugs happen—it can't be helped. They are a normal part of software development. Although TDD can help reduce the number of bugs, it can't eliminate them. One of the side effects of using TDD to develop code is that when you are done, you have a suite of unit tests that you can easily run any time you want to check the state of the code. This framework is very useful when trying to find the source of a bug.

When a bug is discovered, the first thing that needs to be done is to understand how to reproduce the bug in the development environment. Although it may be easy to reproduce the bug manually, it is better to create a new unit test that simulates the conditions of the bug. Creating a unit test for each bug is a good idea for a number of reasons. First, manually setting up the conditions needed to reproduce the bug can be tedious and error prone if the setup has to be done a number of times in order to find the source of the bug. Second, in some cases it is hard, if not impossible, to set up the condition of the bug manually, so using a unit test is the only way, since the testing framework allows you to simulate almost any condition. Third, adding a unit test for this bug means that this new test will be part of the normal unit test suite, which means that any reoccurrence of the bug will be immediately found.

Once you create a unit test that reproduces the conditions of the bug, you should be able to use the test to start tracking down the source of the bug. The error message or stack trace from the unit test should give you a clue as to which class and/or method is causing the bug. You can also run the unit tests through your IDE's debugger if you need more detailed information on the conditions that cause the bug.

Some of the time you will have to write a series of unit tests to zero in on the cause of a bug. For example, let's say a bug is found in the user interface. So you write a unit test to simulate the user input that causes the bug. This leads you to discover that the problem is caused by the data returned to the JSP by the servlet. You now write a unit test for the servlet that calls it using the conditions found in the bug. This unit test may lead you to the cause of the bug or just help define the next test you need to write to zero in on the bug. In either case, using this process will provide a simple, methodical way to isolate the cause of the bug and understand the problem with the original design of the code.

Most bugs are caused by a misinterpretation of the requirements or missing requirements. In this case, writing the unit tests and fixing the bugs help improve the requirements. In this fashion, as bugs are found and unit tests are added, the test suite becomes a set of requirements of higher and higher fidelity. Writing a unit test for a bug may also lead you to write a family of tests to test for bugs that are similar to the one discovered. This may help discover fundamental underlying problems and fix them before they would have normally been discovered.

Using Tests to Improve Performance and Scalability

Although performance testing is usually done only on a finished application in a controlled environment, it can be useful to carry out some performance testing as the application is being developed. The testing done during development should just be some gross measurements of some key operations to ensure that the code developed will have no performance surprises.

Performance testing usually involves measuring the response time for a certain operation. In some respects, the writing of unit tests already measures some performance aspects of the application being developed. This is because the test suite usually reports how long it takes to run. So if you do some refactoring, and the test suite takes 30% longer to run, then you have some indication that the refactoring you've done has hurt the performance of the application. Of course, to make useful measures of performance, you need to measure it on a finer level than the test suite. Performance tests run in the development environment only really measure relative performance and give no indication of actual performance. But measuring relative performance is useful when trying to measure the effect of refactoring on the performance of a critical piece of code.

For example, let's say that you have a method that is used to perform a query on a database and return a result set. The format of the query, the size of the table, the size of the index, etc., all have an effect on how fast the query can be performed. If you are trying to optimize this query, creating a performance test will help you measure the effect each factor has on performance and guide you to the best solution.

There are a number of different tools that can be used to measure performance, but one of the easiest (and cheapest) ones to use is JUnitPerf (http://www.clarkware.com/software/JUnitPerf.html). JUnitPerf is a set of test decorators for JUnit that lets you measure the performance and scalability of your application. For more information on JUnitPerf, see the sidebar "JUnitPerf Overview."

JUNITPERF OVERVIEW

JUnitPerf provides a set of test decorators for JUnit that can be used to create performance and load tests.

TimedTest

Performance tests can be created by using JUnitPerf's `TimedTest` test decorator. A `TimedTest` basically runs a single unit test and measures the time it takes to complete. If the time it takes to complete a test is greater than a specified maximum elapsed time, then the test will fail; otherwise, it will pass. In this way, you can set a limit on how long it can take for a single test to run, so as you refactor the code, the `TimedTest` will allow you to ensure that the refactoring did not degrade performance below a certain level.

For example, let's say that you want to create a test to measure the performance for displaying the football picks for a certain user. We already created a test to make sure that the picks are displayed correctly, so all we have to do is use this test as part of a `TimedTest`. We do this by creating a test suite as follows:

```
public static Test suite()
{
    TestSuite suite = new TestSuite();
    Test testCase = new PlayerPickServletTester("testDisplayPlayerPicks");

    long maxElapsedTime = 1000;
    Test timedTest = new TimedTest(testCase, maxElapsedTime);
    suite.addTest(timedTest);
    return suite;
}
```

As you can see, the way to create a `TimedTest` is to first create a `Test` from any working test. You then create a `TimedTest` using the created `Test` and a max elapsed time (specified in milliseconds). When the test gets run, it will run the test to completion. If the test completes quicker than the max elapsed time, then the test passes; otherwise, it fails. If the test passes, it reports its elapsed time (i.e., how long it took to run). After you run the `TimedTest` on a system, you can use this elapsed time as a relative measure of performance for the method being tested. You can then update the max elapsed time to be closer to the average elapsed time that you see when you run the test. In this way, if the performance degrades, the test will fail, and you can investigate the cause.

One known limitation of JUnitPerf is that the elapsed time reported by a `TimedTest` is not a true measure of performance of the method being tested, since the elapsed time reported includes the time for the `setup()` and `teardown()` methods of the test. This is not a major problem, since JUnitPerf is not meant to be a full-fledged performance-monitoring tool and is bested used to measure relative performance.

LoadTest

JUnitPerf's `LoadTest` test decorator can be used to simulate a set of concurrent users running a particular unit test. This allows you to do some simple load testing of your application. To demonstrate how a load test works, we are going to create a `LoadTest` for the `testDisplayPlayerPicks` method like we did for `TimedTest`. Again, all we have to do is to use the `LoadTest` test decorator as part of the `suite()` method for a `TestCase` as follows:

```
public static Test suite()
{
    TestSuite suite = new TestSuite();

    Timer timer = new ConstantTimer(1000);
    int numUsers = 10;
    int iterations = 2;
    long maxElapsedTime = 20000;

    Test testCase = new PlayerPickServletTester("testDisplayPlayerPicks");
    Test loadTest = new LoadTest(testCase, numUsers, iterations, timer);
    Test timedTest = new TimedTest(loadTest, maxElapsedTime);
    suite.addTest(timedTest);
    return suite;
}
```

As you can see, creating a LoadTest is similar to creating a TimedTest. You first create a Test and then use that Test to create a LoadTest. There are a couple of different ways to create a LoadTest. You can specify just the Test and number of users, or if you want to have each user run multiple iterations of the test, then you can specify the number of iterations. Also, if you want to stagger the time each user executes the test to slowly ramp up the load, you can specify a Timer that delays the start of the test for each user by a specified time. JUnitPerf provides two timer classes: ConstantTimer, which provides a constant delay, and RandomTimer, which provides a random delay.

In the example, we have used all four arguments to create the LoadTest. We could have just added the LoadTest created to the suite, but instead what we have done is to use the LoadTest to create a TimedTest. In this way, when the load test is run, we know that not only can the application handle the load, but also that it completed in a certain period of time. This will help us to ensure not only that the application is scalable, but also that performance doesn't suffer as we refactor the code.

Besides testing response time for time-critical operations, it's also important to do some load testing as the application is being developed. This helps to ensure that it will be scalable once it is put into production. There will be no way to measure the *true* scalability of the application until it is finished and tested in a controlled environment, but adding a few load tests while the application is being developed will ensure that there will be no major issues that will prevent the application from being scalable.

This is especially important in J2EE applications where the application will be used by many people simultaneously. Most of the tests that are used to develop an application with TDD simulate just one user at a time, so it is useful to have a few tests where multiple users hit the application at the same time. This will help you uncover problems with shared resources like databases, message queues, etc. For example, in the Football Pool application, it would be useful to have a couple of tests where 5 or 10 users hit the same web page at the same time to make sure there are no problems with simultaneous access to the database. Again, one of the easiest tools to use to do simple load testing is JUnitPerf. There is no reason to create performance and scalability tests for every part of the application, but it can be useful to create them for certain key areas where performance and scalability are critical. These tests will help you measure the factors that affect performance and scalability and guide you to the optimum solution.

Refactoring Tests As the Code Evolves

One of the hardest things about using TDD is the maintenance of the tests. Sometimes a requirement change or a change in architecture can generate a lot of changes to both the tests and code of a project. This can be frustrating, but it is important to remember that maintaining the tests is an important part of the TDD process because the tests are needed for regression testing among other things. The topics in this chapter should help you create an environment that makes it easier to maintain the tests, but every project is a little different, so it is hard to cover all the possible problems that can occur with maintaining a large number of tests. So if you find it hard to maintain the tests as the project evolves, then take the time to analyze your test environment and determine the source of the problem. Also, take the necessary actions to improve the test environment. Although some people think of tests as second-class code in the TDD environment, the tests are as important as the code. Like all collections of code, including test code, it's important to continually look for ways to improve how code is developed as well as to improve the development environment itself.

Summary

In this chapter, we have taken a step back from the discussions of the normal day-to-day process of TDD to look at what can be done to make the process more efficient. Most of the discussions have centered on the test environment. We have discussed topics like how to better organize the tests, how to improve code coverage, etc. All these topics should help you improve your test environment and make the tests easier to maintain. Of course, every project is different, so how you apply these techniques will vary; the main point of the chapter is that it is important to take the time to constantly refine the TDD process to fit it to your environment and make it as efficient as possible.

This chapter ends the technical discussion of TDD. Chapter 8 will talk about how to transition from a normal development environment to a TDD environment and also how to motivate people to switch to TDD.

CHAPTER 8

■■■

Transitioning to Test-Driven Development

You gotta believe

—Tug McGraw

In the middle of the 1973 baseball season, the New York Mets were in last place in their division, 12½ games out. After the All-Star break, manager Yogi Berra called a team meeting to try to motivate them out of last place. At the meeting, Tug McGraw, a slightly eccentric relief pitcher with a good sense of humor, came up with the now infamous phrase, "You gotta believe." Tug would walk off the pitcher's mound, slap his glove against his thigh, and yell out "You gotta believe" to no one in particular. Although the phrase was kind of taken as a joke coming from a relief pitcher on a last place team, it became the rallying cry for the Mets. As Tug kept slapping his glove against his thigh and yelling out "You gotta believe," he attracted the attention of his team, the fans, and the media. As the phrase caught on, it motivated the players, and the Mets started playing better. By the end of August, they were only 6½ games out of first place, and on the last day of the season, they were in first place and eventually won the National League pennant. The amazing rise of the Mets from last to first has become one of the best examples of the power of motivation.

The point that I'm trying to make with this story is that motivation is an important force not only in sports, but also in software development. Creating good software is more than making good logical decisions—there is an emotional context to it. If you don't believe this, just think back to some of the design "discussions" you have had with other developers. Since you are reading this book, I know that you are interested in TDD and hopefully have been convinced by the preceding chapters that TDD is a way to improve the development of software. At this point, I hope that I have motivated you to give TDD a try and start transitioning from your current development process to one that uses TDD. Of course, you are only one person, so in order to transition from your current development process to one that uses TDD, you have to convince the other members of your team to use TDD (i.e., you are going to have to motivate them to believe in TDD).

This may not be easy, because most people have certain beliefs about how software should be created, and it's hard to change those beliefs. No matter how many arguments are made to convince them that TDD can improve software development, most people are not willing to try it. They are not willing because of fear. They fear that TDD will be too hard to learn, that it won't work, and that if they try it and fail, they will be worse off than before. Most people hate change and would rather continue along the tried-and-true path even if that path has a lot of potholes.

The purpose of this chapter is to give you hints on how to transition from your current development environment to a TDD environment. This will involve a few basic steps: convincing other people that TDD will work, teaching the skills needed to practice TDD, and putting TDD into practice in your development environment. Most of the book has been about explaining the skills of TDD, so there is not much more to say about that. The rest of this chapter will focus on how to convince other people to use TDD and how to transition from your current environment to one that uses TDD.

The upcoming section on convincing other people to use TDD will show you how to sell the ideas of TDD to others who don't believe in the value of TDD. This will involve some salesmanship as well as persistence.

The later section on transitioning from your current environment to one that uses TDD will give you a few hints on how to make the transition without too much disruption to your current software project.

Convincing People to Use TDD

Although programming is computer science, it's not yet an exact science. Unlike driving a car, there is no exact right or wrong way to create software. Although some articles and books will say that they can teach you the best way to develop software, those books are wrong because developing software is a complex process. There is no one methodology, set of tools, or process that will work for every software project. For example, if you are developing the software necessary to control a spacecraft, it needs to be developed in a well-structured, methodical way with lots of testing to ensure that no critical bugs exist. However, if you are developing a web site that is not yet well defined, a simple, more iterative approach might be best.

Developing software is a risky venture. It's almost impossible to properly budget and schedule. According to a Gartner study, 30% of all projects fail to achieve their desired goals, and as many as 70% are late or over budget. Clearly, there is a need to improve the process, but the question is how. TDD can be part of the answer, but before you can convince people to switch to TDD, you have to understand the problems with your current process. Once you understand the flaws in your current process, you can then understand how to use TDD to improve it and use this knowledge to convince other people that it will work.

Finding the Flaws in Your Current Process

Chances are that if you are not practicing TDD or Extreme Programming (XP), then your process is probably some form of the waterfall model (i.e., analyze the requirements, design the code, write the code, test the code). Of course, if your current process is not well defined, then that is probably part of your problem. Two things are required to produce good software: a well-defined development process and good people. A well-defined development process helps to define the roles and responsibilities of the people involved in the process. It also promotes communication between the different groups. Good developers usually have a lot of experience that lets them anticipate problems and fix them before they occur. Most of the problems with software development are caused by bad communication and bad execution.

In order to understand the flaws in your development process, you should ask yourself some basic questions.

1. What is the main cause of most of the bugs in the software?

    a. Misunderstanding of the requirements

    b. Improper understanding of the deployment environment

    c. Lack of adequate testing

    d. Lack of regression testing

    e. Bad execution of design

    f. Coding errors

    g. Other

2. What is the main cause of schedule delays?

    a. Inadequate requirements

    b. Requirement creep

    c. Change in architecture

    d. Too busy fixing bugs

    e. Other

3. What is your average number of bugs per 1,000 lines of code written?

4. How does your process react to changes in requirements?

5. In what phase of the project (design, coding, integration, etc.) do you have the most problems?

Once you have given some thought to these questions, you should have a little better idea about the problems with your current process. It may take a little research to answer these questions, but it's important to understand the problems with your process before you try to understand if and how TDD can be used to fix the problems.

Fixing the Flaws

Now that you have an idea of what is wrong with your process, you can take a look at TDD and decide how best to apply it to help you fix the problems. Once you find problems in your process that can be fixed with TDD, you will have a way to prove that adopting TDD practices will improve development. This will help you convince people to use TDD.

For example, question 1 in the last section asked what is the main cause of bugs in the software. If your answer is *lack of adequate testing* or *lack of regression testing*, then you can argue that using TDD can fix this problem because the number of tests created when using TDD will help improve test coverage and provide a good set of regression tests.

If you continue to analyze the problems with your development environment, you should be able to come up with a number of ways that TDD can be used to improve it.

Now that you have a good idea of what the flaws in your current process are and how you think they can be fixed using TDD, you should be able to make good arguments for using TDD. Of course, as mentioned before, it usually takes more than a good argument to convince people to change the way they develop software; you have to find a way to make them believe that TDD will work.

To do this will usually take a little salesmanship. You may want to make a presentation to your department to explain the benefits of TDD. This will get people to start thinking about TDD and allow you to start a dialogue about it. After this, you will have to continue to be an advocate of TDD and continue to talk with people who don't believe in it and slowly convince them. You also have to continue to improve your knowledge of TDD by experimenting with the testing frameworks and reading relevant articles so that you get a deeper understanding of TDD. This will help you better understand how to apply it to your project and make better arguments for TDD.

Convincing people to try something new is never easy, but with a little time and patience, you should be able to convince enough people to give you the critical mass you need to start using TDD on your project.

If all else fails, then the best way to convince people that TDD works is to just do it. Although TDD works best when all the developers on a project are practicing it, there is no reason why a single developer can't start using it to develop code. Once you do this, you will be able to put TDD into practice on your project and perfect the skill you need to prove it works. With this concrete proof that it works on your project, it should be easier to convince other people to use it.

Making the Transition

Transitioning from your current development process to a TDD one needs to be done in a controlled manner. If you try to make the change too quickly, you will throw your development process into a chaos that will be hard to recover from. You also need to make sure you have a few things in place before you start the transition. This section will present a couple suggestions to help make the transition to TDD a little easier.

Preparing for the Transition

Before you can implement TDD, you should spend time thinking about some of the details of how you plan to use it on your project. You need to decide things like

- What tools and testing frameworks will be used

- How the developers will acquire the skills needed to practice TDD

- How the tests will be organized

- How the tests will be run

- What changes need to be made to the build process to use TDD

- How the introduction of TDD will affect your current process

Some of the decisions you make now may change when you actually start practicing TDD, but thinking about them up front will help you keep your development environment more organized.

Acquiring the Skills

Before you can start practicing TDD, you need to understand it. The fact that you are reading this book means that you have already started acquiring the skills you will need. Books and articles, though useful for gaining knowledge about TDD, are no substitute for experience. You will need experience in two basic areas in order to effectively practice TDD. You need to understand how to use your test frameworks to create effective unit tests, and you also need to understand how to use the TDD process to actually drive the development of your software. The best way to attain these skills is with practice. You can get this practice as you develop software for your project, but you might want to spend some time experimenting on your own before you do this. This will allow you to concentrate on TDD instead of getting caught up in the day-to-day issues of developing software.

The best way to learn how to use a particular testing framework to develop unit tests is to actually use it. The popular testing frameworks like JUnit, HttpUnit, Cactus, etc., all have a lot of information about them and examples of how to use them available in articles, on the web, and in books like this one. See Appendix C in the back of this book for my list of recommended articles, books, and web sites. You should take some of those examples and run them in your development environment. This will help you understand how to set up the testing framework and get familiar with the API. Once you have confidence that you understand how to use the testing framework, you should try and write some simple unit tests for your current software project. This will allow you to work out the details of how to use the testing framework with your actual software project and to develop confidence that you will easily be able to write unit tests for real software.

Learning how to use the TDD process to actually drive the development of code is a little harder than learning how to use a testing framework. Hopefully, the examples and the hands-on exercises in this book have given you some experience with this. Again, there is no substitute for experience, so most of this will have to be learned as you develop your software. One thing that can make the learning process a little easier is to make sure you have a good understanding of patterns and refactoring before you start practicing TDD, because this will help you understand the best way to refactor code and improve its design.

One of the things that you have to remember as you start practicing TDD is that it is a very iterative process, so you don't have to get the code right on the first pass. TDD allows you to discover the design of the code in a slow, incremental fashion, so don't overthink the design of the code. Let the tests show you the design. Once you learn how to let go and let the tests do the work, the process becomes a lot easier. (Don't worry—just keep writing tests and refactoring.)

Acquiring the skills needed to practice TDD will take time away from actual software development and slow the current project down. You should not view this time as wasted time, but as an investment in the future. Also, once developers start writing tests first, you'll be surprised how fast most of them catch on, and how soon it becomes a natural part of the development process. If you are working on a project with a lot of developers, giving them the time and resources that they need to acquire the skills necessary to practice TDD may be prohibitive. In this case, a better approach would be to use mentors to teach the required skills to the development team. The way this would work is that a few senior developers would acquire the skills and then start using TDD. These mentors would then work with the other developers on the team and teach them the skills necessary to practice TDD while they develop code. In this way, the whole team would slowly learn the necessary skills.

Transitioning

Once you have a plan of how TDD will be implemented on your project and have the required skills, you are ready to start using it. The changes that you will have to make to your development environment to move to TDD will not be extensive, so it is possible to introduce TDD to a project and not be too disruptive.

To start the transition, the first thing you need to do is to put the infrastructure in place for building and running the tests. This means that the following things need to be done:

- New directories need to be created to hold the tests that will be created.

- New jars and other support files need to be added to the development environment for the test frameworks that will be used.

- The build has to be updated to build the tests along with the code.

- New tasks need to be added to the build to run the tests.

Once the infrastructure is set up, the next thing you should do is to start writing some tests. At this point, you may just write some unit tests instead of actually trying to drive the development with the tests. This will help you gain experience with writing unit tests in your environment. You should probably start writing unit tests for pieces of code that are particularly buggy, or you could start by writing unit tests that reproduce the bugs that have been found. You should also make sure that you write tests for the different parts of the system like servlets, EJBs, GUI, etc., so you can gain an understanding of how to use the different test frameworks on the different parts of the project.

Once you are comfortable writing unit tests, you can take the next step and start using the tests to drive the development of the code. To do this, you just have to write the test first. It's a subtle change that may seem a bit strange at first, but as you continue to create the tests first, it will seem more natural. As with any new technique, it will take time to learn the new skills and understand how to use them correctly in your environment, so be patient.

If you are working on a project with a lot of developers, you probably want to make the transition gradually by first having only a few developers start practicing TDD. Once they have perfected their skills and adjusted the process to fit the development environment, they can then work with the other developers on the project and slowly teach them how to use TDD.

During the transition to a TDD environment, it is important that there be a lot of communication between the different developers doing the transitioning. It is important that they exchange ideas and support each other so that they can use their collective experience to properly set up and implement a good TDD environment. It is also important to allow the developers the time they need to experiment a little to find the best way to implement TDD on the project. Although this experimentation will take time away from actual development, it will be time well spent. Even after the TDD process has been fully implemented on your project, you will want to occasionally review the process and see if it can be improved. There are always new test frameworks and techniques being developed, so the learning never ends and the process can always be improved.

Summary

At this point, we have come to the end of our discussion of TDD. In this chapter, I have tried to explain a few ways to help you convince people that TDD does work and is worth implementing on your project. I have also tried to give you some hints about how to transition from your current development process to a TDD process. At this point, there is not much left to say except that it is time to stop reading and start doing. This book contains many examples and hands-on exercises that can help you get started. You can also check out the Apress web site for updated code for the book (`http://java.apress.com/book/bookDisplay.html?bID=359`) and the Apress forum (`http://forums.apress.com`) for discussions on this book. Experience is the best teacher, so now that you have read about TDD, it's time to start practicing it.

APPENDIX A

■ ■ ■

Guide to Getting and Using the Source Code for This Book

All the source code for this book as well as the code for the hands-on exercises is available in a zip file. This source code zip file can be downloaded from the Apress web site at `http://java.apress.com/book/bookDisplay.html?bID=359`.

Once you have downloaded the source code zip file, create a new directory on your system and expand the file. Expanding the source code zip file will create a set of directories divided by chapter that contain the source code for the book.

Source Code Organization

Once you have expanded the source code jar file, you should have the directory structure shown in Figure A-1.

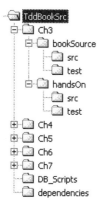

Figure A-1. *Source code directory structure*

If you look at the directory structure, you will see that there is a top-level directory for each chapter in the book in which source code is discussed. Underneath each chapter directory are the bookSource directory, which contains all the test and source code for that chapter of the book, and the handsOn directory, which contains all the test and source code for all the hands-on exercises for that chapter of the book. Each of these directories has two subdirectories: test and src. The test directory contains all the test code, and the src directory contains all the actual source code.

I've included two other top-level directories: DB_Scripts and dependencies. The DB_Scripts directory contains some scripts and data files that can be used to set up the database for the Football Pool application. The dependencies directory is used to hold the dependent libraries needed to compile and run the examples. However, not all of the dependent libraries you need to run the test and source code examples are included in the source code zip file. Most of them need to be downloaded separately. I've listed these dependent libraries and the URLs where they can be found in the next section.

Getting the Dependent Libraries

In order to compile and run the test and source code examples, you will need certain dependent libraries. Table A-1 lists the name of the dependent library, the version used for this book, and the URL where you can find the jar file. As a convenience, you can download all these jar files from the Apress web site at `http://java.apress.com/book/bookDisplay.html?bID=359`. The dependent libraries in the table are grouped by the URL where they can be found.

Table A-1. *Dependent Libraries Used in This Book*

Name	Version	URL
junit.jar	3.8.1	`http://www.junit.org`
j2ee.jar	1.3	`http://java.sun.com/j2ee`
easymock.jar	1.01b	`http://www.easymock.org`
dbunit.jar	2.0	`http://www.dbunit.org`
httpunit.jar	1.5.4	`http://www.httpunit.org`
Tidy.jar	-	Included with the HttpUnit download
js.jar	-	Included with the HttpUnit download
xercesImpl.jar	-	Included with the HttpUnit download
xmlParserAPIs.jar	-	Included with the HttpUnit download
nekohtml.jar	-	Included with the HttpUnit download
jfcunit.jar	2.0.2	`https://sourceforge.net/projects/jfcunit`
jemmy.jar	2.2.4	`http://jemmy.netbeans.org`
cactus-1.6.1.jar	1.6.1	`http://jakarta.apache.org/cactus`
cactus-ant-1.6.1.jar	1.6.1	Included with the Cactus download
commons-httpclient-2.0.jar	2.0	Included with the Cactus download
commons-logging-1.0.3.jar	1.0.3	Included with the Cactus download
aspectjrt-1.1.1.jar	1.1.1	Included with the Cactus download
hsqldb.jar	1.7.2	`http://hsqldb.sourceforge.net`
jakarta-regexp-1.2.jar	1.2	`http://jakarta.apache.org/regexp`
jasper-compiler.jar	2	`http://jakarta.apache.org/tomcat` (Included with the Tomcat download)

Name	Version	URL
jasper-runtime.jar	2	`http://jakarta.apache.org/tomcat` (Included with the Tomcat download)
jboss-common-client.jar	3.2.3	`http://www.jboss.com`
jnp-client.jar	3.2.3	Included with the JBoss download
jdom.jar	-	Included with the JBoss download
junitperf.jar	1.9	`http://www.clarkware.com/software/` `JUnitPerf.html`

Building and Running the Code

An Ant build file (build.xml) is included in the source code zip file. It can be used to build all the source code in each chapter. The build file has two Ant build tasks for each chapter. One Ant task will build the code for the examples shown in the book, and the other task will build the code for the hands-on exercises.

The build file also has two Ant tasks for each chapter that can be used to run the tests for each chapter. One Ant task will run the tests shown in the book, and the other task will run the tests for the hands-on exercises. See the Readme files in each of the chapter directories for details about how to run each of these tasks.

■ ■ ■

Answers to Hands-On Exercises

This appendix contains all the answers for the hands-on exercises. I highly encourage you to try to solve the hands-on exercises on your own before looking at the answers. Working out the solutions on your own will help you truly understand how to practice TDD and reinforce the ideas presented in the text. There are a number of different ways to solve each problem, so each solution presented here is only one possibility. This code can also be downloaded at the Apress web site (see Appendix A for complete download instructions).

Chapter 3 Hands-On Exercise

You're on your own now. It's time to test your knowledge of TDD (and how well I explained it) and try to add some more functionality to the application on your own. Your assignment is to implement the core functionality needed to implement part of Use Case 4 (Administrator Posts Results). You need to implement the behavior necessary to post the results for weekly picks for the football pool. Don't worry about anything to do with the user interface or the actual database implementation at this point.

Solution

Use Case 4 states

> *After the pool is closed, the administrator enters actual scores for each of the games played. Once all scores have been entered, the administrator posts the results. When the results are published, an e-mail is sent to registered players containing the name of the winning player and a URL to the pool results.*

If you decompose this into individual behavior, you get the following:

- The administrator needs a way to post scores for each game in the pool.

- There has to be a way to calculate the winning team for each game after the score has been posted.

- There has to be a way to calculate the winning player after all the games have been posted.

- There has to be a way to store and view results for each week of the pool.

- There has to be a way to send an e-mail to all the players containing the results.

The following tests were created from the required behaviors:

Listing for PoolResultsTester.java

```java
package com.apress.tddbook;

import junit.framework.TestCase;
import junit.framework.Test;
import junit.framework.TestSuite;

import java.util.Vector;

import org.easymock.MockControl;


public class PostResultsTester extends TestCase
{
    private MockControl poolDBMockcontrol;

    public PostResultsTester(String s)
    {
        super(s);
    }

    public void setUp()
    {
        poolDBMockcontrol = MockControl.createControl(PoolDatabase.class);
    }

    /**
     * Test used to ensure the scores can be posted for a game
     */
    public void testPostGameScore()
    {
        Game game = new Game("Kansas City", "Green Bay");
        game.postScore(28, 31);
        int homeScore = game.getHomeTeamScore();
        assertEquals(31, homeScore);
        int awayScore = game.getAwayTeamScore();
        assertEquals(28, awayScore);
        String winningTeam = game.getWinningTeamName();
```

```
        assertEquals("Green Bay", winningTeam);
}


/**
 * Test used to ensure that a football pool can be updated with the scores
 * of the games and that the winning team can be calculated correctly
 */
public void testPostGameScoresToPool()
{
    //Get mock object
    PoolDatabase mockPoolDB = (PoolDatabase)poolDBMockcontrol.getMock();
    //Train mock object
    mockPoolDB.getPoolWithStatus("Open");
    //Create return value for mock method
    Vector mockPoolList = createFbPoolList();
    poolDBMockcontrol.setReturnValue(mockPoolList);
    //Training over. Set the mock to replay trained behavior when called.
    poolDBMockcontrol.replay();

    PoolData poolData = new PoolData();
    //Set PoolDB to mock object
    poolData.set_poolDB(mockPoolDB);
    //Get Pool
    FootballPool pool = poolData.getOpenPool();
    //Post score for some games
    pool.postGameScore(0,28,31);
    pool.postGameScore(3,7,3);
    pool.postGameScore(5,8,31);
    pool.postGameScore(10,14,7);

    //Verify scores were posted correctly
    Vector gameList = pool.getGameList();
    Game game = (Game)gameList.elementAt(0);
    assertEquals(28,game.getAwayTeamScore());
    assertEquals(31,game.getHomeTeamScore());
    assertEquals("Green Bay", game.getWinningTeamName());

    game = (Game)gameList.elementAt(3);
    assertEquals(7,game.getAwayTeamScore());
    assertEquals(3,game.getHomeTeamScore());
    assertEquals("NY Giants", game.getWinningTeamName());

    game = (Game)gameList.elementAt(5);
    assertEquals(8,game.getAwayTeamScore());
    assertEquals(31,game.getHomeTeamScore());
    assertEquals("Cleveland", game.getWinningTeamName());
```

```java
        game = (Game)gameList.elementAt(10);
        assertEquals(14,game.getAwayTeamScore());
        assertEquals(7,game.getHomeTeamScore());
        assertEquals("Buffalo", game.getWinningTeamName());

    }

    /**
     * Test to make sure that the winning player is correctly picked after
     * posting the game scores
     */
    public void testCalcWinner()
    {
        //Get mock object
        PoolDatabase mockPoolDB = (PoolDatabase)poolDBMockcontrol.getMock();
        //Train mock object
        mockPoolDB.getPoolWithDate("2003-09-18");
        Vector mockPoolList = createFbPoolList();
        poolDBMockcontrol.setReturnValue(mockPoolList.elementAt(0));
        mockPoolDB.getAllPicks("2003-09-18");
        poolDBMockcontrol.setReturnValue(createPlayersPicks());
        mockPoolDB.savePoolResults(null);
        poolDBMockcontrol.setMatcher(MockControl.ALWAYS_MATCHER);
        //Training over. Set the mock to replay trained behavior when called.
        poolDBMockcontrol.replay();
        PoolData poolData = new PoolData();
        //Set PoolDB to mock object
        poolData.set_poolDB(mockPoolDB);
        //Calculate the pool results
        PoolResults results = poolData.calcPoolResults("2003-09-18");
        // Check the winner and results for each player to make sure they
        // are correct
        assertEquals("ScottM", results.m_winningPlayersName);
        Vector resultsList = results.m_playerResultsList;
        PlayerResultsData playerResults =
                                (PlayerResultsData)resultsList.elementAt(0);
        assertEquals("EddyC", playerResults.m_playerName);
        assertEquals(9, playerResults.m_correctPicks);

        playerResults = (PlayerResultsData)resultsList.elementAt(1);
        assertEquals("ScottM", playerResults.m_playerName);
        assertEquals(9, playerResults.m_correctPicks);

        playerResults = (PlayerResultsData)resultsList.elementAt(2);
        assertEquals("JenC", playerResults.m_playerName);
        assertEquals(5, playerResults.m_correctPicks);
    }
```

```
/**
 * Test the getPoolResults to make sure we can get a set of Pool results
 * for a Pool
 */
public void testGetPoolResults()
{
    //Get mock object
    PoolDatabase mockPoolDB = (PoolDatabase)poolDBMockcontrol.getMock();
    //Train mock object
    mockPoolDB.getPoolResults("2003-09-18");
    poolDBMockcontrol.setReturnValue(createPoolResults());
    //Training over. Set the mock to replay trained behavior when called.
    poolDBMockcontrol.replay();

    PoolData poolData = new PoolData();
    //Set PoolDB to mock object
    poolData.set_poolDB(mockPoolDB);

    //Get pool results for a particular pool
    PoolResults results = poolData.getPoolResults("2003-09-18");

    //Make sure the results match the expected value
    assertEquals("ScottM", results.m_winningPlayersName);
    Vector resultsList = results.m_playerResultsList;
    PlayerResultsData playerResults =
                            (PlayerResultsData)resultsList.elementAt(0);
    assertEquals("EddyC", playerResults.m_playerName);
    assertEquals(9, playerResults.m_correctPicks);

    playerResults = (PlayerResultsData)resultsList.elementAt(1);
    assertEquals("ScottM", playerResults.m_playerName);
    assertEquals(9, playerResults.m_correctPicks);

    playerResults = (PlayerResultsData)resultsList.elementAt(2);
    assertEquals("JenC", playerResults.m_playerName);
    assertEquals(5, playerResults.m_correctPicks);
}
private Vector createFbPoolList()
{
    Vector poolList = new Vector();
    FootballPool pool = new FootballPool("2003-09-18");
    pool.addGame("Kansas City", "Green Bay");
    pool.addGame("Houston", "Tennessee");
    pool.addGame("Carolina", "Indianapolis");
    pool.addGame("NY Giants", "New England");
    pool.addGame("Chicago", "New Orleans");
    pool.addGame("Oakland", "Cleveland");
```

```
        pool.addGame("Philadelphia", "Dallas");
        pool.addGame("Tampa Bay", "Washington");
        pool.addGame("Miami", "Jacksonville");
        pool.addGame("Pittsburgh", "Denver");
        pool.addGame("Buffalo", "NY Jets");
        pool.addGame("Baltimore", "Arizona");
        pool.addGame("San Francisco", "Seattle");
        pool.addGame("Atlanta", "St. Louis");

        pool.postGameScore(0,28,31);
        pool.postGameScore(1,8,24);
        pool.postGameScore(2,3,17);
        pool.postGameScore(3,21,31);
        pool.postGameScore(4,13,21);
        pool.postGameScore(5,28,35);
        pool.postGameScore(6,28,3);
        pool.postGameScore(7,14,3);
        pool.postGameScore(8,31,28);
        pool.postGameScore(9,13,21);
        pool.postGameScore(10,10,17);
        pool.postGameScore(11,21,7);
        pool.postGameScore(12,3,13);
        pool.postGameScore(13,24,14);
        try
        {
            pool.setTieBreakerGame(13);
        }
        catch (NoSuchGameException e)
        {
            e.printStackTrace();
        }

        poolList.addElement(pool);
        return (poolList);
    }

    private Vector createPlayersPicks()
    {
        Vector pickList = new Vector();
        FootballPool fbPool = (FootballPool)createFbPoolList().elementAt(0);
        Vector gameList = fbPool.getGameList();
        PlayersPicks playerPicks =
                        new PlayersPicks("EddyC", "2003-09-18", gameList);
        for(int i = 0; i < gameList.size(); i++)
        {
            Game game = (Game) gameList.elementAt(i);
            playerPicks.makePick(i, game.getHomeTeam());
```

```
        }
        playerPicks.setTiebreakScore(31);
        pickList.addElement(playerPicks);
        fbPool = (FootballPool)createFbPoolList().elementAt(0);
        gameList = fbPool.getGameList();
        playerPicks =
            new PlayersPicks("ScottM", "2003-09-18", (Vector)gameList.clone());
        for(int i = 0; i < gameList.size(); i++)
        {
            Game game = (Game) gameList.elementAt(i);
            playerPicks.makePick(i, game.getHomeTeam());
        }
        playerPicks.setTiebreakScore(34);
        pickList.addElement(playerPicks);
        fbPool = (FootballPool)createFbPoolList().elementAt(0);
        gameList = fbPool.getGameList();
        playerPicks = new PlayersPicks("JenC", "2003-09-18", gameList);
        for(int i = 0; i < gameList.size(); i++)
        {
            Game game = (Game) gameList.elementAt(i);
            playerPicks.makePick(i, game.getAwayTeam());
        }
        playerPicks.setTiebreakScore(21);
        pickList.addElement(playerPicks);

        return(pickList);
    }
    /**
     * Create a set of Pool results to be used in the tests
     *
     * @return
     */
    private PoolResults createPoolResults()
    {
        Vector resultsList = new Vector();
        PlayerResultsData playerResults = new PlayerResultsData("EddyC", 9);
        resultsList.addElement(playerResults);

        playerResults = new PlayerResultsData("ScottM", 9);
        resultsList.addElement(playerResults);

        playerResults = new PlayerResultsData("JenC", 5);
        resultsList.addElement(playerResults);

        PoolResults results = new PoolResults("2003-09-18", "ScottM", resultsList);
        return(results);
    }
```

```
    public static Test suite()
    {
        TestSuite suite = new TestSuite(PostResultsTester.class);
        return suite;
    }

    public static final void main(String[] args)
    {
        junit.textui.TestRunner.run(suite());
    }
}
```

The following code from Chapter 3 was updated (**new methods and/or code added is in bold**):

Listing for Game.java

```
package com.apress.tddbook;

public class Game
{
    private String _homeTeam;
    private String _awayTeam;
    private String _pickedTeam;
    private int _homeTeamScore;
    private int _awayTeamScore;
    private String _winningTeamName;

    Game(String awayTeam, String homeTeam)
    {
        _homeTeam = homeTeam;
        _awayTeam = awayTeam;
    }

    String getHomeTeam()
    {
        return _homeTeam;
    }

    String getAwayTeam()
    {
        return _awayTeam;
    }

    String getWinningTeamName()
    {
        return _winningTeamName;
    }
```

```java
    int getHomeTeamScore()
    {
        return _homeTeamScore;
    }

    int getAwayTeamScore()
    {
        return _awayTeamScore;
    }
    String getPickedTeam()
    {
        return _pickedTeam;
    }

    public void set_pickedGame(String pickedGame)
    {
        _pickedTeam = pickedGame;
    }

    public void postScore(int awayTeamScore, int homeTeamScore)
    {
        _homeTeamScore = homeTeamScore;
        _awayTeamScore = awayTeamScore;
        if (homeTeamScore > awayTeamScore)
        {
            _winningTeamName = _homeTeam;
        }
        else if( awayTeamScore > homeTeamScore)
        {
            _winningTeamName = _awayTeam;
        }
        else //tie game
        {
            _winningTeamName = "tie";
        }
    }
}
```

Listing for PoolData.java

```java
package com.apress.tddbook;

import java.util.Vector;

public class PoolData
{
    /** Handle to the database access methods */
```

```java
PoolDatabase m_poolDB;
public PoolData()
{

}
/**
 * Get the currently open football pool. There should be only one pool. If there
 * is more than one pool then this is an error
 *
 * @return the currently open football pool or null if there are no open
 * pools or more than one open football pool
 */
public FootballPool getOpenPool()
{
    FootballPool fbPool = null;
    Vector poolList = m_poolDB.getPoolWithStatus("Open");
    if(poolList.size() == 1)
    {
        fbPool = (FootballPool)poolList.elementAt(0);
    }
    return(fbPool);
}

public void savePlayersPicks(PlayersPicks playerPicks)
{
    m_poolDB.savePlayersPicks(playerPicks);
}
public PlayersPicks getPlayersPicks(String playersName, String poolDate)
{
    return(m_poolDB.getPlayersPicks(playersName, poolDate));
}
public void updateFootballPool(FootballPool pool)
{
    m_poolDB.updatePool(pool);
}

/**
 * Calcuate the winner of the weekly football pool given the date of
 * the pool. This method assumes that the scores have been
 * posted for the pool for this date
 *
 * @param date
 * @return    PoolResults or null if there is a problem with the calculation
 */
public PoolResults calcPoolResults(String date)
{
    int mostCorrectPicks = 0;
```

```java
        Vector resultsList = new Vector();
        //Get the Football Pool for the specified date
        FootballPool pool = m_poolDB.getPoolWithDate(date);
        //Get all the player picks for the specified date
        Vector pickList = m_poolDB.getAllPicks(date);
        // For each set of player picks calculate the correct number of picks
        //Also calculate the most number of correct picks
        for(int i = 0; i < pickList.size(); i++)
        {
            PlayersPicks picks = (PlayersPicks)pickList.elementAt(i);
            PlayerResultsData playerResults = calcResults(picks, pool);
            resultsList.addElement(playerResults);
            if(playerResults.correctPicks > mostCorrectPicks)
            {
                mostCorrectPicks = playerResults.correctPicks;
            }
        }
        String winner =
                findPoolWinner(mostCorrectPicks, pickList, pool, resultsList);

        //Create Pool Results
        PoolResults results = new PoolResults(date, winner, resultsList);
        //Store results in database
        m_poolDB.savePoolResults(results);
        //Return results
        return(results);
}
/**
 * Pick the winner of the pool based on the number of correct picks in
 * the tiebreaker
 *
 * @param pickList
 * @param resultsList
 * @return
 */
public String findPoolWinner(int mostCorrectPicks, Vector pickList,
                                    FootballPool pool, Vector resultsList)
{
    Vector bestPlayerList = new Vector();

    //First go through the resultList and find all the players with the
    // mostCorrectPicks
    for(int i = 0; i < resultsList.size(); i++)
    {
        PlayerResultsData results =
                            (PlayerResultsData) resultsList.elementAt(i);
        if(results.correctPicks == mostCorrectPicks)
```

```
            {
                bestPlayerList.addElement(results.playerName);
            }
        }
        //If the list contains only one name then that person is the winner
        if(bestPlayerList.size() == 1)
        {
            return((String)bestPlayerList.elementAt(0));
        }
        else // Else we have to use the tiebreaker score
        {
            return(getTieBreakWinner(bestPlayerList, pickList, pool));
        }
    }
    /**
     * Take a list of player names and picks and return the name of
     * the player with the tiebreaker score
     * closest to the combined score of the tiebreak game
     *
     * @param bestPlayerList
     * @param pickList
     * @return
     */

    private String getTieBreakWinner(Vector bestPlayerList, Vector pickList,
                                                  FootballPool pool)
    {
        String winnersName = "Nobody";
        int closestTieBreakScore = 10000;

        // Find combined score of tiebreak game
        Vector gameList = pool.getGameList();
        Game tieBreakGame = (Game)gameList.elementAt(pool.getTieBreakerGame());
        int actualTieBreakScore = tieBreakGame.getHomeTeamScore() +
                                              tieBreakGame.getAwayTeamScore();


        // Find player with tiebreak score closest to actual tiebreak score
        for(int i = 0; i < bestPlayerList.size(); i++)
        {
            String playersName = (String)bestPlayerList.elementAt(i);
            PlayersPicks picks = findPlayersPicks(playersName, pickList);
            int tieBreakDiff = actualTieBreakScore - picks.getTiebreakScore();
            if((tieBreakDiff > 0) && (tieBreakDiff < closestTieBreakScore))
            {
                winnersName = playersName;
                closestTieBreakScore = tieBreakDiff;
```

```java
            }
        }
        return(winnersName);
    }


    /**
     * Find the set of players picks given a player's name
     *
     * @param playersName
     * @param pickList
     * @return
     */
    private PlayersPicks findPlayersPicks(String playersName, Vector pickList)
    {
        PlayersPicks picks = null;

        for(int i = 0; i < pickList.size(); i++)
        {
            picks = (PlayersPicks)pickList.elementAt(i);
            if(picks.getPlayersName().equals(playersName))
            {
                return(picks);
            }
        }
        // If we get here then the players picks were not found so return null
        return(null);
    }
    public Vector getAllPicks(String date)
    {
        Vector pickList = new Vector();

        return(pickList);
    }


    public PoolResults getPoolResults(String date)
    {
        return(m_poolDB.getPoolResults(date));
    }
    public PoolDatabase get_poolDB()
    {
        return m_poolDB;
    }


    public void set_poolDB(PoolDatabase _poolDB)
    {
        this.m_poolDB = _poolDB;
    }
}
```

```java
/**
 * Given a set of player picks and a football pool this method calculates
 * the number of correct picks made by the player and returns
 * the results in a PlayerResultsData object
 *
 * @param picks
 * @param pool
 * @return
 */
private PlayerResultsData calcResults(PlayersPicks picks, FootballPool pool)
{
    Vector gameList = pool.getGameList();
    int numCorrectPicks = 0;

    for(int i = 0; i < gameList.size(); i++)
    {
        Game game = (Game) gameList.elementAt(i);
        String winningTeamName = game.getWinningTeamName();
        if(winningTeamName.equals(picks.getPickedTeam(i)))
        {
            numCorrectPicks++;
        }
    }
    return(new PlayerResultsData(picks.getPlayersName(), numCorrectPicks));
}
}
```

Listing for PlayerPicks.java

```java
package com.apress.tddbook;

import java.util.Vector;

public class PlayersPicks
{
    private Vector _gameList = new Vector();
    private String _playersName;
    private String _poolDate;
    private int _tiebreakScore;

    public int getTiebreakScore()
    {
        return _tiebreakScore;
    }
```

```java
public void setTiebreakScore(int tiebreakScore)
{
    _tiebreakScore = tiebreakScore;
}


public PlayersPicks(String playersName, String poolDate, Vector gameList) {
    _gameList = gameList;
    _playersName = playersName;
    _poolDate = poolDate;
}



public void makePick( int gameNum, String pickTeam ) {
    Game game = (Game)_gameList.elementAt(gameNum);
    game.set_pickedGame(pickTeam);
}



public String getHomeTeam( int i ) {
    Game game = (Game)_gameList.elementAt(i);
    return game.getHomeTeam();
}



public String getAwayTeam( int i ) {
    Game game = (Game)_gameList.elementAt(i);
    return game.getAwayTeam();
}

public String getPickedTeam( int i ) {
    Game game = (Game)_gameList.elementAt(i);
    return game.getPickedTeam();
}

public int size(){
    return(_gameList.size());
}
public String getPlayersName(){
    return _playersName;
}
public String getPoolDate(){
    return _poolDate;
}
}
```

Listing for FootballPool.java

```java
package com.apress.tddbook;


import java.util.Vector;
public class FootballPool {
    private Vector gameList = new Vector();
    private int _tieBreakerGame;
    private String m_poolDate;
    private String m_status = "Unknown";

    public FootballPool(String poolDate) {
        m_poolDate = poolDate;
    }


    public void addGame( String awayTeam, String homeTeam ) {
        gameList.addElement(new Game(awayTeam, homeTeam));
    }


    public String getHomeTeam( int i ) {
        Game game = (Game)gameList.elementAt(i);
        return game.getHomeTeam();
    }


    public String getAwayTeam( int i ) {
        Game game = (Game)gameList.elementAt(i);
        return game.getAwayTeam();
    }

    public int size(){
        return(gameList.size());
    }
    public int getTieBreakerGame() {
        return _tieBreakerGame;
    }
    public Vector getGameList(){
        return gameList;
    }
    /**
     * Set the status of the pool to open
     */
    public void openPool(){
```

```java
        m_status = "Open";
    }

    public String getStatus() {
        return(m_status);
    }
    /**
     * Post the score for a given game
     * @param gameNum Game number to post score for
     * @param awayTeamScore score of the away team
     * @param homeTeamScore score of the home team
     */
    public void postGameScore(int gameNum, int awayTeamScore, int homeTeamScore)
    {
        Game game = (Game)gameList.elementAt(gameNum);
        game.postScore(awayTeamScore,homeTeamScore);
    }
    public void setTieBreakerGame( int num ) throws NoSuchGameException {
        if((num < 0) || (num > gameList.size()) ){
            throw(new NoSuchGameException());
        }
        _tieBreakerGame = num;

    }
}
```

Listing for PoolDatabase.java

```java
package com.apress.tddbook;

import java.util.Vector;


public interface PoolDatabase
{
    public Vector getPoolWithStatus(String status);
    public void savePlayersPicks(PlayersPicks picks);
    public PlayersPicks getPlayersPicks(String name, String poolDate);
    public void updatePool(FootballPool pool);
    public Vector getAllPicks(String date);
    public FootballPool getPoolWithDate(String date);
    public void savePoolResults(PoolResults results);
    public PoolResults getPoolResults(String date);
}
```

The following new code was created as a result of the tests.

Listing for PoolResults.java

```
package com.apress.tddbook;

import java.util.Vector;

public class PoolResults
{
    public String poolDate;
    public String winningPlayersName;
    public Vector playerResultsList;

    public PoolResults(String date, String winner, Vector resultsList)
    {
        poolDate = date;
        winningPlayersName = winner;
        playerResultsList = resultsList;
    }
}
```

Listing for PoolResultsData.java

```
package com.apress.tddbook;

public class PlayerResultsData
{
    public String playerName;
    public int correctPicks;

    PlayerResultsData(String name, int correctPicks)
    {
        playerName = name;
        this.correctPicks = correctPicks;
    }
}
```

Chapter 4 Hands-On Exercise: Problem 1

Before you move on to developing JSPs using TDD, it's time to test your knowledge of servlet development using TDD and try to add some more functionality to the application on your own. Your assignment is to implement the servlet needed to implement part of Use Case 4 (Administrator Posts Results). You need to implement the behavior needed to post the results for weekly picks for the football pool. Don't worry about how the servlet will pass the data to the JSP; just use the core classes developed in this chapter and the hands-on solutions from Chapter 3 to develop a servlet that will get the data you need to post the pool results.

Solution

The behavior to solve this problem is pretty straightforward. Given pool data, all the servlet has to do is retrieve the results from the database using the PoolData class.

The following test was created from this behavior.

Listing for PlayersResultsServletTester.java

```java
package com.apress.tddbook.servlets;

import org.easymock.MockControl;
import junit.framework.TestCase;
import junit.framework.Test;
import junit.framework.TestSuite;
import com.apress.tddbook.PoolData;
import com.apress.tddbook.PoolResults;
import com.apress.tddbook.PlayerResultsData;
import com.meterware.servletunit.ServletRunner;
import com.meterware.servletunit.ServletUnitClient;
import com.meterware.servletunit.InvocationContext;
import com.meterware.httpunit.WebRequest;
import com.meterware.httpunit.PostMethodWebRequest;

import javax.servlet.http.HttpServletRequest;
import javax.servlet.http.HttpSession;
import java.util.Vector;

public class PlayersResultsServletTester extends TestCase
{
    private MockControl poolDataMockcontrol;

    public PlayersResultsServletTester(String s)
    {
        super(s);
    }

    public void setUp()
    {
        poolDataMockcontrol = MockControl.createControl(PoolData.class);
    }

    public static Test suite()
    {
        TestSuite suite = new TestSuite(PlayersResultsServletTester.class);
        return suite;
    }
```

```java
// Test to make sure that the servlet can return the pool results
// for a given date
public void testGetPoolResults()
{
    //Get mock object
    PoolData mockPoolData = (PoolData) poolDataMockcontrol.getMock();
    //Train mock object
    mockPoolData.calcPoolResults("2003-09-18");
    poolDataMockcontrol.setReturnValue(createPoolResults());
    //Training over. Set the mock to replay trained behavior when called.
    poolDataMockcontrol.replay();

    ServletRunner sr = new ServletRunner();
    sr.registerServlet("PlayerResultsServlet",
                        PlayerResultsServlet.class.getName());
    ServletUnitClient sc = sr.newClient();
    WebRequest request =
        new PostMethodWebRequest("http://localhost/PlayerResultsServlet");
    request.setParameter("poolDate", "2003-09-18");

    try
    {
        InvocationContext ic = sc.newInvocation(request);
        PlayerResultsServlet playerResultsServlet =
                                (PlayerResultsServlet) ic.getServlet();
        assertNull("A session already exists",
                    ic.getRequest().getSession(false));
        HttpServletRequest presultsServletRequest = ic.getRequest();
        HttpSession servletSession = presultsServletRequest.getSession();
        servletSession.setAttribute("PoolData", mockPoolData);
        PoolResults results =
                    playerResultsServlet.getResults(presultsServletRequest);

        //Make sure the results match the expected value
        assertEquals("ScottM", results.winningPlayersName);
        Vector resultsList = results.playerResultsList;
        PlayerResultsData playerResults =
                                (PlayerResultsData) resultsList.elementAt(0);
        assertEquals("EddyC", playerResults.playerName);
        assertEquals(9, playerResults.correctPicks);

        playerResults = (PlayerResultsData) resultsList.elementAt(1);
        assertEquals("ScottM", playerResults.playerName);
        assertEquals(9, playerResults.correctPicks);

        playerResults = (PlayerResultsData) resultsList.elementAt(2);
        assertEquals("JenC", playerResults.playerName);
```

```
                assertEquals(5, playerResults.correctPicks);
        }
        catch (Exception e)
        {
            fail("Error testing PlayerResultsServlet Exception is " + e);
            e.printStackTrace();
        }
    }

    /**
     * Create a set of pool results to be used in the tests
     *
     * @return
     */
    private PoolResults createPoolResults()
    {
        Vector resultsList = new Vector();
        PlayerResultsData playerResults = new PlayerResultsData("EddyC", 9);
        resultsList.addElement(playerResults);

        playerResults = new PlayerResultsData("ScottM", 9);
        resultsList.addElement(playerResults);

        playerResults = new PlayerResultsData("JenC", 5);
        resultsList.addElement(playerResults);

        PoolResults results = new PoolResults("2003-09-18", "ScottM", resultsList);
        return(results);
    }
    public static final void main(String[] args)
    {
        junit.textui.TestRunner.run(suite());
    }
}
```

The following code from Chapter 4 was updated (**new methods and/or code added is in bold**):

Listing for PoolDatabase.java

```
package com.apress.tddbook;

import java.util.Vector;


public interface PoolDatabase
{
    public Vector getPoolWithStatus(String status);
```

```
    public void savePlayersPicks(PlayersPicks picks);
    public PlayersPicks getPlayersPicks(String name, String poolDate);
    public void updatePool(FootballPool pool);
    public Vector getAllPicks(String date);
    public FootballPool getOpenPool();
    public FootballPool getPoolWithDate(String date);
    public void savePoolResults(PoolResults results);
    public PoolResults getPoolResults(String date);
}
```

Listing for PoolData.java

```
package com.apress.tddbook;

public interface PoolData
{
    FootballPool getOpenPool();
    void savePlayersPicks(PlayersPicks playerPicks);
    PlayersPicks getPlayersPicks(String playersName, String poolDate);
    PoolDatabase get_poolDB();
    void set_poolDB(PoolDatabase _poolDB);
    public PoolResults calcPoolResults(String date);
}
```

Listing for PlayersResultsServletTester.java

```
package com.apress.tddbook;

import java.util.Vector;

public class PoolDataImpl implements PoolData
{
    /** Handle to the database access methods */
    PoolDatabase _poolDB;
    public PoolDataImpl()
    {

    }
    /**
     * Get the currently open football pool. There should be only one pool. If there
     * is more than one pool then this is an error
     *
     * @return the currently open football pool or null if there are no open
     * pools or more than one open football pool
     */
    public FootballPool getOpenPool()
```

```
{
    FootballPool fbPool = null;
    Vector poolList = _poolDB.getPoolWithStatus("Open");
    if(poolList.size() == 1)
    {
        fbPool = (FootballPool)poolList.elementAt(0);
    }
    return(fbPool);
}

public void savePlayersPicks(PlayersPicks playerPicks)
{
    _poolDB.savePlayersPicks(playerPicks);
}
public PlayersPicks getPlayersPicks(String playersName, String poolDate)
{
    return(_poolDB.getPlayersPicks(playersName, poolDate));
}
public PoolDatabase get_poolDB()
{
    return _poolDB;
}

public void set_poolDB(PoolDatabase _poolDB)
{
    this._poolDB = _poolDB;
}

public PoolResults calcPoolResults(String date)
{
    int mostCorrectPicks = 0;

    Vector resultsList = new Vector();
    //Get the Football Pool for the specified date
    FootballPool pool = m_poolDB.getPoolWithDate(date);
    //Get all the player picks for the specified date
    Vector pickList = m_poolDB.getAllPicks(date);
    // For each set of player picks calculate the correct number of picks
    //Also calculate the most number of correct picks
    for (int i = 0; i < pickList.size(); i++)
    {
        PlayersPicks picks = (PlayersPicks) pickList.elementAt(i);
        PlayerResultsData playerResults = calcResults(picks, pool);
        resultsList.addElement(playerResults);
        if (playerResults.correctPicks > mostCorrectPicks)
        {
            mostCorrectPicks = playerResults.correctPicks;
```

```java
        }
    }
    String winner =
            findPoolWinner(mostCorrectPicks, pickList, pool, resultsList);

    //Create Pool Results
    PoolResults results = new PoolResults(date, winner, resultsList);
    //Store results in database
    m_poolDB.savePoolResults(results);
    //Return results
    return (results);
}


/**
 * Pick the winner of the pool based on the number of correct picks and
 * the tiebreaker
 *
 * @param pickList
 * @param resultsList
 * @return
 */
public String findPoolWinner(int mostCorrectPicks, Vector pickList,
                             FootballPool pool, Vector resultsList)
{
    Vector bestPlayerList = new Vector();

    // First go through the resultList and find all the players with
    // the mostCorrectPicks
    for (int i = 0; i < resultsList.size(); i++)
    {
        PlayerResultsData results =
                        (PlayerResultsData) resultsList.elementAt(i);
        if (results.correctPicks == mostCorrectPicks)
        {
            bestPlayerList.addElement(results.playerName);
        }
    }
    //If the list contains only one name, then that person is the winner
    if (bestPlayerList.size() == 1)
    {
        return ((String) bestPlayerList.elementAt(0));
    }
    else // Else we have to use the tiebreaker score
    {
        return (getTieBreakWinner(bestPlayerList, pickList, pool));
    }
}
```

```java
/**
 * Take a list of player names and picks and return the name of the player
 * with the tiebreaker score closest to the combined score
 * of the tiebreaker game
 *
 * @param bestPlayerList
 * @param pickList
 * @return
 */

private String getTieBreakWinner(Vector bestPlayerList, Vector pickList,
                                                FootballPool pool)
{
    String winnersName = "Nobody";
    int closestTieBreakScore = 10000;

    // Find combined score of tiebreak game
    Vector gameList = pool.getGameList();
    Game tieBreakGame = (Game) gameList.elementAt(pool.getTieBreakerGame());
    int actualTieBreakScore = tieBreakGame.getHomeTeamScore() +
                                        tieBreakGame.getAwayTeamScore();


    // Find player with tiebreak score closest to actual tiebreak score
    for (int i = 0; i < bestPlayerList.size(); i++)
    {
        String playersName = (String) bestPlayerList.elementAt(i);
        PlayersPicks picks = findPlayersPicks(playersName, pickList);
        int tieBreakDiff = actualTieBreakScore - picks.getTiebreakScore();
        if ((tieBreakDiff > 0) && (tieBreakDiff < closestTieBreakScore))
        {
            winnersName = playersName;
            closestTieBreakScore = tieBreakDiff;
        }
    }
    return (winnersName);
}

/**
 * Find the set of players picks given a player's name
 *
 * @param playersName
 * @param pickList
 * @return
 */
private PlayersPicks findPlayersPicks(String playersName, Vector pickList)
{
```

```java
    PlayersPicks picks = null;

    for (int i = 0; i < pickList.size(); i++)
    {
        picks = (PlayersPicks) pickList.elementAt(i);
        if (picks.getPlayersName().equals(playersName))
        {
            return (picks);
        }
    }
    // If we get here, then the players picks were not found so return null
    return (null);
}

public Vector getAllPicks(String date)
{
    Vector pickList = new Vector();

    return (pickList);
}

public PoolResults getPoolResults(String date)
{
    return (m_poolDB.getPoolResults(date));
}

public PoolDatabase get_poolDB()
{
    return m_poolDB;
}

public void set_poolDB(PoolDatabase _poolDB)
{
    this.m_poolDB = _poolDB;
}

/**
 * Given a set of player picks and a football pool this method calculates
 * the number of correct picks made by the player and returns the results
 * in a PlayerResultsData object
 *
 * @param picks
 * @param pool
 * @return
 */
private PlayerResultsData calcResults(PlayersPicks picks, FootballPool pool)
{
```

```
        Vector gameList = pool.getGameList();
        int numCorrectPicks = 0;

        for (int i = 0; i < gameList.size(); i++)
        {
            Game game = (Game) gameList.elementAt(i);
            String winningTeamName = game.getWinningTeamName();
            if (winningTeamName.equals(picks.getPickedTeam(i)))
            {
                numCorrectPicks++;
            }
        }
        return (new PlayerResultsData(picks.getPlayersName(), numCorrectPicks));
    }
}
```

The following new servlet was created as a result of the tests:

Listing for PlayersResultsServlet.java

```
package com.apress.tddbook.servlets;

import com.apress.tddbook.PoolResults;
import com.apress.tddbook.PoolData;

import javax.servlet.http.HttpServlet;
import javax.servlet.http.HttpServletRequest;

public class PlayerResultsServlet extends HttpServlet
{
    /**
     * Return the pool results for a particular pool given the date.
     * If there are no results for the specified pool date or if there
     * is no pool for that date then null is returned
     *
     * @param request
     * @return PoolResults for the specified date or null if no results or pool
     */
    public PoolResults getResults(HttpServletRequest request)
    {
        PoolData poolData = (PoolData)request.getSession().getAttribute("PoolData");
        PoolResults results =
                    poolData.calcPoolResults(request.getParameter("poolDate"));
        return(results);
    }
}
```

Chapter 4 Hands-On Exercise: Problem 2

It's time to test your knowledge of JSP development using TDD by trying to add some more functionality to the application on your own. Your assignment is to implement the JSP needed to display the data of the servlet developed in the previous hands-on exercise. Your first step should be to turn to the visual design of the results page shown in Chapter 2 (Figure 2-6) and determine the HTML elements needed to render the page. Then develop a test for the JSP page using the JSPDispatcherServlet. After you develop the test, use it to create the dynamic JSP for the results page.

Solution

The JSP that is used to display the pool results is simple; it just shows the name of the winner of the pool for the given week and then shows a table with the correct picks for each player. Figure B-1 shows what the results page should look like.

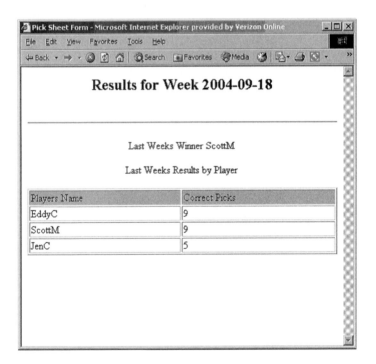

Figure B-1. *Pool Results page*

The following test was created to test the JSP and added to the PlayersResultsServletTester class:

```
/**
 * Test to make sure that the JSP page displays the pool results properly
 */
public void testPoolResultPageJSP()
    {
```

```
            ServletRunner sr = new ServletRunner();
            sr.registerServlet("JSPDispatcherServlet",
                            JSPDispatcherServlet.class.getName());
            ServletUnitClient sc = sr.newClient();
            WebRequest request =
             new PostMethodWebRequest("http://localhost/JSPDispatcherServlet");
            request.setParameter("poolDate", "2003-09-18");
            request.setParameter("JSPPage", "/ResultPage.jsp");
            try
            {
                InvocationContext ic = sc.newInvocation(request);
                JSPDispatcherServlet jspDispServlet =
                                        (JSPDispatcherServlet) ic.getServlet();
                assertNull("A session already exists",
                            ic.getRequest().getSession(false));
                HttpServletRequest jspDispRequest = ic.getRequest();
                HttpSession servletSession = jspDispRequest.getSession();
                servletSession.setAttribute("poolResults", createPoolResults());
                jspDispServlet.doGet(jspDispRequest, ic.getResponse());
                WebResponse response = sc.getResponse(ic);


                assertNotNull("No response received", response);

                WebTable resultsTable = response.getTables()[0];
                assertEquals(2, resultsTable.getColumnCount());
                assertEquals(4, resultsTable.getRowCount());
                assertEquals("ScottM", resultsTable.getTableCell(2,0).asText());
                assertEquals("9", resultsTable.getTableCell(2,1).asText());
            }
            catch (Exception e)
            {
                System.out.println("Error getting reponse Exception is " + e);
                e.printStackTrace();
            }
        }
```

The following JSP was created as a result of the test:

Listing for ResultPage.jsp

```
<%@ page import="java.util.Vector,
                com.apress.tddbook.PoolResults,
                com.apress.tddbook.PlayerResultsData"%>

<HTML><HEAD><TITLE>Pick Sheet Form</TITLE>
<BODY text=#000000 bgColor=#FFFFFF background="" ;>
<%
```

```
    System.out.println("ResultPage JSP is executing...");

%>
<FORM name=theForm action=http://localhost:8080/FootBallPool/PlayerResultsServlet
    method=post >
<CENTER>
<h2><%out.println("Results for Week " + request.getParameter("poolDate")); %>
</h2>
<BR>
<HR>

<DIV align=center>
<CENTER>
<p>Last Weeks Winner
        <%
            PoolResults poolResults =
                            (PoolResults)request.getAttribute("poolResults");

            out.println(" " + poolResults.winningPlayersName);
        %>
        </p>
        <p align="center">Last Weeks Results by Player</p>
        <div align="left">
          <table border="1" width="100%">
            <tr>
              <td width="50%" bgcolor="#C0C0C0">Players Name</td>
              <td width="50%" bgcolor="#C0C0C0">Correct Picks</td>
            </tr>
            <%
                        PlayerResultsData results;

              for(int i = 0; i < poolResults.playerResultsList.size(); i++)
              {
                 results =
                 (PlayerResultsData)poolResults.playerResultsList.elementAt(i);
                 out.println("<tr>");
                 out.println("<td width='50%'>" + results.playerName + "</td>");
                 out.println("<td width='50%'>" + results.correctPicks + "</td>");
                 out.println("</tr>");
              }
          %>

            </table></CENTER></DIV>

        </body>
</html>
```

Chapter 4 Hands-On Exercise: Problem 3

It's time to test your knowledge of JSP/servlet development using TDD by trying to add some more functionality to the application on your own. Your assignment is to complete the development of the servlet/JSP needed to implement part of Use Case 4. You need to finish implementing the behavior needed to post the results for weekly picks for the football pool. Use the code developed in the previous hands-on exercise to create a test that does an end-to-end test of the servlet and allows you to complete the development of the servlet.

Solution

Finishing the implementation of Use Case 4 is just a matter of putting the servlet and JSP developed in the previous exercises together. The following test was added to the PlayerResultsServletTester first to test the completed servlet/JSP:

```
public void testDisplayPoolResultsWithRealJSP()
    {
        //Get mock object
        PoolData mockPoolData = (PoolData) poolDataMockcontrol.getMock();
        //Train mock object
        mockPoolData.calcPoolResults("2003-09-18");
        poolDataMockcontrol.setReturnValue(createPoolResults());
        //Training over. Set the mock to replay trained behavior when called.
        poolDataMockcontrol.replay();

        ServletRunner sr = new ServletRunner();
        sr.registerServlet("PlayerResultsServlet",
                        PlayerResultsServlet.class.getName());
        ServletUnitClient sc = sr.newClient();
        WebRequest request =
            new PostMethodWebRequest("http://localhost/PlayerResultsServlet");
        request.setParameter("poolDate", "2003-09-18");
        try
        {
            InvocationContext ic = sc.newInvocation(request);
            PlayerResultsServlet playerResultsServlet =
                                    (PlayerResultsServlet) ic.getServlet();
            assertNull("A session already exists",
                    ic.getRequest().getSession(false));
            HttpServletRequest presultsServletRequest = ic.getRequest();
            HttpSession servletSession = presultsServletRequest.getSession();
            servletSession.setAttribute("PoolData", mockPoolData);
            playerResultsServlet.doGet(presultsServletRequest, ic.getResponse());
            WebResponse response = sc.getResponse(ic);

            assertNotNull("No response received", response);

            WebTable resultsTable = response.getTables()[0];
```

```
        assertEquals(2, resultsTable.getColumnCount());
        assertEquals(4, resultsTable.getRowCount());
        assertEquals("ScottM", resultsTable.getTableCell(2, 0).asText());
        assertEquals("9", resultsTable.getTableCell(2, 1).asText());
    }
    catch (Exception e)
    {
        fail("Error getting reponse Exception is " + e);
        e.printStackTrace();
    }
}
```

The following methods were added to the PlayerResultsServlet to get the test to pass:

```
public void doGet(HttpServletRequest request, HttpServletResponse response)
        throws ServletException, IOException
{

    PoolResults poolResults = getResults(request);
    request.setAttribute("poolResults", poolResults);
    RequestDispatcher dispatcher =
                getServletContext().getRequestDispatcher("/ResultPage.jsp");
    dispatcher.include(request, response);
    return;
}

public void doPost(HttpServletRequest request, HttpServletResponse response)
        throws ServletException, IOException
{
    doGet(request, response);
}
```

Chapter 5 Hands-On Exercise

You're on your own now. It's time to test your knowledge of GUI development using TDD to add some more functionality to the application on your own. Your assignment is to add the functionality needed to allow the Admin GUI to add a new pool to the list of available football pools. This means that you will have to develop the tests and code needed to get the New Pool button working on the main GUI as well as develop the tests and code needed to get the New Pool dialog box shown in Figure 5-2 working. This may require adding more methods to the FBPoolServer and FBPoolServerStub classes as well as adding other classes to the project.

Solution

Adding the ability for the Admin GUI to create a new football pool means implementing the part of Use Case 2 that deals with adding a new pool. This basically means that you have to implement the behavior of the New Pool dialog box shown in Chapter 5 (Figure 5-2). If you decompose the use case, besides creating the dialog box, you get the following behaviors:

- There has to be a way to get the list of available teams for a given week.

- There has to be a way to add a new game with the selected home and away teams.

- There has to be a way to delete a selected game.

- There has to be a way to save the new pool when the OK button is clicked.

- There has to be a way to set the tiebreak game.

The following new JFCUnit tests were added to `AdminGUITester` from the required behaviors:

```java
/**
 * Test to make sure that the New Pool dialog box can be displayed
 */
public void testNewPoolDialog()
{
    Window appWindow = helper.getWindow("Football Pool Administrator");
    assertNotNull("Unable to get main window", appWindow);
    JButton newPoolButton = (JButton) helper.findNamedComponent(JButton.class,
                                        "NewPoolButton", appWindow, 0);
    assertNotNull("Unable to find New Pool button", newPoolButton);
    helper.enterClickAndLeave(new MouseEventData(this, newPoolButton));
    //Get dialog box
    List dialogList = helper.getShowingDialogs();
    //There should only be one dialog box showing
    JDialog dialog = (JDialog) dialogList.get(0);

    //Check the dialog box to make sure it contains the expected components
    JList teamList = (JList) helper.findComponent(JList.class, dialog, 0);
    assertNotNull("Unable to find team list", teamList);
    JTable gameTable = (JTable) helper.findComponent(JTable.class, dialog, 0);
    assertNotNull("Unable to find gameTable", gameTable);
    JButton addHomeGameButton = (JButton)
            helper.findNamedComponent(JButton.class, "addHomeTeamButton",
                                        dialog, 0);
    System.out.println("Button 1 is " + addHomeGameButton.getText());
    assertNotNull("Unable to find addHomeGame Button", addHomeGameButton);
    dialog.dispose();
}

/**
 * Test to make sure that the Team Name List in the New Pool dialog box
 * contains the correct list of teams
 */
public void testNewPoolDialogPopulateTeamNameList()
{
    JDialog dialog = null;
```

```java
        try
        {
            Window appWindow = helper.getWindow("Football Pool Administrator");
            assertNotNull("Unable to get main window", appWindow);
            JButton newPoolButton =
             (JButton) helper.findNamedComponent(JButton.class, "NewPoolButton",
                                                              appWindow, 0);
            assertNotNull("Unable to find New Pool button", newPoolButton);
            helper.enterClickAndLeave(new MouseEventData(this, newPoolButton));
            //Get dialog box
            List dialogList = helper.getShowingDialogs();
            //There should only be one dialog box showing
            dialog = (JDialog) dialogList.get(0);

            //Check the team name list to make sure it is the right size and
            // contains the correct team names
            JList teamList = (JList) helper.findComponent(JList.class, dialog, 0);
            assertNotNull("Unable to find team list", teamList);
            ListModel model = teamList.getModel();
            assertEquals(30, model.getSize());
            assertEquals("NY Giants", model.getElementAt(0));
            assertEquals("Green Bay", model.getElementAt(1));
            // ...
        }
        // No matter if we pass or fail the test we need to close the dialog
        // so that other tests can bring up a fresh dialog box.
        // If we don't do this then the other tests might fail.
        finally
        {
            if (dialog != null)
            {
                dialog.dispose();
            }
        }

    }


    /**
     * Test to make sure that a user can add a new game in the New Pool dialog box
     */
    public void testNewPoolDialogAddGame()
    {
        JDialog dialog = null;
        try
        {
            Window appWindow = helper.getWindow("Football Pool Administrator");
            assertNotNull("Unable to get main window", appWindow);
```

```java
        JButton newPoolButton =
                    (JButton) helper.findNamedComponent(JButton.class,
                                        "NewPoolButton", appWindow, 0);
        assertNotNull("Unable to find New Pool button", newPoolButton);
        helper.enterClickAndLeave(new MouseEventData(this, newPoolButton));
        //Get dialog box
        List dialogList = helper.getShowingDialogs();
        //There should only be one dialog box showing
        dialog = (JDialog) dialogList.get(0);

        //Click the Add Home Team and Add Away team buttons then
        // check the game table to make sure the game was added
        JList teamList = (JList) helper.findComponent(JList.class, dialog, 0);
        assertNotNull("Unable to find team list", teamList);
        JTable gameTable = (JTable) helper.findComponent(JTable.class,
                                                            dialog, 0);
        assertNotNull("Unable to find gameTable", gameTable);
        JButton addHomeGameButton =
                    (JButton) helper.findNamedComponent(JButton.class,
                                    "addHomeTeamButton", dialog, 0);
        System.out.println("Button 1 is " + addHomeGameButton.getText());
        assertNotNull("Unable to find addHomeGame Button", addHomeGameButton);
        JButton addAwayGameButton =
                    (JButton) helper.findNamedComponent(JButton.class,
                                    "addAwayTeamButton", dialog, 0);
        System.out.println("Button 2 is " + addAwayGameButton.getText());
        assertNotNull("Unable to find addAwayGame Button", addAwayGameButton);

        //Select home team
        teamList.setSelectedIndex(1);
        //Click Add Home Team button
        helper.enterClickAndLeave(new MouseEventData(this, addHomeGameButton));
        awtSleep(5000);
        //Select away team
        teamList.setSelectedIndex(4);
        //Click Add Away Team button
        helper.enterClickAndLeave(new MouseEventData(this, addAwayGameButton));
        //Check game table to make sure game was added
        awtSleep(5000);
        int rowCount = gameTable.getRowCount();
        assertEquals("Green Bay", gameTable.getValueAt(rowCount - 1, 0));
        assertEquals("Chicago", gameTable.getValueAt(rowCount - 1, 1));
    }
// No matter if we pass or fail the test we need to close the dialog
// so that other tests can bring up a fresh dialog box.
// If we don't do this then the other tests might fail.
finally
```

```
        {
            if (dialog != null)
            {
                dialog.dispose();
            }
        }
    }

    public void testNewPoolDialogDeleteGame()
    {
        JDialog dialog = null;
        try
        {
            Window appWindow = helper.getWindow("Football Pool Administrator");
            assertNotNull("Unable to get main window", appWindow);
            JButton newPoolButton =
                            (JButton) helper.findNamedComponent(JButton.class,
                                            "NewPoolButton", appWindow, 0);
            assertNotNull("Unable to find New Pool button", newPoolButton);
            helper.enterClickAndLeave(new MouseEventData(this, newPoolButton));
            //Get dialog box
            List dialogList = helper.getShowingDialogs();
            //There should only be one dialog box showing
            dialog = (JDialog) dialogList.get(0);

            //Click the Add button then check the game table to make sure
            // the game was added. After the addition, delete the game and make
            // sure the game table is empty
            JList teamList = (JList) helper.findComponent(JList.class, dialog, 0);
            assertNotNull("Unable to find team list", teamList);
            JTable gameTable = (JTable) helper.findComponent(JTable.class,
                                                            dialog, 0);
            assertNotNull("Unable to find gameTable", gameTable);
            JButton addHomeTeamButton =
                            (JButton) helper.findNamedComponent(JButton.class,
                                            "addHomeTeamButton", dialog, 0);
            assertNotNull("Unable to find addHomeGame Button", addHomeTeamButton);
            JButton addAwayTeamButton =
                            (JButton) helper.findNamedComponent(JButton.class,
                                            "addAwayTeamButton", dialog, 0);
            assertNotNull("Unable to find addAwayGame Button", addAwayTeamButton);
            JButton deleteGameButton =
                            (JButton) helper.findNamedComponent(JButton.class,
                                            "delGameButton", dialog, 0);
            assertNotNull("Unable to find delete Game Button", addAwayTeamButton);

            //Select home team
```

```
            teamList.setSelectedIndex(1);
            //Click Add Home Team button
            helper.enterClickAndLeave(new MouseEventData(this, addHomeTeamButton));
            awtSleep(5000);
            //Select away team
            teamList.setSelectedIndex(4);
            //Click Add Away Team button
            helper.enterClickAndLeave(new MouseEventData(this, addAwayTeamButton));
            //Check game table to make sure game was added
            awtSleep(5000);
            int rowCount = gameTable.getRowCount();
            assertEquals("Green Bay", gameTable.getValueAt(rowCount - 1, 0));
            assertEquals("Chicago", gameTable.getValueAt(rowCount - 1, 1));

            //Select the first cell of the table
            helper.enterClickAndLeave(new JTableMouseEventData(this, gameTable,
                                                               0, 0, 1));

            //Click Delete Game button
            helper.enterClickAndLeave(new MouseEventData(this, deleteGameButton));
            //Check game table to make sure game was deleted
            awtSleep(5000);
            rowCount = gameTable.getRowCount();
            assertEquals(0, rowCount);
        }
        // No matter if we pass or fail the test we need to close the dialog
        // so that other tests can bring up a fresh dialog box.
        // If we don't do this then the other tests might fail.
        finally
        {
            if (dialog != null)
            {
                dialog.dispose();
            }
        }
    }
}

/**
 * Test to make sure user can correctly set tiebreaker game
 */
public void testNewPoolDialogSetTieBreakGame()
{

    JDialog dialog = null;
    try
    {
        Window appWindow = helper.getWindow("Football Pool Administrator");
        assertNotNull("Unable to get main window", appWindow);
```

```
JButton newPoolButton =
                (JButton) helper.findNamedComponent(JButton.class,
                                "NewPoolButton", appWindow, 0);
assertNotNull("Unable to find New Pool button", newPoolButton);
helper.enterClickAndLeave(new MouseEventData(this, newPoolButton));
//Get dialog box
List dialogList = helper.getShowingDialogs();
//There should only be one dialog box showing
dialog = (JDialog) dialogList.get(0);

//Click the Add then check the game table to make sure
// the game was added. After the addition, delete the game and
// make sure the game table is empty
JList teamList = (JList) helper.findComponent(JList.class, dialog, 0);
assertNotNull("Unable to find team list", teamList);
JTable gameTable = (JTable) helper.findComponent(JTable.class,
                                                    dialog, 0);
assertNotNull("Unable to find gameTable", gameTable);
JButton addHomeTeamButton =
                (JButton) helper.findNamedComponent(JButton.class,
                                "addHomeTeamButton", dialog, 0);
assertNotNull("Unable to find addHomeGame Button", addHomeTeamButton);
JButton addAwayTeamButton =
                (JButton) helper.findNamedComponent(JButton.class,
                                "addAwayTeamButton", dialog, 0);
assertNotNull("Unable to find addAwayGame Button", addAwayTeamButton);
JButton setTieBreakButton =
                (JButton) helper.findNamedComponent(JButton.class,
                                "setTieBreakButton", dialog, 0);
assertNotNull("Unable to find set tie break Game Button",
                addAwayTeamButton);

//Add some games
teamList.setSelectedIndex(1);
helper.enterClickAndLeave(new MouseEventData(this, addHomeTeamButton));
awtSleep(5000);
teamList.setSelectedIndex(4);
helper.enterClickAndLeave(new MouseEventData(this, addAwayTeamButton));
awtSleep(5000);

teamList.setSelectedIndex(3);
helper.enterClickAndLeave(new MouseEventData(this, addHomeTeamButton));
awtSleep(5000);
teamList.setSelectedIndex(5);
helper.enterClickAndLeave(new MouseEventData(this, addAwayTeamButton));
awtSleep(5000);
```

```java
            teamList.setSelectedIndex(7);
            helper.enterClickAndLeave(new MouseEventData(this, addHomeTeamButton));
            awtSleep(5000);
            teamList.setSelectedIndex(9);
            helper.enterClickAndLeave(new MouseEventData(this, addAwayTeamButton));
            awtSleep(5000);

            int rowCount = gameTable.getRowCount();
            assertEquals(3, rowCount);
            //Select the first cell of the table
            helper.enterClickAndLeave(new JTableMouseEventData(this,
                                                    gameTable, 1, 0, 1));
            //Click Delete Game button
            helper.enterClickAndLeave(new MouseEventData(this, setTieBreakButton));
            awtSleep(5000);
            //Check to make sure that the tiebreaker game was set.
            // The tiebreaker game will have an asterisk after it.
            assertEquals("Oakland *", gameTable.getValueAt(1, 0));
            assertEquals("Miami *", gameTable.getValueAt(1, 1));
        }
    // No matter if we pass or fail the test we need to close the dialog
    // so that other tests can bring up a fresh dialog box.
    // If we don't do this then the other tests might fail.
    finally
    {
        if (dialog != null)
        {
            dialog.dispose();
        }
    }
}

/**
 * Test to make sure user can correctly save a new pool once it has been created
 */
public void testNewPoolDialogSaveNewPool()
{
    JDialog dialog = null;
    try
    {
        Window appWindow = helper.getWindow("Football Pool Administrator");
        assertNotNull("Unable to get main window", appWindow);
        JButton newPoolButton =
                    (JButton) helper.findNamedComponent(JButton.class,
                                            "NewPoolButton", appWindow, 0);
        assertNotNull("Unable to find New Pool button", newPoolButton);
        helper.enterClickAndLeave(new MouseEventData(this, newPoolButton));
```

```
//Get dialog box
List dialogList = helper.getShowingDialogs();
//There should only be one dialog box showing
dialog = (JDialog) dialogList.get(0);

//Click the Add button then check the game table to make sure
// the game was added. After the addition, delete the game and make
// sure the game table is empty.
JList teamList = (JList) helper.findComponent(JList.class, dialog, 0);
assertNotNull("Unable to find team list", teamList);
JTable gameTable = (JTable) helper.findComponent(JTable.class,
                                                      dialog, 0);
assertNotNull("Unable to find gameTable", gameTable);
JButton addHomeTeamButton =
                (JButton) helper.findNamedComponent(JButton.class,
                                "addHomeTeamButton", dialog, 0);
assertNotNull("Unable to find addHomeGame Button", addHomeTeamButton);
JButton addAwayTeamButton =
                (JButton) helper.findNamedComponent(JButton.class,
                                "addAwayTeamButton", dialog, 0);
assertNotNull("Unable to find addAwayGame Button", addAwayTeamButton);
JButton okButton =
                (JButton) helper.findNamedComponent(JButton.class,
                                      "okButton", dialog, 0);
assertNotNull("Unable to find OK Button", addAwayTeamButton);

//Add some games
teamList.setSelectedIndex(1);
helper.enterClickAndLeave(new MouseEventData(this, addHomeTeamButton));
awtSleep(5000);
teamList.setSelectedIndex(4);
helper.enterClickAndLeave(new MouseEventData(this, addAwayTeamButton));
awtSleep(5000);

teamList.setSelectedIndex(3);
helper.enterClickAndLeave(new MouseEventData(this, addHomeTeamButton));
awtSleep(5000);
teamList.setSelectedIndex(5);
helper.enterClickAndLeave(new MouseEventData(this, addAwayTeamButton));
awtSleep(5000);

teamList.setSelectedIndex(7);
helper.enterClickAndLeave(new MouseEventData(this, addHomeTeamButton));
awtSleep(5000);
teamList.setSelectedIndex(9);
helper.enterClickAndLeave(new MouseEventData(this, addAwayTeamButton));
awtSleep(5000);
```

```
            int rowCount = gameTable.getRowCount();
            assertEquals(3, rowCount);
            helper.enterClickAndLeave(new MouseEventData(this, okButton));
            awtSleep(5000);
        }
        // No matter if we pass or fail the test we need to close the dialog
        // so that other tests can bring up a fresh dialog box.
        // If we don't do this then the other tests might fail.
        finally
        {
            if (dialog != null)
            {
                dialog.dispose();
            }
        }
    }
}
```

The following code from Chapter 5 was updated (**new methods and/or code added is in bold**):

Listing for FBPoolServer.jsp

```
package com.apress.tddbook.gui.ejbmocks;
import com.apress.tddbook.FootballPool;
import java.util.Vector;
/*
 * This interface is used to define the communucation between the GUI
 * and the stateless session used to manage the football pool
 */
public interface FBPoolServer
{
    /** Get a list of the pools that are defined */
    public Vector getPoolList();
    /** Get all the information about a particular pool */
    public FootballPool getPoolInfo(String poolName);
    /** Get the status of the pool */
    public String getStatus(String poolName);
    /** Set the status of the specified pool to open */
    public void openPool(String poolName);
    /** Get a list of Strings of all the names of the football teams */
    public Vector getTeamNameList();
    /** Add a new football pool to the database*/
    public void addNewPool(FootballPool fbPool);

}
```

Listing for AdminMain.jsp

```
package com.apress.tddbook.gui;

import com.apress.tddbook.gui.ejbmocks.FBPoolServer;
import com.apress.tddbook.gui.ejbmocks.FBPoolServerStub;
import com.apress.tddbook.FootballPool;

import javax.swing.*;
import javax.swing.event.ListSelectionEvent;
import javax.swing.event.ListSelectionListener;
import javax.swing.table.TableColumn;
import javax.swing.table.TableModel;
import java.awt.event.WindowAdapter;
import java.awt.event.WindowEvent;
import java.awt.event.ActionEvent;
import java.awt.*;
import java.util.Vector;

public class AdminMain extends JFrame
{
    JSplitPane sPane = new JSplitPane();
    JLabel listLabel = new JLabel("Pool List");
    JList poolList = new JList();
    JScrollPane listScrollPane = new JScrollPane();
    JButton newPoolButton = new JButton("New Pool");
    JButton closePoolButton = new JButton("Close Pool");
    JButton openPoolButton = new JButton("Open Pool");
    JButton deletePoolButton = new JButton("Delete");
    JLabel gameTableLabel = new JLabel("Week 1 Games");
    JLabel statusLabel = new JLabel("Status:Unknown");
    JLabel closeDateLabel = new JLabel("Closing Date 9-19-2003");
    JTable gameTable = new JTable(14, 3);
    FBPoolServer m_fbPoolServer;

    public AdminMain()
    {
        m_fbPoolServer = getFBPoolServerBean();
        //Initialize GUI components
        initComponents();
        //Populate Pool List
        populatePoolList();

        this.setTitle("Football Pool Administrator");
        this.setName("Football Pool Administrator");
        this.setSize(400, 500);
        this.setVisible(true);
        this.pack();
```

```
}

/**
 * Set up all the components
 */
public void initComponents()
{
    newPoolButton.setName("NewPoolButton");
    openPoolButton.setName("OpenPoolButton");
    statusLabel.setName("StatusLabel");
    statusLabel.setHorizontalAlignment(JLabel.CENTER);

    openPoolButton.addActionListener(new java.awt.event.ActionListener()
    {
        public void actionPerformed(ActionEvent e)
        {
            openPool();
        }
    });

    newPoolButton.addActionListener(new java.awt.event.ActionListener()
    {
        public void actionPerformed(ActionEvent e)
        {
            newPool();
        }
    });
    //Set the table column names
    String colName = gameTable.getColumnName(0);
    TableColumn column = gameTable.getColumn(colName);
    column.setMaxWidth(50);
    column.setHeaderValue("");
    colName = gameTable.getColumnName(1);
    column = gameTable.getColumn(colName);
    column.setHeaderValue("Home Team");
    colName = gameTable.getColumnName(2);
    column = gameTable.getColumn(colName);
    column.setHeaderValue("Away Team");

    JScrollPane tableScrollPane = new JScrollPane();
    JButton editGamesButton = new JButton("Edit Games");
    JButton postScoresButton = new JButton("Post Scores");
    JPanel listPanel = new JPanel();
    JPanel tablePanel = new JPanel();
    JPanel listButtonPanel = new JPanel();
    JPanel tableButtonPanel = new JPanel();
```

```java
listPanel.setLayout(new BorderLayout());
listPanel.add(listLabel, BorderLayout.NORTH);
poolList.setVisibleRowCount(6);
poolList.addListSelectionListener(
        new ListSelectionListener()
        {
            public void valueChanged(ListSelectionEvent e)
            {
                updateGameTable();
            }
        });
listScrollPane.setViewportView(poolList);
listPanel.add(listScrollPane, BorderLayout.CENTER);

listButtonPanel.add(newPoolButton);
listButtonPanel.add(openPoolButton);
listButtonPanel.add(closePoolButton);
listButtonPanel.add(deletePoolButton);

listPanel.add(listButtonPanel, BorderLayout.SOUTH);

JPanel tableLabelPane = new JPanel();
tableLabelPane.setLayout(new BorderLayout());
tableLabelPane.add(gameTableLabel, BorderLayout.WEST);
tableLabelPane.add(statusLabel, BorderLayout.CENTER);
tableLabelPane.add(closeDateLabel, BorderLayout.EAST);
tablePanel.setLayout(new BorderLayout());
tablePanel.add(tableLabelPane, BorderLayout.NORTH);
tableScrollPane.setViewportView(gameTable);
tablePanel.add(tableScrollPane, BorderLayout.CENTER);

tableButtonPanel.add(editGamesButton);
tableButtonPanel.add(postScoresButton);

tablePanel.add(tableButtonPanel, BorderLayout.SOUTH);

sPane.setLeftComponent(listPanel);
sPane.setRightComponent(tablePanel);

addWindowListener(new WindowAdapter()
{
    public void windowClosing(WindowEvent e)
    {
        System.exit(0);
    }
});
```

```java
        this.getContentPane().add(sPane);
}


/**
 * Open the currently selected pool
 */
private void openPool()
{
    String poolName = (String) poolList.getSelectedValue();
    if (poolName != null)
    {
        String poolStatus = m_fbPoolServer.getStatus(poolName);
            // Can't open a pool that is already opened
        if (poolStatus.equals("Open"))                    {
            JOptionPane.showMessageDialog(this, "Pool Already Opened",
                                    "Error", JOptionPane.ERROR_MESSAGE);
        }
        else
        {
            m_fbPoolServer.openPool(poolName);
            poolList.clearSelection();
            poolList.setSelectedValue(poolName, true);
        }
    }
    else //Nothing selected show error
    {
        JOptionPane.showMessageDialog(this, "No Pool Selected", "Error",
                                    JOptionPane.ERROR_MESSAGE);
    }
}


/**
 * Open the New Pool dialog box
 */
public void newPool()
{
    NewPoolDialog newPoolDialog = new NewPoolDialog(m_fbPoolServer);
}
public FBPoolServer getFBPoolServerBean()
{
    return (new FBPoolServerStub());
}


/**
 * Fill in the pool list in the GUI with the data from the FBPoolServer
 */
private void populatePoolList()
```

```java
    {
        Vector gameList = m_fbPoolServer.getPoolList();
        poolList.setListData(gameList);
    }


    /**
     * Called when an item in the pool list is selected
     */
    private void updateGameTable()
    {
        String poolName = (String) poolList.getSelectedValue();
        if ((poolName != null) && (poolName.length() > 0))
        {
            FootballPool poolData = m_fbPoolServer.getPoolInfo(poolName);
            //Use selectedPool to create a table model that will be used to
            // populate the table
            TableModel model = new FBGamesTableModel(poolData);
            gameTable.setModel(model);
            String colName = gameTable.getColumnName(0);
            TableColumn column = gameTable.getColumn(colName);
            column.setMaxWidth(50);
            String poolStatus = m_fbPoolServer.getStatus(poolName);
            statusLabel.setText("Status:" + poolStatus);
        }
    }

    public static void exitGUI()
    {
        System.exit(0);
    }

    public static void main(String[] args)
    {
        AdminMain fbAdmin = new AdminMain();
    }
}
```

The following new code was created as a result of the tests:

Listing for NewPoolPanel.java

```java
package com.apress.tddbook.gui;

import com.compaq.zso.AttachLayout;
import com.compaq.zso.Attachments;
import com.apress.tddbook.FootballPool;
import com.apress.tddbook.Game;
import com.apress.tddbook.gui.ejbmocks.FBPoolServer;
```

```java
import javax.swing.*;
import javax.swing.table.TableModel;
import java.util.Vector;
import java.awt.event.ActionEvent;

public class NewPoolPanel extends JPanel
{
    private JLabel poolNameLabel = new JLabel("Name");
    private JTextField poolNameText = new JTextField();
    private JLabel closeDateLabel = new JLabel("Closing Date");
    private JTextField closeDateText = new JTextField();
    private JLabel teamListLabel = new JLabel("Team List");
    private JList teamList = new JList();
    private JTable gameTable = new JTable(13, 2);
    private JButton addHomeTeamButton = new JButton("Add Home Team");
    private JButton addAwayTeamButton = new JButton("Add Away Team");
    private JButton delGameButton = new JButton("Delete Game");
    private JButton setTieBreakButton = new JButton("Set Tie Break Game");

    /** Handle to the EJB */
    FBPoolServer m_fbPoolServer;
    /** New FootballPool object used to store new pool */
    FootballPool m_fbPool = new FootballPool();


    public NewPoolPanel(FBPoolServer fbPoolServer)
    {
        m_fbPoolServer = fbPoolServer;

        initComponents();
    }
    private void initComponents()
    {
        addHomeTeamButton.setName("addHomeTeamButton");
        addAwayTeamButton.setName("addAwayTeamButton");
        delGameButton.setName("delGameButton");
        setTieBreakButton.setName("setTieBreakButton");

        this.setLayout(new AttachLayout());
        Attachments fc = new Attachments();
        fc.topAttachment = fc.ATTACH_CONTAINER;
        fc.topOffset = 5;
        fc.leftAttachment = fc.ATTACH_POSITION;
        fc.leftPosition = 50;

        this.add(poolNameLabel, fc);
```

```
fc.topAttachment = fc.ATTACH_CONTAINER;
fc.topOffset = 5;
fc.leftAttachment = fc.ATTACH_COMPONENT;
fc.leftComponent = poolNameLabel;
fc.rightAttachment = fc.ATTACH_POSITION;
fc.rightPosition = 75;

this.add(poolNameText, fc);

fc.clear();
fc.topAttachment = fc.ATTACH_COMPONENT;
fc.topComponent = poolNameText;
fc.topOffset = 5;
fc.leftAttachment = fc.ATTACH_POSITION;
fc.leftPosition = 50;


this.add(closeDateLabel, fc);

fc.clear();
fc.topAttachment = fc.ATTACH_COMPONENT;
fc.topComponent = poolNameText;
fc.topOffset = 5;
fc.leftAttachment = fc.ATTACH_COMPONENT;
fc.leftComponent = closeDateLabel;
fc.rightAttachment = fc.ATTACH_POSITION;
fc.rightPosition = 75;

this.add(closeDateText, fc);


fc.clear();
fc.topAttachment = fc.ATTACH_COMPONENT;
fc.topComponent = closeDateText;
fc.topOffset = 5;
fc.leftAttachment = fc.ATTACH_POSITION;
fc.leftPosition = 50;
fc.rightAttachment = fc.ATTACH_CONTAINER;
fc.bottomAttachment = fc.ATTACH_POSITION;
fc.bottomPosition = 80;

TableModel model = new NewPoolGamesTableModel(m_fbPool);
gameTable.setModel(model);
gameTable.setRowSelectionAllowed(true);
JScrollPane gameTableScrollPane = new JScrollPane();
gameTableScrollPane.setViewportView(gameTable);
this.add(gameTableScrollPane, fc);
```

```
fc.clear();
fc.topAttachment = fc.ATTACH_COMPONENT;
fc.topComponent = gameTableScrollPane;
fc.topOffset = 5;
fc.leftAttachment = fc.ATTACH_POSITION;
fc.leftPosition = 50;

setTieBreakButton.addActionListener(new java.awt.event.ActionListener()
{
    public void actionPerformed(ActionEvent e)
    {
        setTieBreakGame();
    }
});

this.add(setTieBreakButton, fc);


fc.topAttachment = fc.ATTACH_COMPONENT;
fc.topComponent = closeDateText;
fc.topOffset = 20;
fc.leftAttachment = fc.ATTACH_CONTAINER;
fc.leftOffset = 10;


this.add(teamListLabel, fc);
fc.clear();
fc.topAttachment = fc.ATTACH_COMPONENT;
fc.topComponent = teamListLabel;
fc.topOffset = 5;
fc.leftAttachment = fc.ATTACH_CONTAINER;
fc.leftOffset = 10;
fc.bottomAttachment = fc.ATTACH_CONTAINER;

JScrollPane teamListScrollPane = new JScrollPane();

teamList.setListData(getTeamNameList());
teamList.setVisibleRowCount(14);
teamListScrollPane.setViewportView(teamList);
this.add(teamListScrollPane, fc);

fc.clear();
fc.topAttachment = fc.ATTACH_COMPONENT;
fc.topComponent = teamListLabel;
fc.topOffset = 20;
fc.leftAttachment = fc.ATTACH_COMPONENT;
fc.leftComponent = teamListScrollPane;
```

```java
        fc.leftOffset = 10;

        addHomeTeamButton.addActionListener(new java.awt.event.ActionListener()
        {
            public void actionPerformed(ActionEvent e)
            {
                addNewHomeTeam();
            }
        });

        this.add(addHomeTeamButton, fc);

        fc.topAttachment = fc.ATTACH_COMPONENT;
        fc.topComponent = addHomeTeamButton;
        fc.topOffset = 5;
        fc.leftAttachment = fc.ATTACH_COMPONENT;
        fc.leftComponent = teamListScrollPane;
        fc.leftOffset = 10;

        addAwayTeamButton.addActionListener(new java.awt.event.ActionListener()
        {
            public void actionPerformed(ActionEvent e)
            {
                addNewAwayTeam();
            }
        });

        this.add(addAwayTeamButton, fc);

        fc.topAttachment = fc.ATTACH_COMPONENT;
        fc.topComponent = addAwayTeamButton;
        fc.topOffset = 5;
        fc.leftAttachment = fc.ATTACH_COMPONENT;
        fc.leftComponent = teamListScrollPane;
        fc.leftOffset = 10;

        delGameButton.addActionListener(new java.awt.event.ActionListener()
        {
            public void actionPerformed(ActionEvent e)
            {
                delSelectedGame();
            }
        });

        this.add(delGameButton, fc);

        this.setSize(300,400);
```

```
}

private Vector getTeamNameList()
{
    return(m_fbPoolServer.getTeamNameList());
}


/**
 * Add a new game to the football pool with the selected home team
 */
private void addNewHomeTeam()
{
    Vector gameList = m_fbPool.getGameList();
    // Get last game if home team not defined, then add selected home team.
    // Otherwise add new game with selected home team.
    if(gameList.size() > 0)
    {
        Game lastGame = (Game)gameList.elementAt(gameList.size() -1);
        if(lastGame.getHomeTeam().length() > 0)
        {
            Game newGame = new Game("", (String)teamList.getSelectedValue());
            gameList.addElement(newGame);
        }
        else
        {
            lastGame.setHomeTeam((String)teamList.getSelectedValue());
        }
    }
    else
    {
        Game newGame = new Game("", (String)teamList.getSelectedValue());
        gameList.addElement(newGame);
    }
    TableModel model = new NewPoolGamesTableModel(m_fbPool);
    gameTable.setModel(model);
}
/**
 * Add a new game to the football pool with the selected away team
 */
private void addNewAwayTeam()
{
    Vector gameList = m_fbPool.getGameList();
    // Get last game if home team not defined, then add selected home team.
    // Otherwise add new game with selected home team.
    if(gameList.size() > 0)
    {
        Game lastGame = (Game)gameList.elementAt(gameList.size() -1);
```

```java
                if(lastGame.getAwayTeam().length() > 0)
                {
                    Game newGame = new Game((String)teamList.getSelectedValue(), "");
                    gameList.addElement(newGame);
                }
                else
                {
                    lastGame.setAwayTeam((String)teamList.getSelectedValue());
                }
            }
            else
            {
                Game newGame = new Game((String)teamList.getSelectedValue(), "");
                gameList.addElement(newGame);
            }
            TableModel model = new NewPoolGamesTableModel(m_fbPool);
            gameTable.setModel(model);
    }
    private void delSelectedGame()
    {
        int selectedRow = gameTable.getSelectedRow();
        Vector gameList = m_fbPool.getGameList();
        gameList.removeElementAt(selectedRow);
        TableModel model = new NewPoolGamesTableModel(m_fbPool);
        gameTable.setModel(model);
    }

    private void setTieBreakGame()
    {
        int selectedRow = gameTable.getSelectedRow();
        try
        {
            m_fbPool.setTieBreakerGame(selectedRow);
        }
        catch (Exception noSuchGameException)
        {
            System.out.println("Error setting tie break game exception is " +
                                        noSuchGameException);
        }
        gameTable.updateUI();
    }

    public void savePool()
    {
        m_fbPool.setPoolDate(poolNameText.getText());
        m_fbPoolServer.addNewPool(m_fbPool);
    }
}
```

Listing for NewPoolDialog.java

```
package com.apress.tddbook.gui;

import com.apress.tddbook.gui.ejbmocks.FBPoolServer;

import javax.swing.*;
import java.awt.*;
import java.awt.event.ActionEvent;

public class NewPoolDialog extends JDialog
{
    private NewPoolPanel poolPanel;
    private JButton okButton = new JButton("OK");
    private JButton cancelButton = new JButton("Cancel");

    FBPoolServer m_fbPoolServer;

    public NewPoolDialog(FBPoolServer fbPoolServer)
    {
        m_fbPoolServer = fbPoolServer;
        initComponents();
        this.show();
    }

    public void initComponents()
    {
        okButton.setName("okButton");
        okButton.addActionListener(new java.awt.event.ActionListener()
        {
            public void actionPerformed(ActionEvent e)
            {
                saveNewPool();
            }
        });

        cancelButton.addActionListener(new java.awt.event.ActionListener()
        {
            public void actionPerformed(ActionEvent e)
            {
                closeDialog();
            }
        });

        this.getContentPane().setLayout(new BorderLayout());
        poolPanel = new NewPoolPanel(m_fbPoolServer);
        this.getContentPane().add(poolPanel, BorderLayout.CENTER);
        JPanel buttonPanel = new JPanel();
```

```
            buttonPanel.add(okButton);
            buttonPanel.add(cancelButton);
            this.getContentPane().add(buttonPanel, BorderLayout.SOUTH);

            this.setSize(600, 400);
        }
    public void saveNewPool()
    {
            poolPanel.savePool();
            this.hide();
    }

    public void closeDialog()
    {
            this.hide();
    }
}
```

Listing for NewPoolGamesTableModel.java

```
package com.apress.tddbook.gui;

import com.apress.tddbook.FootballPool;

import javax.swing.table.AbstractTableModel;

public class NewPoolGamesTableModel extends AbstractTableModel
{
    FootballPool m_poolData;

    public NewPoolGamesTableModel(FootballPool poolData)
    {
        m_poolData = poolData;
    }

    public int getRowCount()
    {
        return (m_poolData.getGameList().size());
    }

    public int getColumnCount()
    {
        //There are only always two columns
        return (2);
    }
```

```java
public String getColumnName(int col)
{
    switch (col)
    {
        case 0:
            return ("Home Team");
        case 1:
            return ("Away Team");
        default:
            return ("Unknown");
    }
}

public Class getColumnClass(int col)
{
    return (String.class);
}

public boolean isCellEditable(int row, int col)
{
    switch (col)
    {
        case 0:
            return (false);
        case 1:
            return (false);
        default:
            return (false);
    }
}

public Object getValueAt(int row, int col)
{
    switch (col)
    {
        case 0: // Home Team
            if (m_poolData.getTieBreakerGame() == row)
            {
                // Mark tiebreaker game with asterisk at end of team name
                return (m_poolData.getHomeTeam(row) + " *");
            }
            else
            {
                return (m_poolData.getHomeTeam(row));
            }
        case 1: // Away Team
            if (m_poolData.getTieBreakerGame() == row)
```

```
                {
                    // Mark tiebreaker game with asterisk at end of team name
                    return (m_poolData.getAwayTeam(row) + " *");
                }
                else
                {
                    return (m_poolData.getAwayTeam(row));
                }
            default:
                return ("");
        }
    }


    public void setValueAt(Object p1, int row, int col)
    {

    }
}
```

Chapter 6 Hands-On Exercise: Problem 1

So far, the tests have helped us to implement the three methods of the PoolDatabase interface, but there is still a lot more work to do. The tests developed have only tested the simple default case wherein the database is set up correctly and there are no error conditions. Create a set of tests that will test the following error conditions:

- Try to get a list of open pools from a database with no pools that are open.

- Try to save a set of player picks for a pool date that doesn't exist.

- Try to get a set of player picks for a player who doesn't exist.

Use the tests developed to improve the PoolDatabaseImpl class so it can handle these error conditions.

Solution

For each possible error condition, we need to add a new test to the PoolDataDBTester. The code that follows shows the new tests and supporting methods that were added:

```
/**
     * Test the getPoolWithStatus method of the PoolDatabase with a
     * real database that doesn't have an open pool
     *
     * @throws Exception
     */
    public void testGetFBPoolOpenError() throws Exception
```

```java
{
    // Reset the database contents with the data with no open pool
    IDataSet dataSet = new FlatXmlDataSet(new FileInputStream("dataset3.xml"));
    DatabaseOperation.CLEAN_INSERT.execute(getConnection(), dataSet);
    PoolDatabase poolDB =
            new PoolDatabaseImpl("jdbc:hsqldb:hsql://localhost", "sa", "");

    Vector openPoolList = null;
    try
    {
        openPoolList = poolDB.getPoolWithStatus("Open");
        fail("getPoolWithStatus did not throw correct exception");
    }
    catch (NoPoolFoundException e)
    {
        //If we get here then the correct exception was thrown
    }
}


/**
 * Test the savePlayerPicks of the PoolDatabase with a real DB with a
 * bad football pool
 */
public void testSavePlayerPicksBadPool() throws Exception,
                                                ClassNotFoundException
{
    PoolDatabase poolDB =
            new PoolDatabaseImpl("jdbc:hsqldb:hsql://localhost", "sa", "");

    FootballPool pool = createFbPool();
    PlayersPicks playPicks = createBadPlayersPicks(pool);
    //Save the player picks to the database
    try
    {
        poolDB.savePlayersPicks(playPicks);
        fail("savePlayerPicks did not throw correct exception");
    }
    catch (SavePlayerPickException e)
    {
        //If we get here then the correct exception was thrown
    }
}

public void testGetPlayerPicksBadPlayer() throws Exception,
                                                ClassNotFoundException
{
    // Reset the database contents with the data needed for the test to pass
```

```
    IDataSet dataSet = new FlatXmlDataSet(new FileInputStream("dataset2.xml"));
    DatabaseOperation.CLEAN_INSERT.execute(getConnection(), dataSet);
    String playerName = "FrankG";
    String poolDate = "2003-09-17";
    PoolDatabase poolDB =
            new PoolDatabaseImpl("jdbc:hsqldb:hsql://localhost", "sa", "");
    //Get picks from database
    try
    {
        PlayersPicks picks = poolDB.getPlayersPicks(playerName, poolDate);
        fail("getPlayerPicks did not throw correct exception");
    }
    catch(PicksNotFoundException e)
    {
            //If we get here then the correct exception was thrown
    }
}

private PlayersPicks createBadPlayersPicks(FootballPool fbPool)
{
    Vector gameList = fbPool.getGameList();
    PlayersPicks playerPicks =
                    new PlayersPicks("WayneC", "2004-08-13", gameList);
    for (int i = 0; i < gameList.size(); i++)
    {
        Game game = (Game) gameList.elementAt(i);
        playerPicks.makePick(i, game.getHomeTeam());
    }
    return (playerPicks);
}
private FootballPool createFbPool()
{
    FootballPool pool = new FootballPool("8/13/2004");
    pool.addGame("Kansas City", "Green Bay");
    pool.addGame("Houston", "Tennessee");
    pool.addGame("Carolina", "Indianapolis");
    pool.addGame("NY Giants", "New England");
    pool.addGame("Chicago", "New Orleans");
    pool.addGame("Oakland", "Cleveland");
    pool.addGame("Philadelphia", "Dallas");
    pool.addGame("Tampa Bay", "Washington");
    pool.addGame("Miami", "Jacksonville");
    pool.addGame("Pittsburgh", "Denver");
    pool.addGame("Buffalo", "NY Jets");
    pool.addGame("Baltimore", "Arizona");
    pool.addGame("San Francisco", "Seattle");
    pool.addGame("Atlanta", "St. Louis");
```

```
        return (pool);
    }
```

The following new dataset file, dataset3.xml, was added to be used by the tests:

```
<dataset>
    <POOL  POOL_ID="1"
                DATE="2003-09-17"
                WINNER=""
                STATUS="Closed"/>
     <GAME POOL_ID="1"
                GAME_NUM ="1"
                HOME_TEAM ="Green Bay"
                AWAY_TEAM="Kansas City"/>
    <GAME POOL_ID="1"
                GAME_NUM ="2"
                HOME_TEAM ="Tennessee"
                AWAY_TEAM="Houston"/>
    <GAME POOL_ID="1"
                GAME_NUM ="3"
                HOME_TEAM ="Indianapolis"
                AWAY_TEAM="Carolina"/>
    <GAME POOL_ID="1"
                GAME_NUM ="4"
                HOME_TEAM ="New England"
                AWAY_TEAM="NY Giants"/>
     <GAME POOL_ID="1"
                GAME_NUM ="5"
                HOME_TEAM ="New Orleans"
                AWAY_TEAM="Chicago"/>
     <GAME POOL_ID="1"
                GAME_NUM ="6"
                HOME_TEAM ="Cleveland"
                AWAY_TEAM="Oakland"/>
    <GAME POOL_ID="1"
                GAME_NUM ="7"
                HOME_TEAM ="Dallas"
                AWAY_TEAM="Philadelphia"/>
    <GAME POOL_ID="1"
                GAME_NUM ="8"
                HOME_TEAM ="Washington"
                AWAY_TEAM="Tampa Bay"/>
    <GAME POOL_ID="1"
                GAME_NUM ="9"
                HOME_TEAM ="Jacksonville"
                AWAY_TEAM="Miami"/>
    <GAME POOL_ID="1"
                GAME_NUM ="10"
```

```
                    HOME_TEAM ="Denver"
                    AWAY_TEAM="Pittsburgh"/>
        <GAME POOL_ID="1"
                    GAME_NUM ="11"
                    HOME_TEAM ="NY Jets"
                    AWAY_TEAM="Buffalo"/>
        <GAME POOL_ID="1"
                    GAME_NUM ="12"
                    HOME_TEAM ="Arizona"
                    AWAY_TEAM="Baltimore"/>
        <GAME POOL_ID="1"
                    GAME_NUM ="13"
                    HOME_TEAM ="Seattle"
                    AWAY_TEAM="San Francisco"/>
        <GAME POOL_ID="1"
                    GAME_NUM ="14"
                    HOME_TEAM ="St. Louis"
                    AWAY_TEAM="Atlanta"/>
<PICKS />
</dataset>
```

These tests cause us to make the following changes to the PoolDatabaseImpl class (**changes in bold**):

```
package com.apress.tddbook;

import java.util.Vector;
import java.sql.*;

public class PoolDatabaseImpl implements PoolDatabase
{
    private Connection m_Conn;

    public PoolDatabaseImpl(String dbPath, String userName, String passwd) throws
                                        SQLException, ClassNotFoundException
    {
        Class driverClass = Class.forName("org.hsqldb.jdbcDriver");
        m_Conn = DriverManager.getConnection(dbPath, userName, passwd);
    }

    /**
     * Return a list of football pools with the given status
     *
     * @param status Status to look for
     * @return
     */
    public Vector getPoolWithStatus(String status) throws NoPoolFoundException
    {
```

```java
int poolID;
Date poolDate;
String poolWinner;
String poolStatus;
int gameNum;
String homeTeam;
String awayTeam;

FootballPool fbPool = null;
Vector poolList = new Vector();
//Query pool table to get pool with the given status
String sqlQuery =
        "Select pool_id, date, winner, status from pool where status =
        '" + status + "'";
try
{
    PreparedStatement poolTBStmt = m_Conn.prepareStatement(sqlQuery);
    ResultSet poolTBResults = poolTBStmt.executeQuery();
    boolean morePoolResults = poolTBResults.next();
    //If no results found throw exception so that client knows that
    // no pool was found
    if (!morePoolResults)
    {
        throw new NoPoolFoundException();
    }
    while (morePoolResults)
    {
        poolID = poolTBResults.getInt(1);
        poolDate = poolTBResults.getDate(2);
        poolWinner = poolTBResults.getString(3);
        poolStatus = poolTBResults.getString(4);
        fbPool = new FootballPool(poolDate.toString());
        //Query game table to get games for this poolID
        sqlQuery = "Select game_num, home_team, away_team from game where
                        pool_id = " + poolID + "order by game_num";
        PreparedStatement gameTBStmt = m_Conn.prepareStatement(sqlQuery);
        ResultSet gameTBResults = gameTBStmt.executeQuery();
        boolean moreGameResults = gameTBResults.next();
        while (moreGameResults)
        {
            gameNum = gameTBResults.getInt(1);
            homeTeam = gameTBResults.getString(2);
            awayTeam = gameTBResults.getString(3);
            fbPool.addGame(awayTeam, homeTeam);
            moreGameResults = gameTBResults.next();
        }
        poolList.addElement(fbPool);
```

```
                morePoolResults = poolTBResults.next();
            }
        }
        catch (SQLException e)
        {
            System.out.println("Error getting getting Pool.  Exception is " + e);
            e.printStackTrace();
        }

        return poolList;
    }

    public Vector getAllPoolDates()
    {
        Date poolDate;
        String homeTeam;
        String awayTeam;

        Vector poolList = new Vector();
        //Query pool table to get all pools
        String sqlQuery = "Select date from pool";
        try
        {
            PreparedStatement poolTBStmt = m_Conn.prepareStatement(sqlQuery);
            ResultSet poolTBResults = poolTBStmt.executeQuery();
            boolean morePoolResults = poolTBResults.next();
            while (morePoolResults)
            {
                poolDate = poolTBResults.getDate(1);
                poolList.addElement(poolDate.toString());
                morePoolResults = poolTBResults.next();
            }
        }
        catch (SQLException e)
        {
            System.out.println("Error getting getting Pool.  Exception is " + e);
            e.printStackTrace();
        }

        return poolList;
    }

    /**
     * Get a football pool with the specified date
     *
     * @param poolDateStr Date of the football pool to get
     * @return
```

```java
*/
public FootballPool getPoolWithDate(String poolDateStr)
{
    int poolID;
    Date poolDate;
    String poolWinner;
    String poolStatus;
    int gameNum;
    String homeTeam;
    String awayTeam;

    FootballPool fbPool = null;
    fbPool = new FootballPool();
    System.out.println("Before FB Pool creation");
    fbPool.setPoolDate("2003-09-11");
    System.out.println("Created FB Pool");
    //Query pool table to get find pool with specified date
    String sqlQuery = "Select pool_id,date,winner,status from pool where date =
                            '" + poolDateStr + "'";
    try
    {
        PreparedStatement poolTBStmt = m_Conn.prepareStatement(sqlQuery);
        ResultSet poolTBResults = poolTBStmt.executeQuery();
        boolean morePoolResults = poolTBResults.next();
        if (morePoolResults)
        {
            poolID = poolTBResults.getInt(1);
            poolDate = poolTBResults.getDate(2);
            poolWinner = poolTBResults.getString(3);
            poolStatus = poolTBResults.getString(4);
            poolDateStr = poolDate.toString();
            fbPool = new FootballPool(poolDateStr.toString());
            fbPool.setStatus(poolStatus);
            fbPool.setWinner(poolWinner);
            //Query game table to get games for this poolID
            sqlQuery = "Select game_num, home_team, away_team from game where
                            pool_id = " + poolID + "order by game_num";
            PreparedStatement gameTBStmt = m_Conn.prepareStatement(sqlQuery);
            ResultSet gameTBResults = gameTBStmt.executeQuery();
            boolean moreGameResults = gameTBResults.next();
            while (moreGameResults)
            {
                gameNum = gameTBResults.getInt(1);
                homeTeam = gameTBResults.getString(2);
                awayTeam = gameTBResults.getString(3);
                fbPool.addGame(awayTeam, homeTeam);
                moreGameResults = gameTBResults.next();
```

```java
                }
            }
        }
        catch (SQLException e)
        {
            System.out.println("Error getting getting Pool.  Exception is " + e);
            e.printStackTrace();
        }

        return (fbPool);
    }

    public void setPoolStatus(String poolDate, String status)
    {
        String sqlQuery = "Update pool set status = '" + status +
                                "' where pool_id = " +
                    "select pool_id from pool where date = '" + poolDate + "'";
        try
        {
            PreparedStatement poolTBStmt = m_Conn.prepareStatement(sqlQuery);
            poolTBStmt.execute();
        }
        catch (SQLException e)
        {
            System.out.println("Error updating pool status.  Exception is " + e);
            e.printStackTrace();
        }
    }

    public void savePlayersPicks(PlayersPicks picks) throws SavePlayerPickException
    {
        int poolID;
        String playersName = picks.getPlayersName();
        String poolDate = picks.getPoolDate();
        //Get pool_id for given pool date
        String sqlQuery = "Select pool_id from pool where date =
                                '" + poolDate + "'";
        try
        {
            PreparedStatement poolTBStmt = m_Conn.prepareStatement(sqlQuery);
            ResultSet poolTBResults = poolTBStmt.executeQuery();
            boolean morePoolResults = poolTBResults.next();
            //If no results found throw exception so that client knows that
            // no pool was found
            if (!morePoolResults)
            {
                throw new SavePlayerPickException("No pool found for date "
```

```java
                                                              + poolDate);
        }
        if (morePoolResults)
        {
            poolID = poolTBResults.getInt(1);
            //Insert a row into the pick table for each game
            String insertStr;
            for (int i = 0; i < 14; i++)
            {
                insertStr =
            "Insert into picks (pool_id, user_name, game_num, picked_team) " +
                        "Values(" + poolID + ",'" + playersName + "'," + (i + 1)
                        + ",'" + picks.getPickedTeam(i) + "'" + ")";
                PreparedStatement pickTBStmt =
                                        m_Conn.prepareStatement(insertStr);
                pickTBStmt.execute();
            }
        }
    }
    catch (SQLException e)
    {
        System.out.println("Error saving picks.  Exception is " + e);
        e.printStackTrace();
    }
}

public PlayersPicks getPlayersPicks(String name, String poolDate) throws
                                                PicksNotFoundException
{
    int poolID;
    int gameNum;
    String pickedTeam;
    String homeTeam;
    String awayTeam;
    Game game;
    Vector gameList = new Vector();
    PlayersPicks picks = null;
    //Get pool_id for given pool date
    String sqlQuery = "Select pool_id from pool where date =
                            '" + poolDate + "'";
    try
    {
        PreparedStatement poolTBStmt = m_Conn.prepareStatement(sqlQuery);
        ResultSet poolTBResults = poolTBStmt.executeQuery();
        boolean morePoolResults = poolTBResults.next();
        if (morePoolResults)
        {
```

```
            poolID = poolTBResults.getInt(1);
            //Get the rows from the pick table that match the pool_id and name
            String SelecttStr;
            for (int i = 0; i < 14; i++)
            {
                SelecttStr = "select g.game_num, g.home_team, g.away_team,
                                    p.picked_team from picks p, game g  " +
                            "where g.pool_id = p.pool_id and g.pool_id=" + poolID
                            + " and user_name = '" + name + "'" +
                            " and p.game_num = g.game_num order by game_num";

                PreparedStatement pickTBStmt =
                                    m_Conn.prepareStatement(SelecttStr);
                ResultSet pickResults = pickTBStmt.executeQuery();
                boolean morePickResults = pickResults.next();
                //If no picks found throw exception so that client knows
                // that no picks were found
                if (!morePickResults)
                {
                    throw new PicksNotFoundException();
                }
                while (morePickResults)
                {
                    gameNum = pickResults.getInt(1);
                    homeTeam = pickResults.getString(2);
                    awayTeam = pickResults.getString(3);
                    pickedTeam = pickResults.getString(4);
                    game = new Game(awayTeam, homeTeam);
                    game.set_pickedGame(pickedTeam);
                    gameList.addElement(game);
                    morePickResults = pickResults.next();
                }
                picks = new PlayersPicks(name, poolDate, gameList);
            }
        }
    }
    catch (SQLException e)
    {
        System.out.println("Error saving picks.  Exception is " + e);
        e.printStackTrace();
    }
    return (picks);
    }
}
```

The following new classes were added to get the tests to pass:

Listing for SavePlayerPickException.java

```
package com.apress.tddbook;

public class SavePlayerPickException extends Exception
{
    public SavePlayerPickException(String errorMsg)
    {
        super(errorMsg);
    }
}
```

Listing for NoPoolFoundException.java

```
package com.apress.tddbook;

public class NoPoolFoundException extends Exception
{

}
```

Listing for PickNotFoundException.java

```
package com.apress.tddbook;

public class PicksNotFoundException extends Exception
{

}
```

Chapter 6 Hands-On Exercise: Problem 2

It's now your turn to work on finishing the integration of the PlayerPickServlet by writing an additional Cactus test to test out one of the other behaviors of the servlet. Write a Cactus test to verify that a player can create a set of picks from a set of games for the currently open pool.

Solution

Verifying that a player can create a set of picks for a pool involves adding the following three methods to the PlayerPickIntTester:

```
/**
    * Test to make sure that a player can make a set of picks correctly
    *
    */
    public void beginMakePlayerPicks(WebRequest webRequest)
```

```java
{
    webRequest.addParameter("username", "TimmyC");
    webRequest.addParameter("action", "makePicks");
    webRequest.addParameter("poolDate", "2003-09-17");
    webRequest.addParameter("game_1_pick", "Green Bay");
    webRequest.addParameter("game_2_pick", "Houston");
    webRequest.addParameter("game_3_pick", "Indianapolis");
    webRequest.addParameter("game_4_pick", "NY Giants");
    webRequest.addParameter("game_5_pick", "Chicago");
    webRequest.addParameter("game_6_pick", "Cleveland");
    webRequest.addParameter("game_7_pick", "Dallas");
    webRequest.addParameter("game_8_pick", "Washington");
    webRequest.addParameter("game_9_pick", "Jacksonville");
    webRequest.addParameter("game_10_pick", "Pittsburgh");
    webRequest.addParameter("game_11_pick", "Buffalo");
    webRequest.addParameter("game_12_pick", "Baltimore");
    webRequest.addParameter("game_13_pick", "San Francisco");
    webRequest.addParameter("game_14_pick", "Atlanta");
}


public void testMakePlayerPicks() throws Exception
{
    System.out.println("Starting Test Make Players Picks");
    PlayerPickServlet servlet = new PlayerPickServlet();
    //Set up the init params needed to initialize the database
    config.setInitParameter("dbLocation", "jdbc:hsqldb:hsql://localhost");
    config.setInitParameter("dbUser", "sa");
    config.setInitParameter("dbPass", "");
    servlet.init(config);
    servlet.doPost(request, response);
    System.out.println("Ending Test");
}

public void endMakePlayerPicks(WebResponse response) throws Exception
{
    System.out.println("Ending Make Players Picks");
    PoolDatabase poolDB =
            new PoolDatabaseImpl("jdbc:hsqldb:hsql://localhost", "sa", "");
    System.out.println("Got poolDB");
    PlayersPicks playerPicks = poolDB.getPlayersPicks("TimmyC", "2003-09-17");
    System.out.println("Got picks");
    assertEquals("Green Bay", playerPicks.getPickedTeam(0));
    assertEquals("Houston", playerPicks.getPickedTeam(1));
    assertEquals("Indianapolis", playerPicks.getPickedTeam(2));
    assertEquals("NY Giants", playerPicks.getPickedTeam(3));
    assertEquals("Chicago", playerPicks.getPickedTeam(4));
```

```
        assertEquals("Cleveland", playerPicks.getPickedTeam(5));
        assertEquals("Dallas", playerPicks.getPickedTeam(6));
        assertEquals("Washington", playerPicks.getPickedTeam(7));
        assertEquals("Jacksonville", playerPicks.getPickedTeam(8));
        assertEquals("Pittsburgh", playerPicks.getPickedTeam(9));
        assertEquals("Buffalo", playerPicks.getPickedTeam(10));
        assertEquals("Baltimore", playerPicks.getPickedTeam(11));
        assertEquals("San Francisco", playerPicks.getPickedTeam(12));
        assertEquals("Atlanta", playerPicks.getPickedTeam(13));
    }
```

This leads us to change the doGet() method of the PlayerPickServlet as follows (**changes in bold**):

```
public void doGet(HttpServletRequest request, HttpServletResponse response)
        throws ServletException, IOException
{
    String action = request.getParameter("action");
    System.out.println("Action is " + action);
    if(action == null)
    {
        FootballPool fbPool = getOpenPool(request);
        request.setAttribute("openPool", fbPool);
        RequestDispatcher dispatcher =
            getServletContext().getRequestDispatcher("/PickPage.jsp");
        dispatcher.include(request, response);
    }
    else if (action.equals("makePicks"))
    {
        try
        {
            storePlayersPicks(request);
            System.out.println("servlet complete");
        }
        catch (SavePlayerPickException e)
        {
            throw new ServletException(e.getMessage());
        }
    }
    else
    {
        FootballPool fbPool = getOpenPool(request);
        request.setAttribute("openPool", fbPool);
        RequestDispatcher dispatcher =
            getServletContext().getRequestDispatcher("/PickPage.jsp"");
        dispatcher.include(request, response);
    }
}
```

APPENDIX C

███

References

Bibliography

Alur, Deepak, John Crupi, and Dan Malks. *Core J2EE Patterns: Best Practices and Design Strategies*. Upper Saddle River, NJ: Prentice Hall, 2001.

Astels, David. *Test-Driven Development: A Practical Guide*. Upper Saddle River, NJ: Prentice Hall, 2003.

Beck, Kent. *Test-Driven Development: By Example*. Boston, MA: Addison-Wesley, 2003.

Fowler, Martin et al. *Refactoring: Improving the Design of Existing Code*. Reading, MA: Addison-Wesley, 1999.

Hatcher, Erik and Steve Loughran. *Java Development with Ant*. Greenwich, CT: Manning, 2002.

Massol, Vincent and Ted Husted. *JUnit in Action*. Greenwich, CT: Manning, 2004.

McConnell, Steve. *Code Complete*. Redmond, WA: Microsoft Press, 1993.

Metsker, Steven. *Design Patterns Java Workbook*. Boston, MA: Addison-Wesley, 2002.

Recommended TDD Web Sites

The following table contains a list of web sites that contain information or tools that are useful to the practice of TDD.

Name	URL	Description
JUnit	http://www.junit.org	The main site for the JUnit testing framework. This site also contains a lot of good links to other testing tools as well as links to information on unit testing and TDD.
MockObjects	http://www.mockobjects.com/	A good place for information on mock objects.
TestDriven.com	http://www.testdriven.com	Web site about TDD.
EasyMock	http://www.easymock.org	Web site for the EasyMock mock object framework.

Continued

Name	URL	Description
dbunit.jar	http://www.dbunit.org	Information on the JUnit extension used to test database-dependent code.
httpunit.jar	http://www.httpunit.org	Home of the HttpUnit and ServletUnit testing frameworks.
jfcunit.jar	http://sourceforge.net/projects/jfcunit	Web site for the JUnit extension used to test Swing GUIs.
jemmy.jar	http://jemmy.netbeans.org	Home of the NetBeans extension that can be used to test Swing GUIs.
Java GUI Testing	http://groups.yahoo.com/group/java-gui-testing	Yahoo group focused on the discussion of testing Java GUIs.
Cactus	http://jakarta.apache.org/cactus	Web site for a testing tool that can be used to do in-container testing of server-side code for J2EE applications.
junitperf.jar	http://www.clarkware.com/software/JUnitPerf.html	Web site for a testing tool that can be used to do performance and load testing on an application.

Index